D1534678

WEST'S LAW SCHOOL
ADVISORY BOARD

MEDIATION
IN A NUTSHELL

By

KIMBERLEE K. KOVACH
University of Texas

Mat #40057250

West Group has created this publication to provide you with accurate and authoritative information concerning the subject matter covered. However, this publication was not necessarily prepared by persons licensed to practice law in a particular jurisdiction. West Group is not engaged in rendering legal or other professional advice, and this publication is not a substitute for the advice of an attorney. If you require legal or other expert advice, you should seek the services of a competent attorney or other professional.

Nutshell Series, In a Nutshell, the Nutshell Logo and West Group are registered trademarks used herein under license.

TEXT IS PRINTED ON 10% POST
CONSUMER RECYCLED PAPER

For Eric

*

PREFACE

During the last twenty-five years, the field of mediation has evolved and matured, perhaps far more than those involved in the process envisioned. In most ways, this growth of mediation use has been very encouraging, constructive and valuable. Individuals are learning innovative and creative ways to solve problems. Matters are being resolved expeditiously. Awareness that all problem solving need not be based upon a win-lose, right-wrong paradigm has increased. But along with that progress have also come concerns and unease. Like any maturity in innovation, "growing pains" have emerged. This is particularly true of mediation use as it relates to the courts. Not surprisingly, the last several years have brought us many developments in terms of how and where mediation is conducted as well as expansion of the parameters of practice. These rules, guidelines and policy matters surrounding mediation practice are now found in case law, statutes, court rules, books, law reviews and professional journals.

This book is an attempt to provide a concise, yet comprehensive overview of most of the issues that currently affect mediation practice. Although space did not permit in depth analyses of each of the myriad of issues raised, the reader hopefully will find useful resources through the references, cases and bibliographies at the end of each chapter.

I wish to thank my friends and colleagues who made suggestions with regard to the content and outline of this book. My indebtedness is also extended to all of those whose thoughtful and insightful publications have formed the foundation of the continuing knowledge and further innovation in the field of dispute resolution.

Much appreciation goes to Liz Herre for her outstanding research and editing assistance, as well as words of encouragement.

And, finally, a special expression of gratitude to my wonderful family, for whose presence and support I am eternally thankful.

KIMBERLEE K. KOVACH

Austin, Texas
January, 2003

OUTLINE

_____

OUTLINE

*

TABLE OF CASES

References are to Pages

A

B

C

D

F

G

H

I

P

R

S

T

*

MEDIATION
IN A NUTSHELL

*

CHAPTER 1

MEDIATION DISTINGUISHED FROM OTHER DISPUTE RESOLUTION PROCESSES

A. INTRODUCTION

Mediation is not a new method of dispute resolution, but rather one of multiple origins and backgrounds. While in the United States as well as in many other countries mediation is viewed as an innovative and viable alternative to the use of the court or justice system, mediation is in fact a quite ancient method of dispute resolution. In other cultures, and at an earlier time in the United States, mediation was viewed as the primary method of dispute resolution. Nonetheless, it is important to understand the contemporary alternative dispute resolution (ADR) movement in light of its relationship with modern day courts and legal system perspectives.

Those participating in mediation, whether as mediators, parties or party representatives, should also be familiar with the various other forms of ADR. In some cases, other processes are used in conjunction with mediation, and these combinations may be found in contracts, court rules or orders. The ability

1

to differentiate between and among the processes is also critical in order to accurately describe and discuss process options with parties in dispute. Often litigants need to know differences in dispute resolution approaches in order to choose an appropriate process when urged or required to do so.

Knowledge and understanding of various ADR processes are also important in the event that matters are not resolved through mediation. This way, either the mediator or those representing clients in mediation, generally lawyers, are better able to make decisions about what other dispute resolution methods may be beneficial in reaching a final resolution.

B. TRADITIONAL DISPUTE RESOLUTION METHODS

To be effective in mediation, it is important to first understand the theories and origins of conflict and disputing. Awareness assists mediators and other participants in understanding the perspectives, beliefs and feelings that accompany the parties in mediation. Examining one's own perspective of conflict is an important aspect in understanding common reactions in dispute situations. The orientation and strategies a mediator may utilize during the process may result from that individual's view of conflict. The approaches parties may take in mediation are also, in part, dependant upon their previous experiences with conflict.

1. CONFLICT AND DISPUTING

Conflict will always occur. Conflict can be defined as a situation in which individuals disagree or have differing needs resulting in a tension between them. The word itself is derivative of the Latin *con* (together) and *flegere* (to strike). Conflict assumes many forms ranging from war and adventure games to family disputes, workplace issues or political debates.

Although engagement in conflict can be positive, most people do not come to mediation with positive expectations. A majority of individuals conceive of conflict as something negative. The perception of a win-lose resolution is often the responsible factor. This is, at least in part, a result of the historical common responses to conflict.

2. COMMON RESPONSES

a. Win–Lose, Right–Wrong Paradigms

For most individuals, the initial means of dispute resolution involves a win-lose approach. This is essentially the fight response which has been used throughout history. The underlying theory is that in order to effect a resolution, one side must win and the other must lose. In many instances, an individual's survival instinct leads to the use of this alternative; the response becomes automatic. The media, sports, and even the courts assist in perpetuating this method.

Derivative, but similar to win-lose is the right-wrong paradigm. When engaged in disputing, a party will immediately consider the other to be "wrong" much effort is often spent in trying to maintain one's "right" position and convince the other party or a decision maker of that contention. Often, either no resolution is reached or a higher authority (parent, teacher, court system) makes a decision as to who is wrong. The loser, however, frequently decides to appeal the decision. In those events, no final resolution is reached in a timely fashion.

b. Avoidance

Another common response to conflict is avoidance. Even when directly faced with conflict, many people continue to ignore it and act as if it doesn't exist. While avoidance may be appropriate in some instances, the end result is that the dispute is never confronted, and therefore never resolved. In some cases, for example, when the parties have a continuing relationship, a lingering unresolved conflict can be quite problematic.

C. EMERGENCE OF ADR

As the United States became industrialized and commerce increased, a greater reliance on the court system to resolve all types of disputes evolved. As litigation grew, so too did concern about the ability of the courts to adequately handle all the disputes. Differing perspectives about the appropriate role of courts in society were also voiced.

In 1976, the Pound Conference, sponsored by the American Bar Association, attempted to address issues of cost and delay in the courts. A variety of initiatives resulted, including the experimental use of ADR in the courts and communities. Courts were urged to offer alternatives to litigation, in part, in response to Professor Frank E. A. Sander's call for a multi-door courthouse in his seminal work, *Varieties of Dispute Processing*.

The goals and objectives of ADR were simple; in most cases, ADR offered resolution to the parties without the cost and delay associated with litigation and its trappings. As various jurisdictions throughout the United States experimented with ADR processes, different methods of ADR procedures emerged as the primary process being utilized. Many courts and statutes across the nation now encourage the use of several ADR processes.

D. ADR PROCESSES AND PROCEDURES

Three primary categories of dispute resolution approaches involve the assistance of a third-party neutral. The third party neutral can be one person or several individuals. Within each category are a variety of different processes. A few are mentioned below so that mediation may be clearly distinguished from them. It is also possible to combine another ADR process with mediation and with each other. Examples of the combination or hybrid processes which involve mediation will be examined in Chapter Twelve.

The first of the three primary categories consists of adjudicative processes, where the neutral third party makes a final, often binding, decision as to the outcome of the dispute. The second category includes evaluative processes, where the neutral(s) provide feedback to the disputing parties (and often their lawyers) about the merits and weaknesses of the case. Alternatively, the evaluation may consist of a sample or advisory jury verdict. This type of evaluative feedback is then used by the parties to continue in negotiation, sometimes directly and other times with assistance, to effectuate a final resolution to the matter. In the third category, facilitative processes, the neutral(s) help the disputing parties achieve a mutually satisfactory resolution by assisting in communication, understanding and problem solving.

1.   PRIVATE JUDGING

One ADR tool falling within the adjudicatory sphere is known as private or special judging. This option allows the parties in litigation to hire a retired or former judge to preside over the trial of a case and render a decision. Several states provide statutory guidance for the procedure, also known as "rent-a-judge." In most cases, the parties must agree to take the matter to the private judge. The private judge can either decide all of the issues or just a portion of the case. While private judging resembles traditional litigation, important differences exist including the expertise of the judge, speed of decision making, and flexibility in rules and procedure. In most instances, however, the special judge can preside only over a bench trial, not a jury trial.

2. ARBITRATION

The most common adjudicatory ADR process is arbitration. Historically, arbitration has been used extensively in the commercial and labor arenas. Arbitration use has expanded over the last two decades and now is utilized in matters ranging from securities to employment to all types of consumer matters.

Arbitrations are generally conducted by a sole arbitrator or a panel of three. In the arbitration process, arbitrators listen to typically adversarial presentations of the case and thereafter render a decision, usually called an award. The parties, either through attorneys or pro se, make the presentations to the arbitrators. Arbitration procedures are generally more formal than most other dispute resolution techniques and allow the presentation of evidence. Experts may also be involved. Although strict adherence to rules such as those governing court procedure and evidence rarely apply in arbitration, there are distinct rules that often control the process. Parties may engage in arbitration pursuant to a contract or by an order or rule of the court. The specific type of arbitration is often dependent on how and when the arbitration is arranged.

a.   Private Contractual Arbitration

In private contractual arbitration, the parties agree in advance to arbitrate should a dispute arise, although it is also possible to agree to private arbitration after a conflict occurs. The outcome or award is generally binding and may be considered more binding than court, as very little opportunity for appeal exists. In most instances, the arbitration clause sets forth the obligation to arbitrate along with details surrounding the proceeding such as selection of arbitrator(s), administrative issues, and governing rules of the process. Once a dispute occurs, one party will generally initiate arbitration. Recently arbitration clauses have begun to include a first step of mediation or direct negotiation prior to arbitration.

b.   Variations

Private contractual arbitration may include variations in the manner in which the process is conducted or the method the award is calculated. This occurs generally at the option and agreement of the parties, or alternatively, in accordance with the specific rules chosen to guide the process. In binding arbitration, these variations include final offer arbitration, also known as baseball arbitration, and high-low arbitration. In final offer arbitration, each side submits a proposed award to the arbitrators, who must ultimately choose one or the other. High-low arbitration involves the parties setting the boundaries of the award. Finally, arbitration can be used with mediation, usually termed med-arb, where if an agreement is not reached through mediation, the neutral "changes hats" and issues an arbitration decision. Often criticized, med-arb is discussed more extensively in Chapter Twelve on hybrid process.

c. Court–Annexed Arbitration

Court programs have also used arbitration to expedite settlement of cases. Because the litigants have already involved a court, they retain their right to a trial. Therefore, unless otherwise explicitly agreed to by the parties, court-annexed arbitration must be non-binding. This means that after the arbitrator renders the award, parties remain free to reject it and continue with the lawsuit. In non-binding arbitration, a party rejecting the arbitrator's award may be penalized as an incentive for settlement. For example, suppose that in a court program, the arbitrator renders a non-binding award in the amount of $58,500 for the plaintiff. If the plaintiff rejects the award, and proceeds to trial, he must achieve a better result (sometimes characterized by percentages (e.g. 10%) or he must pay defense costs and attorneys' fees. Negotiating a settlement that varies somewhat from the award is another option available to the parties.

3. NEUTRAL CASE EVALUATION

Neutral case evaluation is a process in which a neutral party provides the lawyers and litigants with feedback relating to the merits of the case.

After each side presents their version of the case to one or more third party neutrals, the strengths and weaknesses of each party's case are evaluated. In doing so, the neutral often predicts what a likely court outcome may be, usually providing a decision in terms of percentages rather than a precise outcome. For example, the plaintiff has an eighty percent likelihood of prevailing on the issue of liability.

The primary purpose of neutral case evaluation is to provide an objective, non-binding, confidential evaluation of the case which may be used by the lawyers and clients to further settlement negotiations. Common terms used to indicate case evaluation include early neutral evaluation (ENE), neutral case evaluation, and moderated settlement conference.

4. SUMMARY JURY TRIAL

Another evaluative procedure is the Summary Jury Trial (SJT). The SJT is a non-binding process, either ordered by the court or requested by the parties, where a judge presides over a very abbreviated trial. During the SJT, after making an opening statement, each attorney summarizes in a narrative manner what the evidence would show if the case went to trial before a "real" jury. In many cases, the court will also permit live testimony, although it is usually very limited in duration. Generally only one witness per side is permitted. The jurors, many of whom may not know that the procedure is for settlement purposes, then render a "verdict" which is used by the parties to assist them in reaching a final settlement of the case.

5. MINI–TRIAL

The mini-trial, a misnomer as it is not at all trial-like, is delineated as a separate and distinct ADR process in many jurisdictions. The mini-trial is technically a hybrid of a number of ADR processes including negotiation, case evaluation, and mediation. Usually reserved for large business disputes, the mini-trial brings together high-level executives, along with counsel. With a focus on business, the pragmatic basis of the process is the realization that it is often mutually beneficial for principals and their companies to resolve matters without protracted litigation. Preservation of the business relationship is generally a key element in the resolution. The neutral expert advisor presides over and guides the process. After several hours of information exchange, the client representatives meet, generally without the lawyers or the neutral, in an attempt to negotiate a resolution. If an agreement is not reached, the neutral may provide an evaluation, as well as engage in a facilitative role in an effort to effectuate a resolution.

6. FACILITATIVE PROCESSES

In the facilitative processes, the neutral does not render a decision or an evaluation. Rather, the neutral provides assistance to the parties, so that they may reach a mutually acceptable agreement. A distinguishing characteristic is that these processes are much less adversarial than adjudicative or evaluative approaches, as one of the goals in facilitation is to reach mutually acceptable resolutions. Three common facilitative processes are mediation, conciliation, and consensus building. These processes will be discussed throughout the remainder of this book.

7.   COMBINATIONS AND HYBRID PROCESSES

Many, if not most, of the ADR processes can be combined with one another in a variety of fashions. In complex cases, there is often a need for mixed approaches. For instance, in a complicated high-dollar construction case, a neutral case evaluation or summary jury trial may help narrow the bargaining range and provide helpful feedback. The parties will then have a more efficient and productive mediation.

Each ADR process, separately or in conjunction with another, can also be used to resolve only a portion of a case or matter. For example, in a personal injury case, parties may be at an impasse on a liability issue, although they can stipulate to the amount of damages. A neutral evaluation or an arbitrator's decision on liability may overcome such an obstacle. A closer examination of the ADR processes used in conjunction with mediation is provided in Chapter Twelve.

E. ELECTING OR SELECTING THE APPROPRIATE PROCESS

As the menu or selection of ADR processes has enlarged, focus has been placed on just how each process assists parties in reaching resolution. Courts, lawyers and ADR program administrators often discuss which process is "best suited" for a particular type of case. Attempts have been made to match ADR processes with specific dispute characteristics. Two questions have been identified as initial considerations: (1) which process would best achieve the client's or a party's goals and objectives; and (2) what would assist in overcoming the barriers in the parties' direct negotiations (Sander & Goldberg). As these issues are considered, a need for prioritization of both goals and barriers may also exist.

Understanding process selection and preparation for the chosen process are very important components of dispute resolution and in particular, representing clients competently. This knowledge is also important for the mediator who may refer the parties to another process if the matter is not settled at mediation. In other cases, a mediator may need to transition to another neutral role, should an agreement not be reached. Several ethical provisions for mediators advise mediators to be cautious about "changing hats" and occupying a different dispute resolution role. Experts hold that this should be done only in extreme cases and only with all participants' knowledge and consent.

Current informal and anecdotal reports indicate that most ADR procedures have been successful in effectuating settlements in a variety of cases. After consideration of the client's objectives and an analysis of the available dispute resolution techniques, it is likely that an appropriate procedure can either be found or designed. Because of its flexible nature and lack of coercion, mediation is often a first step.

References

Frank E.A. Sander, Varieties of Dispute Processing in the Pound Conference: Perspectives on Justice in the Future (A. Leo Levin & Russell R. Wheeler, eds., 1979).

Frank E. A. Sander & Stephen B. Goldberg, Fitting the Forum to the Fuss: A User–Friendly Guide to Selecting an ADR Procedure, 10 Negotiation J. 49 (1994).

Bibliography

Edward Brunet & Charles B. Craven, Alternative Dispute Resolution: The Advocates Perspective (1997).

Morton Deutsch, The Resolution of Conflict: Constructive and Destructive Processes (1973).

Harry T. Edwards, Alternative Dispute Resolution: Panacea or Anathema, 99 Harv. L. Rev. 668 (1986).

Lon Fuller, The Forms and Limits of Adjudication, 92 Harv. L. Rev. 353 (1978).

Stephen B. Goldberg, Frank, E. A. Sander & Nancy H. Rogers, Dispute Resolution: Negotiation, Mediation and Other Processes (3rd ed. 1999).

Joyce L. Hocker & William W. Wilmot, Interpersonal Conflict (4th ed. 1995).

Jacqueline Nolan–Haley, ADR in a Nutshell (2d ed. 2001).

Alan Scott Rau, Edward F. Sherman & Scott R. Peppet, Processes of Dispute Resolution, The Role of Lawyers (3rd ed. 2002).

Judith Resnick, Many Doors? Closing Doors? Alternative Dispute Resolution and Adjudication, 10 Ohio St. J. on Disp. Resol. 211 (1995).

Jack M. Sabatino, ADR as Litigation Lite: Procedural and Evidentiary Norms Embedded Within Alternative Dispute Resolution, 47 Emory L.J. 1289 (1998).

Andrea Kupfer Schneider, Building a Pedagogy of Problem–Solving: Learning to Choose Among ADR Processes, 5 Harv. Negotiation L. Rev. 113 (2002).

Jeffrey W. Stempel, Reflections on Judicial ADR and the Multi–Door Courthouse at Twenty: Fait Accompli, Failed Overture or Fledgling Adulthood, 11 Ohio St. J. on Disp. Resol. 297 (1996).

Thomas J. Stipanowich, The Multi–Door Contract and Other Possibilities, 13 Ohio St. J. on Disp. Resol. 303 (1998).

Katherine Stone, Private Justice: The Law of Alternative Dispute Resolution (2000).

Stephen J. Ware, Alternative Dispute Resolution (2001).

The Handbook of Conflict Resolution (Morton Deutsch & Peter T. Coleman eds., (2000).

CHAPTER 2

THE MEDIATION PROCESS

A. HISTORICAL PERSPECTIVES

Although a detailed, thorough history of mediation is not necessary to gain a full understanding of the process, knowledge of the historical basis and philosophies of mediation can be helpful to students, practitioners, and participants of the process. For instance, when facing differences in approaches of mediators, some of the variation can be traced to the original trainings and philosophies of the process. It is also important to understand that very diverse perspectives of mediation exist.

1. ANCIENT INTERNATIONAL EXAMPLES

It is clear that various forms of mediation are deep-rooted in human interaction. Mediation is broadly defined as a process where an impartial person assists others in reaching a resolution of a conflict or dispute. In fact, there is even some evidence of mediation in deity interaction. References to ancient types of conciliatory approaches are plentiful and are often grounded in a combination of culture and religious teachings.

16

a. Biblical References

In the Judeo–Christian tradition, scriptures provide references to mediation. According to the Bible, Jesus was to serve as the mediator between God and man. (1 Timothy 2:5–6) This idea carried over to the clergy, who often saw their role as mediators between God and the congregation. As a result, many Jewish communities in Biblical times used mediation to resolve religious and political disputes.

b. Greece

In ancient Greece, public arbitration was viewed as a primary dispute resolution method. Upon closer examination, the process was more like a mediation, since the neutral would first try and persuade the parties to reach a voluntary resolution before he would issue a final decision.

c. China

China likely has the longest history of mediation use. Reports of mediation use in China date back over 4,000 years. Much of the Chinese use of mediation is traced to religious and cultural philosophies. Historically, the Chinese have rejected legal remedies, instead placing emphasis on mediation and maintaining relationships based upon moral edicts. Even with legal reforms taking place, mediation remains a primary form of dispute resolution. For example, there are nearly ten million mediators in China, while there are only approximately 110,000 lawyers. (Clark)

2. UNITED STATES

Admittedly, other cultures have had a more extensive history of mediation and facilitation, producing greater experience with informal types of dispute processing than the United States. Yet, for the most part, it is the modern mediation methods of the United States that have recently been looked to as other jurisdictions throughout the world establish mediation projects and programs. In other words, it is this more contemporary use of mediation that is being exported for use in communities, as well as in legalized disputes.

a. Colonial ADR

Early mediation use in the United States took place in the colonies. The use of informal dispute resolution was based, at least in part, upon recognition by the colonists that peaceful coexistence was valuable. The importance of cooperation among the new settlers influenced their decision to use a non-adversarial method for dispute resolution. As commerce and colonization expanded, however, the common law and adversarial system was imported from England to fill needs made apparent by commercialism of the new states. Yet early on, the downside to the litigation system was recognized in United States history as President Lincoln warned, "Discourage litigation. Persuade your neighbors to compromise whenever you can. Point out to them how the nominal winner is often a real loser—in fees, expenses and waste of time."

b. Labor

Initial Congressional legislation which provided for mediation was the Railroad Act in the 1800's and later the Taft–Hartley Act in 1947. The Taft–Hartley Act established the Federal Mediation and Conciliation Service "to prevent or minimize interruptions in the free flow of commerce growing out of labor disputes, to assist parties to labor disputes in industries affecting commerce, to settle such disputes through ... mediation." 29 U.S.C. § 173(a). As a result of such efforts, mediation was used primarily in the collective bargaining arena. In particular, the focus of mediators was to assist in the resolution of labor disputes and community-wide civil rights disputes.

c. Early Centers

In the late 1960s and early 1970s, a number of experimental mediation programs were developed. Many experts believe the origins of the field of community dispute resolution are within the Community Relations Service, a federal program established through the Civil Rights Act of 1964 to prevent violence and encourage constructive dialogue in communities. The Philadelphia Municipal Court Arbitration Tribunal, perhaps the first center established, was created in 1969 through the joint efforts of the American Arbitration Association, the Philadelphia District Attorney, and the local Municipal Court. Disputants were offered the option of binding arbitration for their cases instead of facing a trial.

Other experimental mediation centers were funded by a variety of sources, including the Law Enforcement Assistance Administration (LEAA), a former division of the United States Department of Justice. As centers developed and societal emphasis was placed upon party participation and particularly, individual empowerment, the primary process for dispute resolution became mediation.

i.   Columbus, Ohio Night Prosecutor Program

The City Prosecutor's Office in Columbus, Ohio, with the help of LEAA funding, developed the Night Prosecutor Program (NPP) in 1971. This program provided disputing parties, who made allegations of criminal misdemeanor activity, with the option of mediation. The first mediators used by the project were local law professors, and as the program expanded, law students were trained to serve as mediators. The NPP served as a model for the development of a number of other programs throughout the United States, and eventually the world.

ii.   Rochester, New York

In Rochester, New York, a dispute resolution center focusing primarily on the mediation process was established in 1972. This center was sponsored by the American Arbitration Association, and its immediate goal was to assist families in managing the conflict related to school integration. The Rochester program also served as a model and was the impetus behind the expansion of New York's network of mediation centers.

iii.   San Francisco Boards

The San Francisco Community Board Program differs from a number of other early mediation programs in that it was truly sponsored by the community. Unlike the previously highlighted programs, which were connected in different ways to the legal system, the Community Boards program was a grass roots effort.

d. Pound Conference

In 1976, a number of lawyers, judges, law professors and court administrators came together at the Pound Conference, to examine problems within the current legal system. Two distinct but related developments in mediation resulted from the Pound Conference. The first consisted of the establishment of three experimental "Neighborhood Justice Centers" which paved the way for the creation of hundreds, perhaps thousands of community dispute resolution centers throughout the United States and now the world. The other mediation-related result consisted of efforts to provide ADR options, including mediation, in the court system. This was largely a response to Professor Frank E.A. Sander's work, which called for a "multi-door courthouse," where citizens would be given a number of options for dispute resolution in addition to litigation.

i. Neighborhood Justice Centers

The first three Neighborhood Justice Centers, funded by LEAA, were established in Atlanta, Los Angeles, and Kansas City. The primary goal was to establish model centers for community dispute resolution, where disputes could be resolved before they escalated, thereby reducing demand on the courts. All three centers chose the mediation process, although Kansas City experimented with arbitration as well. The mediators were volunteers, with a variety of backgrounds. The centers tried various approaches to case intake and selection, ranging from police referrals to public awareness efforts. Evaluations of the centers were quite favorable, both in resolving cases and party satisfaction with the process.

Over the last three decades, the growth of community dispute resolution centers has been remarkable. Many states have statewide, as well as local or specialized centers, which provide mediation services.

ii.   Court Programs

Some of the very early programs using mediation in court cases can be traced to work with the community mediation centers. Initially, the Department of Justice evaluated these community mediation programs. When found to be quite successful, an exploration for mediation use in small claims disputes was urged.

Another influence on courts emerged from the involvement of judges and lawyers with the community centers. Some attorneys and judges, inspired by the Pound Conference, began to explore options for court-annexed ADR, especially mediation, indepen-

dent of the centers. This work led to the establishment of court-connected mediation programs.

B. MODERN MEDIATION MOVEMENT: POST POUND

The Pound Conference is noted as the beginning
of the "Modern Mediation Movement." Early mediation use, as described previously in this chapter,
was available, but scant. Since Pound, however, a
vast increase in the use of mediation has occurred.

From 1976 through the early part of the twenty-
first century, mediation has passed through at least
three distinct stages of development. The initial
phase was one of experimentation. From the mid-
seventies through the early eighties, mediation was
tried in experimental projects and pilot programs.
Most of these were community-based, rather than
court-annexed, programs. Use of mediation in small
claims courts, however, was occurring in conjunction with the creation and expansion of many of the
centers. About a decade later came a time of rapid
implementation, where courts and communities
were active in establishing a large number of programs. These programs were generally implemented
without consideration of the numerous legal, ethical, and practical issues that mediation is currently
facing. Finally, over the last few years the mediation profession has been involved in a time of regulation. Many of the legal, policy, philosophical, and
practical issues surrounding mediation use are ripe
for contemplation and decision making. Regulation
in this context covers a wide range of issues. These

include such matters as the management of cases which participate in mediation; how the mediation process is conducted; the conduct of the participants in mediation; and mediator quality control. These matters are discussed further in subsequent chapters.

Since the time of the Pound Conference, phenomenal growth has occurred in both the court-annexed arena as well as in the community mediation centers. This dual expansion, while sharing an origin, has followed somewhat different paths. Hundreds of court programs exist in general jurisdiction state courts throughout the nation. Additional mediation programs exist throughout the federal system at both the trial and appellate court levels. Mediation also takes place in small claims courts, as well as other specialized courts, such as the housing courts in New York City. Use of mediation in criminal law is another growing area. Wide diversity exists in mediation use. Court programs, along with community and specialized applications, continue to evolve. Furthermore, mediation use is now prevalent in government as well as the private sector.

1.   COMMUNITY PERSPECTIVES

Much of the impetus for the proliferation of mediation programs originated within the community mediation centers. The development of these centers came from a variety of sources, and the work at these centers was both at a grass roots level and integrated within the court system. Today there are likely over five hundred community dispute resolution centers in the United States. They handle a variety of cases ranging from the neighborhood barking dog dispute to court-annexed pending litigation cases.

Community mediation is characterized by a number of features. These include the use of trained community volunteers; sponsorship by a private non-profit or public agency with a governing or advisory board; representation of the diversity of the community served; direct access of mediation to the public; the provision of services to the public regardless of the ability to pay; promotion of collaborative community relationships; encouragement of public awareness; intervention during the early stages of the conflict; and providing an alternative to the judicial system at any stage of the conflict. See National Association for Community Mediation, Overview of Community Mediation (1998) (available online at *www.igc.org/nafcm/overview.html*).

Volunteer mediators come from a wide variety of educational and occupational backgrounds, as well as different socioeconomic, racial, and ethnic groups. These volunteers often include lawyers and law students, human resources personnel, CPAs, social workers, businesspersons, retired persons, teachers, urban planners, clergypersons, and community activists.

Community mediation centers are sponsored and funded by an assortment of entities. These may include public and private grants, state bar associations, filing fees for ADR services, and government monies. Funding is often a difficult matter for the centers. As options vary according to state and locality, several centers nationwide lack the necessary funds to operate as actively as they would like. Many of the more successful centers are part of statewide coordination efforts and receive political support. In some states, DRCs have begun to charge for mediation services and mediation training. Most centers continue to rely heavily on volunteers, paying only the full-time staff members.

2. COURT PERSPECTIVES AND ADMINISTRATION

a. Generally

Although immediately following the Pound Conference, primary focus was on the creation of community dispute resolution centers, some minor interest in mediation was demonstrated by lawyers and judges. In particular, in jurisdictions where community centers had been established, local lawyers and judges became active in the work of the centers and knowledgeable about mediation. Curiosity about the possibility of using mediation in pending litigation grew. Activity of state and local bar associations (as outlined below) was also a critical component in the development of court programs.

Now, mediation is utilized in all types of courts: state and federal, trial and appellate. Although current debate surrounds objectives of the process, and different approaches to court-annexed mediation exist, the number of programs continues to grow. A number of court-annexed or connected mediation programs are very organized and employ administrative staff. Others are active, but how mediation is recommended or even mandated is entirely dependant upon each individual judge.

b. Settlement Weeks

The concept behind Settlement Weeks is simple: during the time when the courthouse is not being used for trial, specifically during judicial conferences, courtrooms, jury rooms and other conference rooms can be made available to litigants for settlement discussions. In two different jurisdictions, California and Ohio, the idea of using the courthouse to focus on settlement was the impetus behind the initial establishment of settlement weeks. Since the mid-eighties, settlement weeks have been very successful not only in terms of resolving cases, but also in serving as an introduction to mediation and settlement to a number of people. In a number of jurisdictions, settlement weeks were responsible for the development of early mediation use and the growth of court-connected mediation programs.

Settlement weeks are voluntary in some jurisdictions and statutorily mandated in others. In a number of jurisdictions such as Florida, Texas and California, courts refer or mandate mediation use on a regular basis. As some say, ''Every week is settlement week.'' As a consequence, the need no longer exists for specific settlement weeks to the extent it once did.

c. Family Law Mediation

With the advent of no fault and "do-it-yourself" divorces, family law was ripe for mediation use. These factors, combined with the recognition that an adversarial approach to divorce was not always in the best interests of the parties, led to the implementation of divorce mediation. The late 1970s and early 1980s saw a dramatic increase in the use of mediation to effectuate divorce settlement. As the initial intent of the process was to avoid the court system, early mediators would assist in resolving the terms of the divorce, as well as drafting the documents necessary to finalize the divorce. Mediators were often lawyers or therapists. In instances where the mediator was not a lawyer, this resulted in some claims of unauthorized practice of law. Moreover, concerns arose that the parties did not know their legal rights and that women, in particular, were disadvantaged through the mediation process. (Grillo).

In many states, the first, and in some cases, the only, use of mediation in pending litigation has been in family law cases. Mediation in contested custody matters is mandatory in several states. Currently, several approaches to divorce mediation exist. All types of family restructuring matters may be mediated, including separation and custody matters in same gender relationships, as well as cases involving children's protective services.

3. ROLE OF BAR ASSOCIATIONS

National, state and local bar associations have played a large role in the encouragement of mediation. It was particularly important that the organized bar supported mediation, as many lawyers and judges were initially hesitant about its use in litigation. In a few jurisdictions, some lawyers are still reluctant to use mediation. However, as mediation use is mandated and legal education continues to introduce mediation early in a lawyer's career, increased acceptance is likely.

a. ABA

The American Bar Association (ABA) has been instrumental in promoting the use of mediation, both in court-related matters as well as in community centers. In 1978, the ABA created a committee to examine dispute resolution. The committee, initially considered temporary, was named the Special Committee on Resolution of Minor Disputes. At that time, the idea of using mediation for large litigation matters was not considered. The work of the committee primarily consisted of information dissemination to lawyers and judges, as well as the general public. Over time, however, the committee's focus changed, and it began to provide technical assistance to a number of jurisdictions that demonstrated interest in establishing court-connected dispute resolution programs with primary focus on mediation.

As interest in mediation and ADR increased, the committee recognized the potential for greater involvement by additional members. In 1993, the committee was abolished when the ABA created a separate Dispute Resolution Section, which now boasts over 7,000 in membership. The ABA's Dispute Resolution Section is active in a variety of educational efforts. These include national legal education programs, lobbying efforts, further exploration of mediation use and addressing difficult issues in the field of dispute resolution.

b. State and Local Bar Associations

While the work of the ABA was quite valuable in increasing interest and involvement in mediation among lawyers and judges, it was often those efforts on a local level that really contributed to widespread adoption of many mediation programs. For example, in Texas, the early work of the Houston Bar Association's Committee on Dispute Resolution led to the creation of a Neighborhood Justice Center. Neighborhood Justice Centers were later followed by statewide dispute resolution centers, as well as comprehensive legislation which led to court-annexed projects.

In many locations, committee work became so significant and interest increased so rapidly that the state bar associations created special sections of dispute resolution, which today continue the work started by these small committees. Like the ABA, state and local bar section work involves continuing public awareness efforts. Generally, the sections hold an educational program for members once a year, and they regularly provide assistance to the courts and other practitioners in terms of the development of ADR programs, particularly in the court-annexed arena.

4. LEGAL AND GRADUATE EDUCATION

Prior to the modern mediation movement, negotiation courses were offered in a few law schools, but they were not regarded as a common part of the curriculum. Often negotiation was included as a part of a client interviewing and counseling course. Arbitration was likely studied in the labor law arena, but distinct dispute resolution courses were rare. As interest in mediation surged, activity among academics, primarily those in legal education, grew. Separate law school courses were offered, beginning with a dispute resolution overview and negotiation. Currently, at least 830 dispute resolution courses are offered at 182 ABA accredited law schools. Courses range from the theoretical to the practical. They include selections such as ADR process and policy, mediation, arbitration, advanced dispute techniques, and public policy mediation.

Additionally, there has been a simultaneous focus on clinical, practical legal education. Consequently, the number of schools offering clinical experiences in mediation has also grown. In mediation clinics, law students conduct actual mediations, and a few even provide students the opportunity to represent clients at a mediation. Several law schools offer specializations in Dispute Resolution noted by a separate certificate, and a few law schools offer an L.L.M. degree in dispute resolution.

The interdisciplinary nature of mediation is being increasingly recognized as many of these programs are starting to include courses outside the law school curriculum. In addition, the dispute resolution courses in the law school are frequently made available to graduate students not enrolled in law school. In a number of universities, ADR courses are offered on a cross-disciplinary track. Additionally, several colleges and universities are beginning to offer specialized undergraduate or graduate degrees in conflict resolution.

Mediation can be viewed as a process of creative problem solving. Legal education has recently begun to focus on a more expansive role for the lawyer—one as problem solver. As the role of lawyers expands and evolves to include non-adversarial problem-solving services, many of the principles of mediation will likely be playing an even greater role in the educational sphere.

5. GOVERNMENT

Some of the early work in the public arena involved the Federal Mediation and Conciliation Service. National, state and local governments have also employed mediation in a variety of contexts. Early work in the area at the national level began with the Administrative Conference of the United States. The Administrative Conference was active in the education of federal agencies about dispute resolution options. The Conference also designed programs and assisted a number of agencies in the use of mediation-like processes in their work. Mediation use was included as a dispute resolution tool as well as in a more preventative manner in rule making.

The Department of Justice was also involved in starting pilot programs for ADR in Atlanta, Kansas City, and Los Angeles. Many organizations including governmental agencies at both the state and local level, were initially funded by the Hewlett Foundation. The Foundation allocated funds to various groups involved in the practice or research of mediation. Other states, encouraged by developments in dispute resolution by the ABA and the Neighborhood Justice Centers, began statewide ADR initiatives and set up state offices of Dispute Resolution.

6. PRIVATIZATION

The private sector was active in the promotion of mediation as well. Benefits of saving time and money were highlighted, as businesses and corporations were urged to use mediation and other ADR processes in resolving disputes. While the initial focus was primarily on costs savings, the opportunity to maintain business relationships through mediation use became prominent.

In the business world, a vast array of disputes can benefit from mediation. These include direct business disputes, conflict in employment matters and consumer issues. Today, rather than wait until a dispute has arisen, a number of businesses utilize ADR clauses in contracts, increasingly specifying mediation as the chosen process. The more common uses of mediation clauses are for disputes involving consumers and employees. Often this aspect of mediation use occurs prior to the institution of legal action or as a condition precedent to arbitration.

Privatization of mediation is an important factor in the development of mediation as a separate profession. In many locations, individuals serve as mediators on a full-time basis. Mediation is no longer seen as a corollary practice to law, but instead it is recognized as its own independent profession.

C. BENEFITS OF MEDIATION

The use of mediation is appropriate in so many different and varied contexts; attempting to describe all of them would be nearly impossible. At one time there were certain types of disputes that many experts stated were inappropriate for mediation. Over the last several years, however, mediation has been used effectively in nearly all types of cases and matters. These include matters such as children's protective services cases, bankruptcy cases, large environmental disputes, mass tort claims, and victim-offender matters, including homicides and other serious crimes. In addition to the type of case, many other factors are indicators of mediation use. This widespread acceptance of mediation is due in large part to the numerous advantages of the process. As information about mediation is disseminated and the general public becomes more familiar with the process, knowledge of fundamental benefits can be beneficial to expanded use.

1. TIME AND COST SAVINGS

The legal system can be an appropriate and effective method of dispute resolution, but it is also time and cost consuming. This focus, the cost and delay of litigation, has stimulated court reform, at least in civil cases. In most instances, mediation may provide a more timely resolution. Because mediation is informal and flexible, strict procedures which draw out litigation matters are avoided. Where time is of the essence, particularly in cases where a lawsuit has not been filed, a mediation could take place in a matter of days or even hours. In most instances, a speedy resolution also results in a monetary savings. Parties save the expense for extensive litigation, including costs for experts, depositions, and attorneys' fees. By reaching a prompt resolution, much of the emotional drain from engagement in continual conflict is also avoided.

2. CONFIDENTIALITY AND PRIVACY

The courthouse is a public institution, and when lawsuits are filed, all of the activity of the courtroom is open to the general public. Exceptions do exist, such as in the case of minors, but they are rare. In some cases, the parties may wish to publicize what has happened. For those individuals, the open courtroom is an advantageous and strategic. In many cases, though, the parties would prefer to keep the details of their dispute private. Mediation allows all facets of a matter to be revealed and discussed privately. Individuals who may be uncomfortable discussing personal matters in an open courtroom can be more relaxed in mediation's private setting. Moreover, as will be discussed in greater detail in Chapter Seven concerning confidentiality, the parties are generally assured that the mediator will not make any public disclosures. Institutions and large corporations may also have a keen interest in confidentiality and, for example, may wish to prohibit a party from disclosing the type or amount of settlement.

3. SELF–DETERMINATION

When parties participate in an adjudicative procedure such as trial, arbitration, or administrative hearing, a third party makes the decision for them. A ruling is issued with which they must comply. In mediation, on the other hand, the parties are the final decision makers. A core feature of mediation is that the parties make decisions, including whether they wish to ultimately resolve the matter, as well as the terms of any resolution. This is part of the empowerment ethic inherent in mediation, and it is emphasized in several applications of the process. Because of personal involvement in the process and the resolution, the parties possess a psychological ownership, making it more likely that they will comply with any agreement reached. Most definitions of mediation carefully state that the mediator should not substitute his judgment for that of the parties. Mediator standards, such as codes of ethics, warn against coercion from the mediator and emphasize the need and importance of party self-determination.

4.   AUTHORIZING AND ACKNOWLEDGING FEELINGS AND EMOTIONS

When individuals engage in conflict, whether it be personal or professional, frequently strong emotions and feelings surface. Legal proceedings do not focus on emotion, but instead look at most conflicts through the prism of relevancy, admissibility and procedure. Mediation, however, values the expression, understanding and release of emotions. Mediation presumes that the expression and understanding of a party's emotional needs may be a condition precedent to settlement. Mediation also values basic human expressions, such as an apology or act of forgiveness. Emotional issues may be found in almost every type of dispute, but they are quite common in family law disputes, employment matters, and personal injury cases in which a loved one has been seriously injured or has died.

5.   OPPORTUNITY FOR PRESERVING RELATIONSHIPS

In many cases, the parties who are involved in a conflict have had a long-standing relationship. This association may be personal or professional, intimate or unemotional. Examples of these relationships include neighbors, family members, employment situations, consumers, and businesses. In many instances, the parties, though upset about the dispute, still hope to continue their affiliation. In some circumstances, the nature of the relationship may need modification or alteration, yet it is ultimately preserved. For example, in the family law setting, the parenting role will persist even if the parents are proceeding through a divorce. In the business context, all parties may profit by continuing their association. Mediation provides an opportunity to explore various ways a relationship might continue. Mediators are trained to look for potential mutual as well as complementary interests, and to be considerate of the parties' desire to preserve relationships.

6. POTENTIAL FOR CREATIVE SOLUTIONS

When disputes are resolved through court or another adjudicatory process, the customary result is a judgment in favor of one party and against another. Usually the judgment orders the party against whom it is issued to pay to the other a sum of money. Only in rare instances such as cases where the parties have sought injunctive relief, do courts issue rulings that require that the parties do or not do something. On the other hand, through mediation, the potential for imaginative and creative solutions is much greater. The parties are able to construct solutions more suitable for them; they are not governed by restrictive adherence to the law. Many mediators encourage parties "to think outside the box" and to brainstorm potential options in order to maximize creativity.

7. PROCESS FLEXIBILITY
AND INFORMALITY

Mediation, by design, is flexible. Relatively few rules guide the actions of the mediator with regard to how the process might unfold. As such, mediation is a more informal process. In mediation, parties are encouraged to discuss any issue and to express themselves freely. Few rules direct the specific conduct of the mediator, particularly with regard to tasks, responsibilities and actions. While guidelines do exist, such guidelines are rarely precise or detailed. Mediators often need to make instantaneous decisions about an approach or process modification. Because mediation deals with human nature and individual behavior, the mediator must be adaptable to the various situations he confronts. Individuals are encouraged to discuss a matter or dispute in detail with the mediator. Often, in a formal setting such as a courtroom or a deposition, people are intimidated and hesitate to talk freely. On the other hand, mediation offers the opportunity for informality and maximizes communication and participation. Parties are more at ease, and participate more fully in the process.

8. AVOIDANCE OF LEGAL PRECEDENT

In some cases, lawsuits are brought to change the law or to right a wrong. In those types of lawsuits, it is essential that the court make a ruling and set a precedent. In the majority of lawsuits, however, precedent is not the primary focus. As a result, mediation is often appropriate. In fact, parties may desire to settle a particular dispute in order to avoid setting what may be a negative precedent.

The desire for precedent should not be confused with a "matter of principle." A party may be involved in a conflict because his or her specific principles are involved. A mediator may deal effectively with those personal principles, which are different than a desire to change a body of law or public policy.

D. DISSECTION OF THE MEDIATION PROCESS

In order to become familiar with specific aspects of the mediator's work, it is helpful to break down the process into distinct stages. Examining the various stages or components of the process, as well as the accompanying skills which mediators utilize, may assist in learning both the theoretical and practical aspects of mediation.

Over the years, numerous outlines or views of mediation have evolved. A variety of stages or segments of the mediation process have been outlined. These range from a four or five-stage model to one with ten or more stages. The majority of models, however, set forth similar basic concepts and encompass recognition of the inherent fluidity of the process.

1. STAGES AND COMPONENTS

One view separates mediation into nine distinct stages, with four additional optional components. (Kovach) While each stage is considered important to the mediation process, in some cases the stages overlap or fold into one another. Resolution may be reached without experiencing every stage. Optional stages are listed in parentheses. Employment of these optional stages is quite common, and depends upon the parties, the nature of the matter and the mediator's style.

One basic model is as follows:

Preliminary Arrangements

Mediator's Introduction

Opening Statements by Parties

(Ventilation)

Information Gathering

Issue and Interest Identification

(Agenda Setting)

(Caucus)

Option Generation

(Reality Testing)

Bargaining and Negotiation

Agreement

Closure

The preliminary arrangement stage encompasses everything that occurs prior to the actual mediation session. This includes matters of referral and selection of the mediator, the determination of those attending the mediation, fees and allocation of settlement authority. Decisions about the process itself including the approach of the mediator and role of the lawyers, should also be considered as part of preliminary arrangements. As these preliminary matters set forth the parameters of the process, their impact may be considerable.

During the mediator's introduction, all participants are introduced. The mediator then describes his role, explains the mediation process, and sets out any ground rules that guide the process. The mediator may also identify and briefly discuss the benefits of the process. Legal parameters, such as confidentiality and enforceability of settlement, are outlined. Goals and objectives from the mediator's standpoint are also included, along with housekeeping details.

Following the mediator's introduction, each side presents opening remarks. In making opening statements, the parties and/or their representatives provide an uninterrupted presentation of their views of the case or dispute. This opening statement stage provides a time for parties to fully express and explain to the mediator, and, more importantly, to each other, how they view the dispute in their own words. In most instances, little restriction is placed on the opening statements. In complex, multi-party cases, however, time limits may be necessary.

After all participants and their representatives, if appropriate, provide opening remarks, the mediator undertakes an information gathering process. The parties may also make inquiries of one another. Allocating time for the parties to vent their emotions about the dispute is often another critical component in mediation.

As additional information is disclosed, the mediator attempts to identify exactly what issues are in dispute. The mediator frequently restates the issues in more neutral language, which allows for enhanced communication and understanding, as well as increased openness to options for resolution. Determining the underlying interests of the parties will also be a focus of the mediator's efforts. The mediator may then move the parties toward generating ideas, options, or alternatives that might help resolve the matter. In order to identify some options for resolution, the mediator may request that the parties engage in a brainstorming session where a number of different alternatives may be explored.

Often during these two stages (identifying issues and interests and option generation) the mediator meets privately with each party. This is known as a caucus or private session. The mediator uses the private caucuses to gain additional information from the parties, which may or may not be shared with the other party, depending upon the style of mediator, the mediator's strategy, local practice and custom, and any controlling law.

In complex cases, the mediator may also want to set a detailed agenda. This agenda outlines in a specific order which issues will be addressed. A variety of strategies for agenda setting have been identified, most notably by Christopher Moore. These include discussing easier items first, ranking the items by importance, tackling the most difficult issue first, or alternating issue selection. As with many aspects of mediation, there are benefits, along with disadvantages to each approach. Some require more structure; others allow for increased flexibility. Often more than one strategy is used. (Moore).

Once the potential options for settlement have been identified by the participants and the mediator, a negotiation ensues. During this "give and take" part of mediation, the mediator assists the parties in contemplating trade-offs. As part of this process, the mediator may also engage in "reality testing." Each side is challenged about the realistic possibilities of attaining their goals, which can help them move away from unrealistic positions.

If these negotiations result in an agreement, the mediator will outline it, and in most instances, draft either the complete agreement or a memorandum of settlement. If no agreement is reached, the mediator will usually make some restatement of where the parties are, in terms of potential settlement. The final stage of most mediation is closure, although in some models subsequent action is required by the mediator regarding follow up and enforcement of the agreement.

Although composed of stages, mediation is simultaneously designed to be flexible, and often variation in one or more of the stages is necessary. Some of the stages may overlap, and frequently the mediator must revisit one or more of the stages.

Additional models provide diversity in how the mediation process may be approached. For example, in one of the early works on mediation, Christopher Moore described the process as including twelve stages, five of which take place prior to the actual mediation session. Pre-session events include collecting background information, designing a plan for mediation, and building trust and cooperation.

One of the oldest ongoing programs, the Columbus, Ohio Night Prosecutor Program, which is affiliated with the Center for Dispute Resolution at Capital University Law and Graduate Center, utilizes a seven-stage model of mediation. The stages are Introduction; Problem Determination; Summarizing; Issue Identification; Generation and Evaluation of Alternatives; Selection of Appropriate Alternatives; and Conclusion.

Folberg and Taylor in their work on divorce mediation also use a seven-stage model, consisting of the following components: Introduction; Fact Finding and Isolation of Issues; Creation of Options and Alternatives; Negotiation and Decision Making; Clarification and Writing a Plan; Legal Review and Processing; and Implementation, Review, and Revision. They acknowledge that not all stages will be completed in every case and that other authors and practitioners may divide the stages differently or use different labels. Compared with most models, this version is "bottom heavy." The majority of models do not focus on activity after an agreement is reached. (Folberg & Taylor).

In a legal model of mediation, Professor Dwight Golann divides the stages of mediation into three parts: Joint Session, Private Caucuses, and Moderated Negotiations. In each segment, a number of specific goals and objectives similar to the models discussed earlier are included.

From a pragmatic standpoint, the mediator possesses a great deal of control in how mediation is conducted. The ability to adapt and modify the mediation process is a primary benefit of its use. Some of the most dramatic changes have been within the legal field, where mediation has begun to assume a more legalistic process, looking more like case evaluation or traditional court-conducted settlement conferences. In these instances, much of the focus on parties' interests and creativity is absent. Acknowledging the value of diversity in approaches, many mediators now balance their approach recognizing a need to maintain the mediation process as a separate, unique and distinct dispute resolution method.

2.   SKILLS ESSENTIAL TO MEDIATION

Effective mediators must possess a variety of skills. Some of these can be taught explicitly, while others are more implicit and almost intuitive. At the core of mediation is human interaction. Mediators must enjoy people, respect diversity, and understand the importance of human perceptions. One of the most critical skills involved in mediation is interpersonal communication.

a. Communication

Communication is the foundation of mediation. Often parties are in dispute as a result of faulty or dysfunctional communication. Sometimes no communication has occurred at all. Mediators must not only communicate directly with the parties, but they also serve as an interpreter for communication between the parties, making certain that each party has heard and understood the other's messages.

Communication can be simply defined as the sending and receiving of a message. Most messages are both verbal and nonverbal. During communication, what one party intends when sending the message is not always what the recipient hears or receives. Part of this discrepancy is due to coding and decoding—the specific meaning to the message. Mediators often must decode messages sent between the parties. To more closely examine aspects of communication in mediation, the communication process has been divided into distinct components: Listening, Questioning, Restating, Two–Way Communication, and Non–Verbal Communication.

i. Listening

Listening is an essential component of mediation. Listening serves a number of goals. As the mediator listens to each party discuss the matter, she gains information not only about the dispute but also the potential options for resolution. Listening encourages disclosures. When people know someone is listening, they will generally continue to share information. As the mediator demonstrates listening, he is also modeling skills for the parties who may not have previously been willing to listen to each other.

Listening also meets a fundamental human need: the need to be heard. The mediator lets the parties know that they have been heard through the use of active and interactive listening responses. People often interpret the failure of others to listen as disrespectful and hurtful. People tend to feel more respected when they are confident they have been heard and understood. In many instances, disputants feel the mediation is the first time that someone has taken the time to listen to their story. In essence, it is the first time they have been heard.

ii.　Questioning

In order to gather additional information, the mediator must ask questions. Questioning can also serve additional functions, such as changing the focus of discussion, providing information (by the nature of the question), assisting parties in clarifying objectives, and bringing a matter to closure. Types of questions include open, open-focused, closed, yes/no and leading. Mediators generally begin with open-ended questions in order to elicit a broad view of the matter and underlying needs and interests. As the mediation progresses, more focused and even closed questioning may be used.

iii.   Two–Way Communication

Once the parties have provided their opening remarks, most of the remainder of the mediation involves two-way communication. Two-way communication includes not only dialogue between the mediator and parties, but also conversations the parties may have with each other. As the process transitions from one of information gathering to one where options are developed, the manner of communication can be critical.

iv.   Restating and Reframing

In his role as interpreter for the parties, the mediator attempts to remove any negativity in the language used. A statement may be phrased less negatively, while retaining accuracy with regard to the content of the message. One way this is accomplished is through the use of restating and reframing. Although the two terms are sometimes used interchangeably, each may provide assistance in somewhat different ways.

When a mediator *restates* what a party (or their representative) has said, the primary purpose is to let the party know that he has been heard, and simultaneously state the situation again in more neutral language. Often a reflective type of approach is used, whereby the mediator focuses on the party's interests, removing blaming or accusatory language.

For example, if a dispute involving loud music and noise in an apartment complex is framed as "the problem with late night music," as opposed to that "terrible, loud noise," the parties might begin to consider options such as turning down the volume or not playing music after certain hours. One statement of the issue is more accusatory and presents a personal challenge, while the other framing suggests less personal circumstances for discussion.

In *reframing*, the mediator tries to place the disputed issues of the parties in more neutral manner, in such a way that the parties begin to focus on potential outcomes. Often, the way a problem is framed will guide the parties in their consideration of alternatives for resolution.

Framing the problem differently may lead to additional possible solutions. For example, if instead the discussion centers around helping Party A sleep at night, ideas such as ear plugs or sound proofing might result. In the context of litigated cases, a specific sum of money may be reframed as compensation, which then allows the parties to consider things of value in addition to money. In many instances, mediators will attempt to broadly frame the problem, in order to encourage a larger number of options.

v.   Non–Verbal Communication

A great percentage of communication is nonverbal. If mediators fail to pay astute attention to nonverbal communication, much opportunity for gaining information and understanding will be lost.

Nonverbal communication may take place in several channels of expression. The two most common are kinesics or body language, and paralinguistics, the vocal portion of the message other than the words. These include such aspects of speech such as pace, volume, tone and pitch of the voice.

b.   Analysis and Interpretation

As mediators listen and gather information, they must also analyze what the parties are saying. Analysis in this sense may include some legal analysis, so the mediator will be able to reality test some of the parties' contentions. As a mediator actively listens, she also analyzes and interprets the content of the messages. Such analysis and interpretation occurs concurrently on many levels. A mediator may analyze part of the message as it relates to a legal issue in the dispute. While at the same time, another part of the message may be interpreted as a strong emotional point such as profound disappointment, betrayal, pride or an absence of respect. In essence, the mediator is analyzing and interpreting both the objective and subjective content of messages.

In other instances, a mediator listens carefully for information that identifies a non-monetary interest; these include a need for an apology, an expression of regret, or some acknowledgment of the hardship a party has experienced. Simultaneously, the mediator is interpreting the non-verbal messages in an attempt to identify sensitive or "hot button" issues. A party's failure to express emotion may suggest the need for additional trust building. Often a party may be more open to communicate important feelings in the private caucus. Such analysis is not intended for the mediator to form a judgment, but rather to ensure that the mediator understands the full text, import and meaning of the communication.

c. Reality Testing

Reality testing is a technique of asking questions of the parties and their representatives, often causing them to rethink a position, objective or opinion. Mediators must often ask difficult questions in order to stimulate a new perspective on the part of the participants. Additionally, mediators often consider the contingencies involving the workability of the agreement, as people can be unrealistic with regard to their objectives in mediation.

In using these questions, mediators are careful to not embarrass a party, even those with impracticable and naïve expectations. Much of reality testing is accomplished in private sessions or caucuses. For example, in a neighborhood dispute Party A may insist that Party B (with whom he has a dispute) move away from the neighborhood. The mediator knows that B has lived in the neighborhood for nearly thirty years, is close to work and school, and the market for home sales is not good. Asking questions which lead A to realize that the suggested option is unworkable may assist A in generating and considering other options.

In court-annexed mediation, reality testing often involves consideration of the underlying lawsuit and the potential of prevailing at trial. Often parties come into the mediation very confident of their case. In fact, some of this psychological bias contributes to the failure of direct negotiations. (Birke & Fox) Mediators will ask direct and specific questions to move the parties toward reconsideration of their strong perspectives and positions.

Fisher and Ury in the seminal book, *Getting to Yes*, first suggested a consideration of one's BATNA, the Best Alternative to a Negotiated Agreement, as a part of reality testing. Since then, additional considerations have evolved, and part of the mediator's task is to encourage the parties to also consider their WATNA, Worst Alternative to a Negotiated Agreement, or perhaps LATNA, Likely Alternative to a Negotiated Agreement.

d. Organization

Another valued skill in mediation is organization. Organization encompasses a number of skills, ranging from sorting through information involved in the dispute to discovering information necessary for determining solutions.

When people are involved in a dispute or conflict, they may not be focused on records of the event. Disorganization or a lack of awareness of relevant or necessary documents such as contracts or receipts can be problematic. Mediators will often assist the parties in focusing on these matters by requesting that they bring their documents to the mediation. Mediators may also assist in organizing what documents are available, or sorting through figures with the parties. Such organization is often essential to the parties' understanding of the matter, as well as any ultimate resolution.

Often individuals in dispute are not communicating effectively. While basic communication skills such as listening may be absent, the difficulty may also be part of a lack of organization with regard to the information exchange.

Process organization is another component of the mediator's work. When engaged in conflict, people often think they are communicating, but in reality may be talking apples and oranges. They do not hear or understand one another. By setting forth and maintaining the structure of the process, a mediator can lend organization to the communication. Moreover, individuals process information differently; for some, it may be more scattered and auditory. These people would be able listen and process information. Others are more visual and must be able to see and visualize information before they may comprehend, process, or understand it. Structuring the information for the parties in a way most suitable for each person's processing is often necessary so that each can gain an understanding of the other's perspective.

e. Counseling and Calming Skills

While mediation is certainly not therapy, and the mediator should guard against trying to psychoanalyze the parties, using therapeutic listening and calming techniques may be beneficial to the process. Many times individuals in mediation simply want someone to listen to them; others need to express emotion. Mediators often demonstrate empathic listening, while simultaneously guarding against appearing to agree with the content of what a party says.

On one hand, venting emotions is often necessary. Mediators, however, must be careful to not allow an emotional outburst to become uncontrollable. Appreciating emotions and allowing some venting is often helpful in moving toward resolution, but destructive interaction is not. Being able to calm the party, while retaining neutrality is a valuable skill for the mediator to possess.

f. Recognition of Cultural Diversity

Today's world is very diverse. Culture is recognized and valued as part of a person's identity. While culture is a difficult concept to describe in an accurate way, mediators must be aware of the impact that a party's culture may have on mediation participation. Culture is often based upon nationality, gender, age, and religion, but it may also be based on more subtle aspects such as occupation. The legal culture is one example. Subcultures may also exist within a culture. Examples may include African Americans under-thirty or the legal culture of a particular locality. Knowledge of some of the nuances of a particular culture may assist the mediator to know when and how to modify the process. One aspect of culture that has a particular impact upon the mediation process is communication.

Much cultural diversity exists in terms of communication. For example, eye contact in most Western cultures is a sign that you are listening to the speaker. In other cultures, however, direct eye contact may be viewed as insulting or demonstrating a lack of respect for the individual. Mediators should try to obtain some knowledge about any particular culture that might impact the mediation. The more the mediator can ascertain prior to the session, the better able he will be to adjust the process to allow for cultural needs and differences.

In some cases, part of the dispute involves lack of a realization or recognition of another person's cultural differences. When the mediator discovers this, it may be helpful to explore with one party his perceptions and attempt to ascertain the underlying beliefs or reasons for his viewpoint. In some instances, mediators actively assist the parties in acknowledging and understanding the differences in perceptions as well as cultural differences not previously realized.

3. JOINT PROCESS OR SEPARATE SESSIONS

One area of debate among mediators concerns the use of the caucus, or private session. Some mediators, most often those from a community or empowerment philosophy, were trained to facilitate communication and understanding between the parties, while all parties remained together. Only in rare instances would a mediator separate the parties and meet with each one independently. On the other hand, in court-annexed mediation, a presumption of private caucusing exists. This is due in part to initial training based more upon the labor and collective bargaining model of mediation, where private caucuses are used almost exclusively.

Like many of the approaches to mediation, there are advantages as well as disadvantages to each method. With an approach that does not utilize a caucus, direct communication between the parties may be enhanced. Opportunities to repair or establish trust among the participants may be increased. In the brainstorming session, the ability to cross-fertilize and stimulate thinking while all parties are together can be helpful to the process. Likewise, in negotiating the final resolution, the mediator may find it more efficient to meet with all participants rather than going from one party to the other. With joint meetings, there is less of a chance that mediators may misinterpret a comment or share information which was to be kept confidential.

A caucus approach offers the opportunity for the parties to share information that they were hesitant to disclose in front of the other party. Private meetings allow time for trust building between the mediator and the parties. People are frequently more willing to disclose personal matters and tell "secrets" when meeting privately with the mediator. Meeting separately with each party also allows the mediator to be more direct with the individual. This may include confronting the person about their negotiation style or their participation in the process. Mediators often analyze these factors when deciding whether to caucus, and the decision is often based upon the needs and dynamics of the case.

Two approaches exist regarding the confidential aspect of the caucus. In some cases, all information shared in the caucus is considered confidential, except that information a party explicitly tells the mediator can be shared. In other cases, absolute confidentiality is not assured. Sharing of information is at the discretion of the mediator.

4.   A NO STAGE PERSPECTIVE OF MEDIATION

Another view of mediation is one where no stages exist in which to break down the process. The work of these mediators proceeds without regard to particular tasks or goals. A mediator may merely go about attempting to forge a resolution. In the process, the mediator may utilize a variety of different approaches to gather information. Mediators who utilize this approach are often quite intuitive and rely on their "gut" to guide the process. Although this type of mediation is less structured, when the parties are committed to the process, it may be effective. Alternately, situations exist where parties may need the structure that a more planned process provides.

E.   MEDIATION'S UNIQUE FOCUS ON INTERESTS

In many definitions, mediation is described as a move away from a focus on the right-wrong dichotomy. Instead mediation offers a perspective for problem solving that is concerned with the parties' needs and interests. In most other dispute resolution processes, there remains a strong emphasis on a determination or consideration of factual matters based upon evidence. In mediation, while some discussions of a potential court or other outcome may be included, a primary theoretical foundation of the process is the focus on the parties' underlying interests.

1.   PHILOSOPHICAL

Mediation as a method of dispute resolution not only attempts to resolve a problem or conflict without resort to adjudication, but attempts to do so by centering on what people really want or what means the most to them in terms of the ultimate outcome. For example, a car accident victim may claim a desire or a need for money, but may also want an acknowledgment of injury or an apology. When lawsuits are filed, the focus of outcome is usually narrowed as only money can be recovered. In mediation, however, many types of non-monetary resolutions are possible.

In providing a focus on interests, mediation offers a unique perspective in terms of a method for dispute resolution. Because it is the parties who must inform the mediator and the other participants about what it is they really desire, the parties themselves take a very active part in the process. Often part of the mediator's role is to assist the parties in clarifying and prioritizing their real interests. With a focus on interests, opportunities for creative, mutually satisfactory resolutions are enhanced.

2. PRAGMATIC

In some cases, despite the attempt of the mediator to focus on the parties' interests, the parties are not forthcoming with necessary information. In some instances, the parties may not know or may not have identified their real interests. In other cases, particularly litigation matters in which the focus has been on a right-wrong or win-lose outcome, movement away from such paradigms may be difficult, if not impossible. One recent study made an attempt to ascertain the likelihood of relationship repair and other integrative solutions in "legal mediations." In less than twenty percent of the cases, a relationship repair occurred. In over thirty percent of the cases, however, the agreement included at least one integrative (non-monetary) term. (Golann) Even in those instances where the mediation process resembles more traditional settlement negotiation and may not include "joint gains," the parties are nonetheless more satisfied, due in large part to their participation in the process. (Baruch Bush) While mediation philosophy has a focus on interests, from a practical standpoint, the parties must be willing to engage in such explorations and discussions.

F. MEDIATION'S POTENTIAL IN TRANSACTIONAL MATTERS

Mediation is most often considered in the context of conflict and dispute resolution. When mediation is considered before a dispute arises, it is usually in terms of a pre-dispute clause, which suggests or mandates that the parties use mediation if and when a conflict arises. When individuals negotiate a transaction, for example the sale of a home, purchase of a car or partnership agreement, they occasionally reach an impasse. This ultimately results in the deal falling through. Consequently, the house is not purchased, or the sale of the widget chip not consummated. When negotiators in transactions reach an impasse, the assistance of a mediator can be beneficial.

To date, however, little work has been done with regard to mediation use in transactions. Articles are scarce and few mediators have actively marketed their business as assisting with transactional matters. Yet a review of the negotiation literature, particularly those addressing barriers and difficulties in negotiation, appear to have applicability in the negotiation of transactions as well as disputes. Likewise, articles demonstrating the mediator's assistance in negotiation have dual application. As time passes, additional use of mediation in commercial transactions is likely.

G. VARIATIONS AND ADAPTATIONS
OF MEDIATION

As mediation use increases, particularly in varied contexts, needs for adaptations and modifications in approaches may exist. Variations in approaches have been recognized early on. For example, Folberg & Taylor noted several modifications from a general model, some based in part upon the mediator's style or approach, while other adaptations depend upon the type of dispute. Some of these also emphasized a particular aspect of the mediator's role. For example, the scrivener model is a passive method of mediating where the mediator relies on the parties' abilities to resolve their own conflict. Although a mediator using this style may restate the parties' thoughts and ideas, he does not actively intervene. Another style, shuttle mediation, involves the mediator going back and forth between separate caucus sessions. Muscle mediation is a method by which mediators urge or even coerce parties to settlement. In therapeutic mediation the mediator's focus is on understanding the underlying conflict and resolving the emotional aspects of the dispute.

Other versions of mediation styles have been identified as well. For example, Alfini categorized three distinct approaches to mediation as Trashing, Bashing and Hashing. The trashing methodology involves legally evaluating the parties' positions; bashing techniques focus on generating settlement options; hashing refers to a more flexible approach to mediation, depending on the needs and interests of the parties. (Alfini)

Finally, one of the more controversial explorations of the diversity in mediation approaches revolves around what has become widely known as the evaluative-facilitative debate. Professor Riskin identified mediator orientation by a graph which contains four quadrants, as illustrated below. (Riskin) Riskin's Grid examines different mediator techniques depending on whether the mediator defines the problem broadly or narrowly and whether the mediator assumes an evaluative or facilitative role.

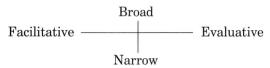

Broad

Facilitative ———————— Evaluative

Narrow

Many of the questions raised since the publication of Riskin's Grid was publicized address whether evaluation can be part of mediation, what it means to mediate, and who should make those critical decisions. Much has been written about these issues, and a great deal of literature examining the various viewpoints is currently available. (Kovach & Love)

As various and conflicting views of mediation have evolved, attempts to regulate the type and style of mediation have resulted. While different approaches are appreciated and may offer consumers of mediation diversity, such variations might also be problematic for the general public by causing confusion with regard to what is expected in the process. One suggested option is to require that the mediator inform the parties of the style of mediation that will be used. Another option is to ascertain what approach the parties desire or what exactly the parties want to accomplish through the mediation process. As mediation use increases and educational efforts continue, people will be increasingly comfortable with variety in the use and methods of mediation.

References

James J. Alfini, Trashing, Bashing and Hashing It Out: Is This the End of "Good Mediation," 19 Fla. St. U. L. Rev. 47 (1991).

Robert A. Baruch Bush, "What Do We Need a Mediator For?" Mediation's "Value–Added" for Negotiators, 12 Ohio St. J. on Disp. Resol. 1 (1997).

Richard Birke & Craig R. Fox, Psychological Principles in Negotiating Civil Settlements, 4 Harv. Negotiation L. Rev. 1 (1999).

Kevin C. Clark, The Philosophical Underpinning and General Workings of Chinese Mediation Systems: What Lessons Can American Mediators Learn?, 2 Pepp. Disp. Resol. L.J. 117 (2002).

Roger Fisher & William Ury, Getting to Yes: Negotiating Agreement Without Giving In (1991).

Jay Folberg & Alison Taylor, Mediation: A Comprehensive Guide to Resolving Conflicts Without Litigation (1984).

Dwight Golann, Mediating Legal Disputes: Effective Strategies for Lawyers and Mediators (1996).

Dwight Golann, Is Legal Mediation a Proces of Repair—or Separation? An Empirical Study and Its Implications, 7 Harv. Negotiation Rev. 301 (2002).

Trina Grillo, The Mediation Alternative: Process Dangers for Women, 100 Yale L.J. 1545 (1991)

Kimberlee K. Kovach, Mediation: Principles and Practice (2000).

Kimberlee K. Kovach & Lela P. Love, Mapping Mediation: The Risks of Riskin's Grid, 3 Harv. Negot. L. Rev. 71, 93 (1998).

Christopher Moore, The Mediation Process: Practical Strategies for Resolving Conflict (2d ed. 1996).

Leonard Riskin, Understanding Mediators' Orientations, Strategies and Techniques: A Grid for the Perplexed, 1 Harv. Neg. L. Rev. 7 (1996).

Primary Cases

Bibliography

James J. Alfini et al., Mediation Theory and Practice (2001).

Charles B. Craver, Effective Legal Negotiation and Settlement (2001).

Joseph P. Folger & Robert A. Baruch Bush, Transformative Mediation and Third Party Intervention: Ten Hallmarks of a Transformative Approach to Practice, 13 Mediation Q. 263 (1996).

Carol J. King, Burdening Access to Justice: The Cost of Divorce Mediation on the Cheap, 73 St. John's L. Rev. 375 (1999).

Murray S. Levin, The Propriety of Evaluative Mediation: Concerns About the Nature and Quality of an Evaluative Opinion 16 Ohio St. J. on Disp. Resol. 267 (2001).

Dan McGillis, A Brief History of the Evolution of Community, Community Mediation Programs: Developments and Challenges, National Institute of Justice, US Department of Justice, July, 1997.

Sally E. Merry & Susan Silbey, Mediator Settlement Strategies, 8 L. & Policy 7 (1986).

Robert B. Moberly, Mediator Gag Rules: Is It Ethical for Mediators to Evaluate or Advise? 38 S. Tex. L. Rev. 669 (1997).

Cao Pei, The Origins of Mediation in Traditional China, 54 Disp. Resol. J. 32 (1999).

Edith B. Primm, The Negotiation Justice Center Movement, 81 Ky. L.J. 1067 (1992–93).

Donna M. Stringer & Lonnie Lusardo, Bridging Cultural Gaps in Mediation, 56 Disp. Resol. J. 29 (2001).

Joseph B. Stulberg, Facilitative Versus Evaluative Mediator Orientations: Piercing the "Grid" Lock, 24 Fla. St. U. L. Rev. 985 (1997).

Carrie–Anne Tondo, Rinarisa Coronel, & Bethany Drucker, Note, Mediation Trends: A Survey of the States, 39 Fam. Ct. Rev. 431 (2001).

American Bar Association Section of Dispute Resolution Directory of Law School Dispute Resolution Courses and Programs (2000).

Community Mediation: A Handbook for Practitioners and Researchers (Karen Grover Duffy, James W. Grosch and Paul V. Olczak, eds. 1991).

CHAPTER 3

MEDIATION AS FACILITATION OF NEGOTIATION

Mediation is quite often considered to be the facilitation of a negotiation. A mediator essentially intervenes in an unresolved negotiation. The disputing parties are, for a variety of reasons, unable to reach an agreement without the assistance of an outside neutral person. The mediator's role is to assist with or facilitate their negotiation. Because the bulk of the mediator's work involves diagnosing, and then repairing difficulties in negotiation, it is imperative that mediators possess a working knowledge of the negotiation process.

A. UNDERSTANDING NEGOTIATION

A noticeable increase in the understanding of the variety of dimensions of negotiation has been seen in the last several decades. Until the last twenty-five or so years, the art and science of negotiation consisted primarily of specific tactics, strategies and attitudes that were thought to be effective. Negotiation was often not considered a process with distinct stages and essential elements. Although some literature existed, the majority was focused on "winning" the negotiation—on getting more. The literature provided specific tactics that one could employ to gain advantage over the other person. But how and why certain tactics worked, and why others did not, was not frequently examined in any great detail.

More recently, a great deal of research has been undertaken in an attempt to further appreciate the many nuances of negotiation. These topics range from aspects of culture and gender to the psychological dimensions of the process. With the increased focus on dispute resolution generally, a corresponding proliferation of negotiation courses and educational efforts has been observed. An examination of negotiation may include matters such as a categorization of stages, underlying theories, negotiation styles and tactics, and additional factors that may impact the particular approaches taken and results achieved.

1.   A MULTI–STAGE PROCESS

Negotiation, like any activity when dissected, can be broken down into distinct stages. A closer examination of the various stages or phases assists the mediator in understanding the sequence of the negotiation process. While not all phases proceed in a systematic manner in each negotiation, it is helpful to use a stage model outline as a focal point. Awareness of the phases can also assist the mediator in recognizing what may have been overlooked in terms of process points when the negotiation does not proceed as expected or desired.

One very basic view of negotiation consisting of six stages is taken from Gifford's *Legal Negotiation*. These stages are as follows:

1. Planning and preparation

2. Establishing initial relationships between negotiators

3. Opening offers or initial proposals

4. Information exchange

5. Narrowing of differences

6. Closure

While the description of these stages is essentially self-explanatory, in many instances, the phases do not exactly proceed as outlined. In many cases, information exchange may occur in some form, albeit limited, prior to opening offers or proposals. In terms of the negotiation of legal matters, litigation in particular, information is exchanged in the filing of a petition or answer. Offers or demands are not "put on the table" until minimal, or even nearly all discovery is completed. Most other stages are usually present in any given negotiation, although the period of time allocated to each will vary considerably. As the negotiation proceeds through these stages, it is not uncommon that one reason or another will dictate a return back to an earlier phase.

In *A Practical Guide of Negotiation*, Thomas F. Guernsey provides a more detailed analysis of additional stages which relate to the intricacies of the activities of the negotiation. These additional stages include the following:

- Preparation and planning
- Ice breaking
- Agenda control
- Information bargaining
- Proposals, offers, demands
- Persuasions/justifications
- Concessions/reformulation
- Crisis: resolution or deadlock
- Closing
- Memorialization

As discussed earlier, in many circumstances, the stages are not as discrete as listed above. Early models of negotiation generally assumed an adversarial approach to the process. Now expanding knowledge and theory provide an array of ways to examine negotiation. Overlap exists between the theoretical basis, types, styles and strategies of negotiation. For instance, depending on her style, a negotiator may prefer to use a particular type of negotiation tactic or strategy. When involved in a particular type of negotiation with a distinct theoretical basis, one might find certain styles more effective than others. For example, an exclusively integrative approach usually calls for a collaborative style. Expert negotiators are able to modify their styles depending upon a number of factors including the styles and strategies of the other parties, the subject matter, and the context of the negotiation.

2. FUNDAMENTAL THEORIES

There are a number of basic theories which have been used to describe the negotiation process. The term *theory* is used to explain the way the process is viewed, or type of general approach taken. Often choice of theory will then dictate the specific style employed, especially if planned in advance.

Distinct types or underlying premises of negotiation have been identified. Most of these theories can be understood by contrasting two approaches to negotiation. Two primary theories of negotiation have been explored in detail: the dichotomy of negotiation as either distributive or integrative, and the negotiation process as either positional or principled.

In a distributive (also termed linear) negotiation, the parties view the possible outcome as a "fixed pie". The matter is considered to involve limited resources (usually money) to be distributed or about which to negotiate. A direct conflict of interest between the parties results. An adversarial, competitive style is most often observed.

Integrative negotiations involve the exploration of a number of options, many of which are not in direct conflict with one another. There is an "expanded pie," which provides an opportunity for mutual gain in the negotiation. The interests of the parties are varied and room for creativity exists. A more collaborative problem solving approach is often used in integrative negotiations. While these approaches to negotiation are often viewed as distinct, some experts consider them as segments in the same negotiation. In cases where the parties are at an impasse in a distributive mode, usually concerning the payment of money, mediators make attempts to search for integrative potential. Examples of more integrated considerations include matters such as apologies or a company changing policies with regard to harassment issues.

Another way of examining the negotiation process concerns whether the approach is viewed as positional or principled, terms first used in *Getting to Yes*. In positional bargaining, the parties align themselves with a position and spend a great deal of effort defending it. The parties sometimes do not focus on what they really want. Rather, they remain stuck on their position, and focus on its support. Principled negotiators, on the other hand, attempt to identify underlying interests and alternatives for settlement. Rather than a single answer solution, the principled negotiator looks for several possible solutions that might satisfy everyone's interests. The objective is achieving a final resolution that satisfies everyone.

While many mediation educators and trainers strongly urge mediators to steer the parties toward an integrative, principled approach, by searching for integrative potential, in some cases this may not be possible. Mediators, therefore, must be aware of all the variables in negotiation and be prepared to utilize diverse approaches depending upon where the parties are in their efforts.

A key task for the mediator is to assess the type of negotiation the parties are using. Far more difficult for the mediator is to change or influence the specific stylistic approaches of the negotiators. Additional theories of negotiation have been identified including a rights-focused versus interest-based negotiation and adversarial versus problem solving negotiation.

3.   PERSONAL STYLES

Style can be used to describe the personal adaptation or approach that a negotiator may take. While certain styles are more common in particular approaches, style may also depend upon the personality type of the individual negotiator. Sophistication, education and experience of the negotiator are additional factors.

Nearly thirty years ago, Professor Gerald Williams conducted a study of two primary lawyer negotiating styles. He identified lawyers involved in negotiating a settlement of a personal injury case as either competitive or cooperative, and attempted to determine which style was more effective. The results demonstrated that neither style alone was the determining factor for effectiveness, but rather that other factors such as reputation and preparation were more critical in terms of rating effectiveness. (Williams) Since that time, a third category of style, a collaborative approach, has gained recognition. This style is can be considered an extension of the cooperative approach, as it extends perhaps a step further, as the parties actively interact with each other to find acceptable and integrative solutions.

A subsequent study has recently been conducted to follow up on Williams' efforts. Professor Schneider identified negotiation approaches as either problem solving or adversarial. She then inquired about the perception of effectiveness of lawyers as assessed by their peers in the Milwaukee and Chicago Bar Associations. Results showed that the overwhelming majority of problem solving negotiations were noted as effective, whereas only nine percent of adversarial approaches were thought to be successful. (Schneider)

Another way of looking at personal techniques in negotiation is determining whether they are competitive, accommodating or avoiding. Accommodating is similar to cooperative, whereas the avoider refuses to engage in the process at all. (Mnookin) Personal style adapts over time, and may also change depending upon the personal style of the other negotiator.

4.   TACTICS AND STRATEGIES

Negotiation tactics and strategies, often interrelated, have been examined by a number of authors and negotiation experts. Generally, tactics are the identifiable, specific conduct or behaviors of a negotiator designed to achieve a specific result. One prevalent tactic is the lack of authority. Negotiators will engage the other party, and after obtaining a commitment will claim they lack the authority to make the final decision in an attempt to generate additional concessions.

Strategies encompass overall plans or approaches that negotiators may utilize. Most of the identifiable tactics are designed for the competitive distributive approach to negotiation. It is helpful for mediators to be able to identify when they are in use, and in particular when they are used negatively as they are usually counter-productive to reaching a resolution. Some mediators are quite active in assisting the parties when they are utilizing tactics and strategies which, while useful in an adversarial setting, may not be productive in the mediation process.

B. THE MEDIATOR'S ROLE IN DIAGNOSING PROBLEMS IN NEGOTIATIONS

Many times parties or their representatives experience difficulties in negotiating a resolution to a dispute. A number of reasons have been identified that may better explain these problems including lack of communication, unrealistic expectations, psychological biases, and a variety of cognitive barriers. A critical element of the mediator's role is to first diagnose, if possible, why the parties are unable to reach a resolution or settlement through a direct negotiation.

1. PARTICULAR PROBLEMS IDENTIFIED

While one can never be exactly sure of what may be occurring during a mediation, there are several particular problems or difficulties in negotiation which mediators readily observe. When certain approaches present specific obstacles to the mediation, the mediator is sometimes able to change dynamics so that a more productive process will emerge.

a. Deficient or Partisan Information

Lack of information often presents difficulties in negotiation. Without specific and necessary pieces of information, parties may be unwilling to come to any decision about a matter. Some participants are explicit in their demand for particular information, while others are not as forthcoming. In some instances, individuals may not want the information, since it may force them to reevaluate their contentions.

Focusing on only biased information also creates obstacles in negotiation. This contributes to an inability to see another's point of view. Overconfidence in one's own position is also common. Often lawyers go into a negotiation with a preconceived notion of what the amount of settlement should be. This is sometimes referred to as the 'value of the case'. Interestingly, in reality, there is rarely one value of the case; there are usually several, based upon differing perspectives. In shorthand, what is termed the 'value of the case' is that value which the lawyer predicts, sometimes with certainty, and at other times with doubt, regarding what a court's outcome may be. Without accurate information, however, it is difficult to ascertain an objective value.

b. Purely Distributive Focus

Another problem stems from the perception and belief that the negotiation must be distributive. Even in instances of an enlarged pie, where additional value has been recognized, negotiators must still reach agreement on how the pie is to be distributed. Much of the early literature as well as the general public's common understanding of negotiation focuses on the distributive approach. A purely distributive focus results in overuse of adversarial, and competitive tactics. Stalemates often result.

c. Psychological Impacts

A number of psychological barriers in negotiations have been identified. Some of these account for a party's unrealistic expectations regarding the potential outcome of a matter. For example, in lawsuits, the concept of anchoring heuristics is common, whereby parties learn what others in a similar situation may have achieved in terms of a verdict or settlement, and they then set their expectation as the same, even though many differences between the matters may exist. (Birke). Once that amount or number is "set" there is often considerable difficulty for them to consider a different result.

Another psychological barrier involves perspective bias. Whatever information is available, is often viewed from a self-interested standpoint. This may result in a party overestimating what the desired outcome should be. A related matter concerns over-commitment. In this instance, once a party commits to a certain viewpoint or outcome, internal pressures to be consistent makes change quite difficult.

Additionally, an individual's responses to and comfort with risk are cognitive functions that affect negotiation. People who are risk adverse are much more likely to settle for a known quantity. Those who appreciate risk will likely take their chances in a different forum if not completely satisfied with the proposed outcome. In other instances, people who are on the paying end are often loss adverse. These people will not agree to something if they perceive it to be a loss. (Mnookin).

d. Principal–Agent Difficulties

Where an agent represents a principal in a negotiation, the opportunity for conflict or disagreement on the "same side of the table" is present. While an agent can provide expertise in the process, as well as the subject matter of the negotiation, there are also difficulties or conflicts that may surface. The agent and principal may have different views with regard to the outcome of the negotiation. The agent, having expertise in a specific area, may decide what norms to apply. For example, the lawyer may determine the legal outcomes that should be achieved in negotiation. Yet, the principal may have other interests and needs.

e. Lack of Skill and Knowledge

Many people come to mediation without any real theoretical or practical knowledge about the negotiation process. This can be a problem for those who do not like to negotiate, and instead, would rather avoid conflict. In mediation, these people are not inclined to actively participate.

Another problem relates to the tendency to perceive disputes in a right-wrong paradigm. This contributes to the inability of individuals to maintain focus and concentrate on finding a resolution or reaching a settlement. Instead, they concentrate on and remain locked into proving their point. Often they are unable to consider other alternatives or resolutions.

While these examples include some of the more common difficulties in negotiation, additional problems may confront the mediator in the cases he mediates. For instance, situations involving class actions or other multi-party disputes can powerfully change dynamics as the number of parties increases. Cultural differences, such as age, gender or nationality, can also profoundly effect the negotiation process and if not addressed may result in impasses as well.

2. SPECIFIC STRATEGIES FOR OVERCOMING OBSTACLES

As previously discussed, part of what a mediator attempts to do is repair the difficulties in the parties' negotiation. Once the mediator determines the nature of the problem, he then guides the parties away from these impediments.

One of the more common obstacles that confronts the mediator is the lack of an absolute authority or an absent decision maker. This is addressed in detail in Chapter Five and in many cases can be prevented or rectified by the mediator before the mediation begins. When lack of information or particularly one-sided data leaves the parties intensely focused on their own positions, mediators often encourage the parties to listen to the other side and seriously consider the dispute from another perspective.

In cases where the parties are unfamiliar with negotiation, a mediator can serve the role of educator. In some instances, she may assist the parties in formulating offers or demands. In others, she will identify the need for certain types of information and provide assistance in the information exchange. Assisting the parties in a transition from a positional to a more principled approach or from an adversarial to a more problem solving focus is another method mediators utilize.

Where psychological aspects present barriers to the settlement, a mediator may first need to search for additional information from a party. By questioning the party regarding his interests, needs, and desires, the mediator might discover underlying issues that need to be addressed before a resolution can be considered. This may involve matters that are sensitive to a party, the need for emotional release, or the desire for an apology.

In the case of anchoring, where the parties are stuck on a particular number, the mediator helps them reassess their position. Examining the underlying foundation for a settlement figure can also help move the parties toward considering alternative solutions.

Use of a decision tree is another way that mediators assist the parties in understanding their options. Decision tree analysis requires the application of a number of probabilities and percentages, considering the likelihood that they will occur. Decision trees can be relatively simple or in other cases, quite complex. The creation of a decision tree produces not only the expected case value, but also forces the lawyer and client to systematically think through the consequences of litigation. In terms of lawsuits, decision trees may be specific, focused only on the likelihood of the result at trial. In other cases, the tree and its branches consider the total costs involved in projected outcomes, which include non-monetary matters, such as relationships, psychological impact and social concerns.

When the parties remain entrenched in a purely distributive negotiation, a mediator's task is often to explore the possibility of an integrative or principled method by moving toward and maintaining emphasis on interests and options. Such an approach, however, is not always successful. In such cases where parties remain entrenched in a distributive mode, the mediator may take an active role in helping the parties reevaluate their positions. An honest reassessment of one's chances of prevailing in court or another adjudicatory process often produces movement toward settlement. Decision trees are useful at this juncture. Although parties usually consider their BATNA, the Best Alternative to a Negotiated Agreement, the mediator also asks about the party's WATNA, the Worst Alternative to a Negotiated Agreement. These can be critical elements in moving the parties toward resolution.

Any number of additional difficulties also present themselves as potential barriers to settlement. Ultimately, these problems can be as diverse as the people themselves. They may relate to gender, culture, race, socio-economic status, past history, or stereotypes. Whatever the circumstance, the mediator must recognize the difficulty and address the issue, directly or indirectly, in order to help repair it.

C. ETHICAL ISSUES IN NEGOTIATION

Because mediators facilitate negotiation, the ethical considerations that impact negotiators also influence the mediation process. By virtue of their role, mediators observe and may need to address the ethical issues that may arise during the process. Mediators may also assist in educating mediation participants, especially lawyers, about limitations on positional or adversarial bargaining.

Much debate surrounds the parameters of ethical behavior for negotiators, particularly those engaged in legal negotiations. On one hand, traditionally legal negotiation has taken place in an adversarial climate, and thus the behavior of the negotiators, whether lawyers or clients, tends to take on a more strategic, aggressive and competitive posture. This has been the more accepted view of legal negotiation and is supported by the Model Rules of Professional Conduct which allow puffing, noting that normal conventions in negotiations include deception.

On the other hand, as mediation and collaborative and problem solving negotiation gain use and acceptance, there may be a trend toward a more cooperative, honest and respectful approach to negotiation. (Cohen). This movement away from zealous adversarial representation is also supported by the call for more professionalism in the legal field and the encouragement of civility in the practice of law. Commentators note that changing to a more ethical negotiation process would necessitate conduct different from that acceptable in the context of adversarial situations. (Alfini, Kovach). Although the ABA had the opportunity to change this rule in its review of the rules through its Ethics 2000 Commission, it failed to do so.

Because no definite rules currently exist, other than some statutes calling for good faith in the context of mediation, no concrete guidance has been provided to negotiators, and the mediators who assist them.

References

James J. Alfini, Settlement Ethics and Lawyering in ADR Proceedings: A Proposal to Revise Rule 4.1 19 N. Ill. U. L. Rev. 255 (1999).

Richard Birke & Craig R. Fox, Psychological Principles in Negotiating Civil Settlements, 4 Harv, Negotiation L. Rev. 1 (1999).

Roger Fisher & William Ury, Getting to Yes (1981); Roger Fisher, William Ury & Bruce Patten, Getting to Yes (2d ed. 1991).

Donald G. Gifford, Legal Negotiation (1989).

Thomas F. Guernsey, A Practical Guide of Negotiation (1996).

Kimberlee K. Kovach, New Wine Requires New Wineskins: Transforming Lawyer Ethics for Effective Representation in a Non–Adversarial Approach to Problem Solving: Mediation 28 Fordam Urb. L. J. 935 (2001).

Robert H. Mnookin, Scott R. Peppet, and Andrew S. Julenillio, Beyond Winning: Negotiating to Create Value in Deals and Disputes (2000).

Robert H. Mnookin, Why Negotiations Fail: An Exploration of Barriers to the Resolution of Conflict, 8 Ohio St. J. Disp. Resol. 235 (1993).

Andrea Kupfer Schneider, Shattering Negotiation Myths: Empirical Evidence on the Effectiveness of Negotiation Style, 7 Harv. L. Negotiation Rev. 143 (2002).

Gerald S. Williams, Legal Negotiation and Settlement (1983).

Cases

Rizzo v. Haines, 555 A.2d 58 (Pa.1989).

Bibliography

Robert S. Adler & Elliot M. Silverstein, When David Meets Goliath: Dealing With Power Differentials in Negotiations 5 Harv. Negotiation L. Rev. 1 (2000).

William J. Breslin & Jeffrey Z. Rubin, Eds., Negotiation Theory and Practice (1991).

Jennifer Gerarda Brown, The Role of Hope in Negotiation, 44 UCLA L. Rev. 1661 (1997).

Jonathan R. Cohen, When People are the Means; Negotiating with Respect, 14 Geo. J. Legal Ethics 739 (2001).

Charles B. Craver, Effective Legal Negotiation and Settlement (1993).

Roger Fisher & Scott Brown, Getting Together: Building Relationships as We Negotiate (1989).

Clark Freshman, Adele M. Hayes and Greg C. Feldman, The Lawyer–Negotiator as Mood Scientist: What we Know and Don't Know About How Mood Relates to Successful Negotiation, 2002 J. Disp. Resol. 1 (2002).

See Ronald J. Gilson & Robert H. Mnookin, Disputing Through Agents: Cooperation and Conflict Between Lawyers in Litigation, 94 Colum. L. Rev. 509 (1994).

Jonathan Hyman, Negotiation Methods and Litigation Settlement Methods in New Jersey: "You Can't Always Get What You Want," 12 Ohio St. J. on Disp. Resol. 253 (1997).

Russell Korobkin, Aspirations and Settlement, 88 Cornell L. Rev. 1 (2002).

Russell Korobkin, A Positive View of Legal Negotiation, 88 Geo. L. J. 1789 (2000).

Russell Korobkin & Chris Guthrie, Psychological Barriers to Litigation Settlement: An Experimental Approach, 93 Mich. L. Rev. 107 (1994).

David A. Lax and James K. Subenius, The Manager as Negotiator (1986).

Carrie Menkel–Meadow, Ethics, Morality and Professional Responsibility in Negotiation in Dispute Resolution Ethics—A Comprehensive Guide, Edited by Phyllis Bernard and Bryant Garth, ABA Section of Dispute Resolution, 2002.

Carrie Menkel–Meadow, Toward and the View of Legal Negotiation: The Structure of Problem–Solving, 31 UCLA L. Rev. 754 (1984).

Scott R. Peppet, Can Saints Negotiate? A Brief Introduction to the Problems of Perfect Ethics in Bargaining, 7 Harv. Negotiation L. Rev. 83 (2002).

Charles B. Wiggins & L. Randolph Lowry, Negotiation and Settlement Advocacy: A Book of Readings (1997).

Douglas H. Yarn, Lawyer Ethics in ADR and the Recommendations of Ethics 2000 to Revise the Model Rules of Professional Conduct: Considerations for Adoption and State Application 54 Ark. L. Rev. 207 (2001).

CHAPTER 4

GETTING TO THE MEDIATION

While mediation is being used with greater frequency and continues to gain familiarity and acceptance, it is still not the default paradigm for dispute resolution. One significant and vital consideration is how matters, disputes or lawsuits get to mediation in the first place. To examine this more closely, issues surrounding referrals, legal constraints, policy concerns, and practical matters must be addressed.

Many people seek legal advice and commence lawsuits when confronting a dispute or conflict. Although mediation is used before lawsuits are filed, primarily in contractual matters, the bulk of mediation use is subsequent to the filing of a lawsuit. While public awareness of mediation is increasing, mediation is not often the first process considered when individuals consider dispute resolution.

Much debate has taken place regarding the propriety of mandatory versus voluntary mediation. The debate centers around whether parties should be compelled by a contract or by a court to attend mediation. On one hand, mediation, by its very nature is a voluntary process, and to mandate or coerce its use is viewed as philosophically inconsistent. Proponents of this position believe that parties will voluntarily decide to participate in mediation. However, a difficulty with this approach is that all parties must agree to mediate. If one party is reluctant to try mediation, the mediation does not occur. As mediation gains familiarity in the legal system, it is likely that more litigants or their lawyers will decide to voluntarily undertake mediation, lessening the need for a mandatory approach.

A court mandate can get reluctant or hesitant parties to the mediation table. For example, in pending court cases, many lawyers were initially reluctant to try mediation, and were not inclined to suggest it to opposing counsel. One primary concern was that such a suggestion would be interpreted as a sign of weakness or as having an ineffective case. When courts required mediation however, lawyers had no choice; their fear that discussing mediation would be misinterpreted was alleviated. The belief that the initial impetus for mediation should come from outside of the dispute, especially from a higher authority, such as a court, is often the basis for mandatory mediation schemes.

Despite the tension in these conflicting philosophies, courts throughout the United States have made decisions to direct cases to mediation. A variety of different approaches to mediation referral has resulted, often depending on the local legal culture and mediation experience in a specific jurisdiction.

In addition to voluntary participation, there are three methods that compel parties in a dispute to

attend mediation: pre-dispute contract, court rule
or order and legislation.

A. VOLUNTARY APPROACHES

Anyone involved in a dispute or conflict may
volunteer to involve a mediator in an effort to reach
a resolution. One difficulty, however, is getting the
other side to agree to such an approach. Mediation
centers have been quite effective in expanding the
use of voluntary mediation. Dispute Resolution Centers, (DRCs) many of which were originally known
as Neighborhood Justice Centers, are generally non
profit or quasi-governmental entities which provide
dispute resolution services—primarily mediation—
at little or no cost. Such centers now operate in a
variety of settings and also serve important public
education and awareness functions.

1. COMMUNITY OR NON–LITIGATION MATTERS

Parties in disputes may agree to mediation if they
are aware of the process and possess a sincere
desire to resolve the matter. The parties themselves
may contact a local community or dispute resolution center and request that a mediation be scheduled. While such initiations are beneficial and
should be encouraged, in reality, no one can compel
the other party to appear at mediation. Many centers, however, when contacted by one party, try to
"sell "the process to the other party. Mediation is
explained in an effort to make the party more

comfortable with the process. Such attempts are educational in nature and often do result in participation in mediation. However, even when parties voluntarily agree to participate, no way exists to assure that the parties will actually appear at the mediation, as there is no consequence for failure to attend.

2. SUBTLE SUGGESTIONS AND ENCOURAGEMENT

While technically voluntary programs, some early centers used subtle, and in some cases, not so subtle methods to persuade parties to attend mediation. For example, some centers included letters from a prosecutor's or district attorney's office in their correspondence suggesting that further legal action might be taken if the party failed to appear for mediation. While this tactic was criticized by some as misleading and unnecessarily coercive, others justified this approach. They argued that since most individuals were not aware of the mediation option, they needed a push or "jump start" to get into the process. The safeguard was that any party could always walk away once there; coercion to attend was, and is not, coercion to settle.

3. COURT–RELATED MATTERS

DRCs have also been effective in assisting courts in the establishment of dispute resolution programs. In some jurisdictions, center staff have provided initial technical assistance and training for the courts and mediators. In others, the community center serves as the administrative arm of a court-annexed mediation program. In still other situations, these centers oversee a roster of mediators which the court may use.

In voluntary court-related or court-annexed mediation, judges or court personnel generally encourage the use of mediation, but do not go as far as to order or mandate that the litigants participate in the process. Essentially two philosophies surround this issue. Some policy makers, such as judges, lawyers, court administrators, and mediation program personnel are of the opinion that mediation should be a completely voluntary process. This includes whether or not to participate in the first place. Parties are free to choose if to go, when to go, and who to select as a mediator. Dispute resolution centers or courts provide the parties information about mediation and may offer volunteer mediators for those who do not wish to pay private mediators.

In contrast, court-mandated or required mediation is where the court actually orders the litigants and their attorneys to attend mediation. (See Section C, *infra*.)

4.   AGREEMENT OF THE PARTIES

In many cases, the execution of a contract before a dispute or conflict has arisen may establish a contractual obligation to mediate. Although this is considered a legal obligation to mediate, it may also be considered voluntary, since the parties initially chose to contract in the first place. Parties may also enter an agreement to mediate after a dispute arises. Apart from the corporate, business or employment context where mediation agreements are seen with greater frequency, individual voluntary use of mediation remains infrequent. Few people immediately think of mediation as a viable option to resolve disputes. An increase in public awareness could assist in additional use of mediation prior to initiating legal action.

Predispute agreements to mediate are likely enforceable, either standing alone or where they establish a condition precedent to taking any other action to resolve the dispute. Most agreements to mediate are understood to compel attendance at mediation, but stop short of dictating specific conduct at the mediation. (Issues surrounding the degree of participation are addressed in detail in the next chapter.)

Post-dispute agreements refer to contracts or agreements to mediate after a dispute arises. In the event one party changes their mind prior to the mediation, little recourse is available. While such agreements, if in writing, are technically enforceable, a party would have to bring a specific enforcement action in court to compel attendance.

B. ISSUES SURROUNDING CONTRACTUAL OBLIGATIONS TO MEDIATE

Although in most instances a written agreement to mediate will be enforced, several matters should be considered. These include methods of contract enforcement, cost, pre-mediation information exchange, and the right to legal representation at mediation.

Many forms of agreements to mediate exist, ranging from a very simple statement that the parties agree to mediate to those setting out a number of details with regard to the mediation itself, as well as options subsequent to mediation. Agreements to mediate may be found in a number of contexts including employment, real estate, consumer, corporate or health care areas.

1.   VOLUNTARY CONTRACTS

The term *voluntary* is used to indicate that no disagreements exist about whether all parties to the contract are familiar with mediation and agree to use mediation as a first step or one step in resolving any future disputes. For example, some businesses, particularly those who have an ongoing relationship, decide that should a dispute arise during the course of transactions, mediation will be used prior to initiating legal action.

If the parties have agreed in advance that any future dispute will be resolved through mediation, the parties have essentially mandated such participation. Chapter Five addresses in detail what such an obligation might entail.

2.   CONTRACTS OF ADHESION

Although allegedly voluntary, some contracts, specifically those of adhesion have become a concern, since the parties usually are not of equal bargaining power. A mediation clause may be included in a very lengthy contract which is signed by an individual who has not read or understood the clause. Two primary areas where adhesion contracts are common are in consumer and employment matters. While concerns have been voiced regarding the use of mediation clauses in these areas, the idea that one party has been disadvantaged is not as compelling as with arbitration clauses. The distinguishing point is that with mediation agreements, the parties still have the option of going to court should an agreement not be achieved through the mediation. This is not the case with contractual arbitration clauses.

Even in those instances where it appears that the parties do not have a real choice, studies find that nonetheless participants are satisfied with the mediation process, and that most disputes are resolved. Other issues, such as the right to counsel, representation, and cost are important considerations in mediation and are often addressed in the contract.

3. ISSUES OF ENFORCEABILITY

In most instances, contracts or agreements to mediate will be enforced. One exception is in the case of pending litigation, where the agreement to mediate was not in writing. In *Kirschenman*, a California Court of Appeals overturned the trial court's sanction against a party for not attending mediation, because the agreement to mediate was oral, and the defendants withdrew consent to mediate prior to the session. (*Kirschenman v. Superior Court,* 1994). Even though the parties are often compelled to mediate, parties are not obligated to come to an agreement or settle their case. In other words, additional options remain available should the parties be unable to agree to a resolution.

Another issue that arises involves methods of enforcing agreements to mediate. In most cases, this will necessitate a court appearance. Two common scenarios often surface. In the first instance, the parties merely do not mediate. One party may then petition a court for specific enforcement of the mediation clause in the contract. In the second situation, the obligation to mediate is a condition precedent to the use of another process, most often either litigation or arbitration. Under these circumstances, if a party proceeds to arbitration or court before complying with the mediation provision, the other party must object and call the court or arbitrator's attention to the mediation requirement. The degree of participation in mediation prior to proceeding to trial or arbitration is an undetermined issue, and is discussed in greater detail in the next chapter.

4.   DRAFTING AGREEMENTS TO MEDIATE

Details that should be considered when drafting agreements to mediate include matters concerning what actions prompt the obligation to mediate, the manner of mediator selection, the location where mediation will be conducted, the appropriate cost division between the parties, and other session details.

As strategies may differ, no one answer is right for every mediation. For example, a debate exists as to whether such details should be considered and decided before a dispute arises, when the parties are perhaps more agreeable, or after the dispute occurs, as more will be known about the nature of the dispute and needs of the parties at that time.

Most agreements allow, but do not mandate the presence of lawyers. Additional matters to be contemplated include the degree of preparation desired and the nature and methods of pre-mediation information exchange. It may also be helpful to consider, in advance, types of enforcement mechanisms and possible remedies for failure to participate in the mediation.

5.   MEDIATOR SELECTION

Assuming that all involved parties agree to mediation, the next step entails locating or identifying a potential mediator. There are many ways to identify a qualified mediator, including receiving referrals by lawyers or friends or using general public information such as telephone directories and the internet. Mediators' fees vary considerably, and additional options, if cost is a concern, include dispute resolution centers and community mediation programs, where mediators may be available at little or no cost to the parties.

C. COURT–ORDERED MEDIATION

The term "mandatory" is often used in conjunction with mediation, to connote that attendance at a mediation session is required. In some instances, however, the term has been confused with a very different issue—the coercion or mandate that the parties reach some agreement or resolution at the mediation. While some confusion about the term remains, "mandatory" is used in the following discussions to describe that a court or statute may demand that the parties "participate" in mediation.

Many times those involved in a dispute would likely benefit by participation in mediation, but are not familiar with the process. Since historically mediation has not been the default paradigm for dispute resolution, parties often need awareness and encouragement. To advance mediation use and simultaneously increase knowledge and awareness of the process, courts began to urge and mandate that parties in litigation participate in mediation. Statutes have also been enacted which compel parties to attend mediation.

Currently, the most common method of compelling parties to mediation involves a court order. As courts became more interested in getting parties to mediation and lawyers were reluctant to suggest it, many courts became advocates for the mediation process. A variety of methods exist by which courts refer pending litigation to mediation.

1. AUTHORITY OF COURTS TO MANDATE MEDIATION

a. Inherent Authority

As courts began to consider mediation, concerns arose regarding their authority to mandate participation in the process. One contention is that judges have inherent authority to require participation in mediation as part of their ability to manage their own caseloads. Another view is that judges are acting within the parameters of the rules that give them the ability to control the court docket. Many believe judges are provided this authority under statutes or rules regulating court procedures. For example, federal judges have had authority to require participation in pre-trial conferences for some time, and in 1983, (Fed.R.Civ.P. 16) was specifically amended to encourage settlement discussions. This is often used as a basis to mandate ADR use. Although a prior concern, very few challenges to this judicial authority exist today, as state legislatures and Congress have enacted specific legislation allowing courts to mandate referrals to a variety of ADR processes. (For further explanation, see the Civil Justice Reform Act of 1990 and the Alternative Dispute Resolution Act of 1998, discussed *infra*.)

b. Statutes

Due in part to concerns about the validity of the courts' ability to refer cases to mediation, a number of states enacted legislation which provides more specific authority to the courts. These statutes allow courts to order mediation without the consent of the parties. Many times, these statutes include additional requirements for attendance and good faith participation, as well as provisions for appropriate sanctions, should a party fail to comply with such mandates. Other statutes provide courts the authority to mandate mediation in specific kinds of cases, often divorce or family law matters. In other instances, statutes enacted strongly encourage the courts to utilize mediation, but stop short of mandating its use.

i.   State

State court systems have approached implementation of mediation use with some variation. In some states, such as Florida, Texas, Indiana, and North Carolina there is widespread use of mediation within the court system. State statutes provide referral authority to the courts, and courts are free to apply the referral process in a number of ways.

ii.   Federal

In several federal courts, initial concerns surrounded the court's authority to mandate ADR procedures. (See *Strandell v. Jackson Co., Ill.*, 1987). Other ADR processes such as summary jury trial and neutral case evaluation, rather than mediation, appeared more prevalent early on. However, as mediation has become more familiar to the bar and the judiciary, its use has increased. This development is also a result of two acts passed by Congress, specifically encouraging ADR use.

1.   Civil Justice Reform Act of 1990

In 1990, Congress enacted the Court Justice Reform Act, which included a provision that encouraged each federal district court to enact a cost and delay reduction plan. It was suggested, and in some cases mandated, that the plans include provisions addressing ADR use. Mediation was one of several ADR processes listed. 28 U.S.C. §§ 471–482 (1992).

2.   Alternative Dispute Resolution Act of 1998

Congress enacted the Alternative Dispute Resolution Act of 1998 to broadly authorize federal district courts to implement ADR programs. 28 U.S.C. §§ 651–658 (Supp. V 2000). Specifically the directive required all federal trial courts to establish an ADR program for litigants and further allowed courts to mandate participation in those programs. The Act did permit existing programs to continue, as long as they proved to be effective. While this particular legislation set no deadline date for implementation and provided no specific structure for the courts to follow, it mandated immediate execution of the Act's provisions. Consequently, it has been an important catalyst for sending many cases to mediation.

Individual courts have also enacted local rules or standing orders, which obligate litigants to consider or participate in mediation. Some court orders mandate mediation use as part of pretrial procedure, while others state that participation in mediation is a condition precedent to retaining a case on the trial docket. An obligation to mediate (or participate in another ADR process) is also included in pretrial scheduling orders. Court rules can also impact the particular method of referral, whether decisions are made on a case-by-case basis or alternatively in groupings of cases.

2.   METHODS OF COURT REFERRAL

Courts utilize numerous methods in making referrals to mediation. Each has advantages as well as drawbacks. The type of method employed by individual courts may depend upon factors such as the local legal culture, structure of court, time allotment, volume of cases, support staff, and the availability of mediators.

a.   Independent Judicial Selective Referral

In this approach, each individual judge is responsible for selecting those cases on his docket which will be sent to mediation. This may occur as lawyers appear before the court at a hearing or for a motion. Alternatively, as the judge reviews the case file, she may make a determination on an individual basis that mediation is appropriate.

b.   Standing Orders or Local Rules Establishing an Obligation to Mediate

In some jurisdictions, the courts have worked together and enacted a local rule or a standing order which requires litigants to participate in mediation. Many federal courts enacted local rules addressing dispute resolution alternatives in response to the Civil Justice Reform Act, as well as the 1998 directive.

c.   Condition Precedent to Trial

Another method of referral is to obligate litigants to mediate before a date for trial is set. This method can be effectuated through a local rule or court directive such as a scheduling order. The requirement may apply to all pending cases, or the court may identify specific types of matters. While this referral method assures that the litigants will mediate, often the mediation occurs late, right before trial.

d.   Opt Out Provisions and Objections

Many courts and statutes have established methods that allow a party to "opt out" of mediation, or alternatively, file an objection with the court when they do not wish to mediate. Some lawyers and judges have been sensitive to, and in some cases, critical of a mediation mandate, and consequently, structured the opt out provision. Most mediation directives in family law cases have specific provisions that allow cases involving domestic violence to be excluded. With some opt out provisions, the parties may simply inform the court or ADR coordinator that mediation is not desired. In other instances, an objection must be filed, and the discretion to order mediation remains with the court.

3. ISSUES SURROUNDING COURT MANDATES

a. Constitutional Concerns

When courts are involved in setting out the requirements to mediate and occasionally the parameters of participation, concern arises that such activity may fall under the rubric of "state action." As a result, constitutional considerations may need to be addressed. For example, Professor Richard C. Reuben contends that when courts are involved in dispute resolution practices, including mediation, it is no longer merely a private matter, but rather part of the public court system. As such, it is necessary, according to Reuben, to assure the presence of constitutional safeguards such as due process protections, qualified right to counsel, right to present and contest evidence, and the impartiality of the neutral. (Reuben).

b. Timing Considerations

One factor which garnered significant attention in the referral of cases to mediation is that of timing. Identifying the time in the life of a dispute that is appropriate for mediation has been an elusive endeavor. Competing concerns exist. On one hand, if mediation takes place early, before suit is filed, the time and monetary savings are greater. In cases that are referred to mediation early, sometimes the parties are less likely to be hardened in their positions. Greater flexibility with regard to potential outcomes exists. Alternatively, many lawyers contend that if a dispute is mediated too soon, there has not been sufficient time to gather the necessary information, participate in discovery, or properly evaluate their case. In some instances, the passage of time is a way to allow parties to "cool off." Emotions lessen and parties are more reasonable. They may be more willing to compromise and entertain alternatives when their emotions have decreased.

c. **Effect on Other Aspects of Litigation**

Participation in court-annexed mediation may have consequences for the pending litigation. Concerns have been raised regarding the effect on litigation strategy, timing of deadlines and information disclosure. Litigators argue that a requirement to mediate compels them to disclose matters about the litigation which, from adversarial, strategic and tactical perspectives may not be beneficial. Despite claims of confidentiality, in most cases, information that is shared with the other parties can be discovered should the case not settle. As a result, some participants decline to make disclosures. Difficulties arise, however, in many situations where mediators are required by ethics or practice standards to encourage the parties to disclose information. Without information exchange, it is very difficult for the mediator to get to the main issues and interests of the dispute, and often information exchange is necessary for settlement.

Another consideration is the time allotted to participate in mediation and the effect upon other deadlines in the case. Many courts have enacted strict scheduling orders in an effort to streamline pretrial matters and drive the case to trial without delay. If mediation is attempted during the course of litigation, it may impact such orders and schedules. If the local rule or statute is unclear, and deadlines are a concern, the best course of action would be to petition the court for a specific ruling.

The running of statutes of limitations is another matter that can be affected by mediation participation. Very few state statutes provide for an automatic tolling of the limitations statute during the time of participation in mediation. In most instances, orders and statutes are silent. As such, if a statute of limitations deadline is an issue, then it is advisable to either reach stipulation or agreement among the parties or obtain a ruling from the court.

d. Mediator Selection Methods and Issues

During the initial stages of court-annexed mediation, courts in some jurisdictions were very active in the selection of individual mediators. Often the court order mandating mediation specifically named the mediator. Such practice raised issues of favoritism and potential judicial ethics violations. While in some cases, particularly complex and difficult matters, courts continue to hand pick the mediator for the parties, in most instances, parties are encouraged to select their own mediator. Courts which take an active role in administering mediation programs may have compiled a list or roster of "approved mediators." The parties are then directed to select a mediator from the list.

Parties may also be more committed to the mediation if they participate in the selection process. And some repeat users, such as insurance companies, have established relationships with particular mediators. "Repeat player" considerations present difficulties as well. Some companies and lawyers may have numerous cases which need to be mediated. For example, with insurance companies as defendants, the concern is that such repeat business may impinge upon the mediator's neutrality. The influence may be subtle or overt in acknowledging the potential for future business. Claimants may be sensitive to the fact that the mediator has mediated over a hundred cases for Brand X Insurance Group. In most cases, mediators are urged to make disclosure to all parties about past mediations. Chapter Six concerning mediator neutrality and Chapter Nine on Ethics examine these issues in greater detail.

e. Cost Considerations

The cost of the mediation is another matter of concern, especially where the court mandates that the parties participate. Simply stated, one party may more easily bear the costs of mediation than the other. For example, a large corporation may have no difficulty with a mediation fee, while an individual may be unable to tolerate such costs. Mediator fees range considerably from type of mediator to type of case and vary among jurisdictions throughout the United States. While one selling point is that mediation costs no more than a deposition, others contend that the court, a public institution, should not be in a position to obligate litigants to increase cost. Another frequently voiced perspective is that mediation will assist the parties in reaching a final resolution, thereby saving the cost of protracted litigation, trial, and perhaps appeal. In most instances, if the parties cannot afford to pay for a private mediator, local dispute resolution centers provide mediators at little or no cost. Some courts also sponsor programs where mediators serve pro bono, or at least must commit to mediating a specific number of cases per year on a pro bono basis.

D. LEGISLATIVELY MANDATED OBLIGATIONS TO MEDIATE

In some states, the legislature has established a requirement of mediation for dispute resolution. In most cases, these provisions are very specific and involve a particular subject matter, such as family law. Alternatively, some legislation requires mediation as the initial means of dispute resolution in specific matters. For example, New York has ordered a hospital mediation system for all disputes arising in the contest of the issuance of orders not to resuscitate. N.Y. Public Health Law § 2972 (1993). Disputes involving medical malpractice must be mediated in Maine (Me. Rev. Stat. Ann. 24 §§ 2851–2859). Alaska requires mediation in breach of warranty suits, (Alaska Stat. § 45.45.355, 1996), and in Oregon, mediation is required for child adoption disputes (1993 Or. Laws 401). As the use of ADR increases, statutes such as these will likely become more common.

E. ARGUMENTS AGAINST MEDIATION USE

While many individuals urge an increase in mediation use, citing the numerous benefits of the process, there are some who contend that mediation can be detrimental, especially when mandated. Examples of the problem include situations where there is an imbalance of power between the parties or where individuals may fare worse in mediation than in an adjudicatory or rule guided process. Because mediation is private and the process flexible, no procedural safeguards exist. This has been a source of controversy.

Although many reasons exist for the use of mediation and its practice has vastly increased over the last two decades, situations remain where mediation may not be preferred. In some instances, courts have ordered the parties to participate anyway, and resolutions have been reached in several of the cases. At other times, courts may consider the objection and excuse the party from participation. A few of the more common objections to mediation use are discussed below.

1. PROCEDURAL CONSIDERATIONS

One concern voiced by critics of mediation is that the process lacks procedural safeguards. Some feel that compelling parties to meet with one another may be detrimental, particularly where the parties are not represented by counsel. Another consideration is that race and culture may dictate that some parties are not treated as fairly as they might be in a courtroom. One contention is that prejudicial attitudes are more prone to be acted upon in informal settings. (Delgado, et al.)

Another procedural objection concerns discovery. In some cases, it is paramount to a realistic consideration of alternatives for settlement that certain information be learned. If it is not, then the parties are unwilling to even consider a proposal of resolution. One solution is that the mediator oversees an informal method of information exchange prior to the mediation session.

Another concern surrounds the issue of procedural justice, particularly in court-annexed cases. The concern is that in mediation, the procedure may not be fair—or at least perceived as fair from the parties' viewpoint. Yet, research indicates that the parties' participation is the key to assurance of procedural justice, or at least their perceptions of justice. One method advocated to assure procedural justice in mediation is party participation. (Welsh).

2. POWER IMBALANCES

In those instances where an imbalance exists between the education or sophistication of the parties, mediation may not be appropriate. One party may emphasize such imbalance to take advantage of the other through the use of mediation. Where one party is more experienced and in a better position to make truly informed decisions, then the other may clearly be at a disadvantage. Some believe that this is a real problem when the parties are not represented, but that the presence of counsel will alleviate the concerns. However, in many cases, even the presence and differences in representation can result in power imbalances.

While some of the mediation literature discusses methods that a mediator may utilize to equalize such imbalances, he may not always be able to do so. Moreover, once a mediator attempts to rectify an imbalance, often it results in a loss of neutrality. (Chapter Six explores these dilemmas in the context of impartiality considerations, informed consent and the appropriateness of social and legal norms in mediation.)

3. UNWILLING AND UNCOOPERATIVE PARTIES

In some instances, one or more of the parties involved in a dispute may be unwilling to go to mediation. The reasons are many, but sometimes the parties are ordered to attend nonetheless. In many of those cases, a resolution is achieved. However, where a court order or contract does not exist, it is unlikely that the parties will participate. By default, this is essentially the most effective method of objection since if a party refuses to participate, it is nearly impossible to engage in the process.

4. NEED FOR PRECEDENT

Certain types of disputes require that a determination be made by an outside third party, such as a court. For a variety of reasons, individuals sometimes have a need for developing case law and setting a precedent. In some instances, however, mediation is specifically used to avoid such a result, although this approach has been criticized. One of the prominent early critics of ADR, Owen Fiss argued that the primary problem or drawback to use of alternative processes is that they ignore the role of the courts in the adjudication process. (Fiss). While some subject matters dictate a need to establish precedent, whether by rule of law or by practice methods, most cases are suited to a less formal resolution.

F. LAWYERS OBLIGATION TO ADVISE CLIENTS ABOUT MEDIATION

Many individuals consult an attorney when involved in a dispute or controversy. A requirement that lawyers advise clients about mediation is one way to increase both awareness and use of the process. Although this idea remains somewhat controversial and is by no means a settled issue, lawyers should be aware that the possibility of such a requirement exists.

1. CURRENT ETHICAL RULES

The ABA Model Rules of Professional Conduct, as well as several state codes, have many provisions regarding the lawyer-client relationship. While not explicit, several of these provisions suggest an implicit obligation to advise a client about ADR. For example, ABA Model Rule 3.2 calls for "reasonable efforts to expedite litigation." Many believe this rule creates an obligation for attorneys to inform their clients about ADR. Consideration of dispute resolution alternatives is also viewed as a necessary part of client decision making; clients need information with which to make informed choices (Cochran).

2.   SPECIFIC PROVISIONS

Several states, such as Colorado and Texas, have established provisions that direct lawyers to advise their clients about mediation. These provisions are not included in disciplinary rules, but rather in professionalism mandates. Most are aspirational in nature. Provisions include terminology that a lawyer "should," rather than "shall," advise her client about ADR. Other statements contain qualifying language, such as "when appropriate," so that such an obligation is not absolute, but rather left to the lawyer's judgment.

3.   PROPOSED RULES

In 1997, the American Bar Association established the Ethics 2000 Commission, which had as its task the review of the Model Rules of Professional Conduct. The ABA Section of Dispute Resolution, as well as several individuals, during this reconsideration of the Model Rules urged the Commission to add a provision suggesting or mandating that lawyers advise clients about ADR options, including mediation. Initially, the commission rejected the idea of a requirement. The final draft of the report, however, does include a provision that calls for some consideration of alternate dispute resolution. Furthermore, it would not be surprising to see additional rules requiring such counseling at the state level when disciplinary boards look to reconsider ethical rules.

4.   INFORMATION DISCLOSURE AND DECISION MAKING

One important issue which arises when considering an obligation to counsel clients about mediation is the extent of the discussion with the client. On one hand, mere mention of a mediation alternative to the client may be sufficient, particularly if the client is knowledgeable about mediation. At the other extreme, if a client is completely unaware of mediation, then a detailed description and cost-benefit analysis of mediation use and settlement may be appropriate.

Throughout legal ethics, discussion continues over the allocation of decision making between the lawyer and the client. One guideline is the means-ends dichotomy. The lawyer alone can make decisions concerning the specific means of achieving a result as long as it is consistent with the ends desired by the client. In the context of mediation, it would seem that the final decision with regard to mediation use would remain in the purview of the client, particularly if settlement is a desired objective. On the other hand, many lawyers contend that they are in a better position to make the decision because they are more knowledgeable about methods of settlement. Issues concerning allocation of decision making also exist with regard to how the mediation is conducted, including the extent of information to disclose, choice of mediator, strategy in negotiation and final outcome.

5. CONSEQUENCES OF FAILURE TO ADVISE

As requirements to advise clients regarding ADR emerge, corollary issues surround the consequences of the lawyer's failure to advise. If specific rules are enacted, the next consideration is enforcement. For instance, if a requirement to advise has been enacted, then appropriate disciplinary action may be taken by a governing bar association, should a grievance be lodged against the lawyer.

a. Disciplinary action

Disciplinary action against lawyers is taken when a violation of a specific rule is established. Currently, this may be difficult, as few states have specific mandates regarding dispute resolution. Yet, if rules are established in the future, then procedures for enforcement will necessarily follow.

b. Legal Negligence or Malpractice

It is possible that a legal negligence claim may be brought against a lawyer for the failure to advise about mediation. This would essentially be a new cause of action, as no reported cases currently exist. Anecdotal reports suggest that the few cases which have been filed have settled without a trial.

Failure to advise *about* mediation as a potential cause of action should be distinguished from the situation where the lawyer advises the client to not settle *during* the mediation. This is a separate issue that concerns different ethical violations, such as failure to advise a client about settlement offers. (See *Rizzo v. Haines,* 1989).

G. PRE–MEDIATION CONDUCT AND CONCERNS

Once a decision is made to participate in mediation, whether voluntary or mandated, the next vital step is that of preparation and planning. Many of the events which lead up to the mediation may have a significant influence on what occurs during the session. Mediators, as well as the participants, engage in the preparation and planning process. In the private sector, preparatory efforts are often managed by the mediator who helps guide the participants and the lawyers in the process. Planning in this context includes administrative matters such as the location and time of the session. Methods for information exchange with the other side and the mediator are also addressed. In the public court-sponsored or community programs, many of the administrative matters are handled by staff members rather than the individual mediator.

1. ORGANIZATIONAL MATTERS

Administrative matters include setting the date and time of the mediation; determining the amount of time allotted for the session; and deciding whether it will be one mediation session or multiple sessions. For example, in some divorce mediations, the process is divided into one hour sessions which occur once a week for a period of several weeks until the matter is resolved. In large complex cases, such class actions, several full days of mediation may need to be scheduled. Still in other cases, only a few hours will be allotted for the mediation. Timing allocations are determined by the mediator, participants or administrative personnel.

The location for the mediation in another matter which is determined and communicated in advance. In court programs, mediations may take place in the courthouse, perhaps in a jury room that is not occupied. In the private sector, most mediators have office space or rent conference rooms. In community programs, mediation occurs at the program office. Alternatively, if a program is a run by government entity, official buildings are often available. One of the most important factors in location determination is to assure that the site is a neutral one.

Part of pre-mediation planning also includes identifying any special needs the parties may have. Identification of who will attend the mediation and ensuring that the parties necessary to make decisions will be present is another critical element of planning. Specific seating arrangements may also be considered in advance of the session.

2.   PREPARATION

Adequate and comprehensive preparation is an extremely valuable and necessary ingredient to a beneficial mediation experience. This is true for the mediator as well as the parties and their representatives.

a.   Mediator

Part of the mediator's preparation includes the mechanical details outlined above. A mental component to preparation is also necessary. This involves gathering information about the case and the participants, as well as focusing on the mediation the day of the session. In terms of pre-mediation information exchange, many mediators request some type of document usually called a pre-mediation submission or memorandum. Requiring the parties provide these documents may be considered part of participation in mediation. (See Chapter Five.) The amount of information provided to the mediator by way of these documents varies, depending upon the nature of the case and whether the parties are represented by counsel. In a matter where no lawsuit exists, the parties themselves may submit a brief outline or statement about the case. In other instances, this information may be acquired through the program itself and relayed to the mediator right before the session.

Debate exists about how much information the mediator should acquire in advance of the session. On one hand, the mediator needs to be somewhat knowledgeable about the matter. On the other hand, too much information may lead to possible bias and premature judgments.

It is also critical that mediators engage in mental preparation. Important mental preparation involves being ready to listen carefully, analyze information and remain neutral. In all cases, the mediator should think through what types of information, as well as the extent and detail of information, he is seeking. Additionally, during the preparation stages, the mediator might consider how to deal specifically with the lawyers and their clients and the expectations he has from each. The mediator also prepares to explain in his introductory remarks how the process will proceed.

b. Participants

The mediation participants, both parties and representatives, also spend some time in preparation in advance of the mediation. Drafting pre-mediation documents assists the participants in their focus and preparation. One component of preparation involves deciding what information to provide to the mediator and what information will be disclosed to the other parties. Preparation may also include learning about the mediation process itself.

Where the parties are represented by lawyers at mediation, determining the role of the lawyer vís a vís the client is another critical aspect to mediation preparation. Time should also be spent in considering what types of possible resolutions are desirable. On the other hand, rigid decisions with regard to potential outcomes are generally not advised. Flexibility and the ability to consider a variety of creative solutions are often key elements to a successful mediation. Consideration should also be given to what the possible desired outcomes are for the other parties.

Use of documents, graphs and videos should also be considered in advance. Time and effort should appropriately be devoted to the planning and preparation components of mediation, just as they would any other procedure that results in a final disposition of the case. In most instances, matters settle at mediation.

References

Robert F. Cochran, Jr., Legal Representation and the Next Steps Toward Client Control: Attorney Malpractice for the Failure to Allow the Client to Control Negotiation and Pursue Alternatives to Litigation, 47 Wash. & Lee L. Rev. 819 (1990).

Robert F. Cochran, Jr., Professional Rules and ADR: Control of Alternative Dispute Resolution Under the ABA Ethics 2000 Commission Proposal and Other Professional Responsibility Standards, 28 Fordham Urb. L. J. 895 (2001).

Richard Delgado et.al., Fairness and Formality: Minimizing the Risk of Prejudice in Alternative Dispute Resolution, 1985 Wis. L. Rev. 1359.

Owen Fiss, Against Settlement, 93 Yale L. J. 1073 (1984).

Richard C. Reuben, Constitutional Gravity: A Uniting Theory of Alternative Dispute Resolution and Public Civil Justice, 47 UCLA L. Rev. 949 (2000).

Nancy A. Welsh, Making Deals in Court–Connected Mediation: What's Justice Got to do With it? 79 Wash. U. L. Q. 787 (2001).

Primary Cases

Kirschenman v. Superior Court, 36 Cal.Rptr.2d 166 (Cal. Ct.App.1994).

Strandell v. Jackson County, Ill., 838 F.2d 884 (7th Cir. 1987).

Rizzo v. Haines, 555 A.2d 58 (Pa.1989).

In re Atlantic Pipe Corporation, 304 F.3d 135 (1st Cir. 2002).

Bibliography

James J. Alfini & Catherine G. McCabe, Mediating in the Shadow of the Courts: A Survey of the Emerging Case Law, 54 Ark. L. Rev. 171 (2001).

Marshall J. Breger, Should an Attorney Be Required to Advise a Client of ADR Options?, 13 Geo. J. Legal Ethics 427 (2000).

John Cooley, Mediation Advocacy (1996).

Caroline Harris Crowne, Note, The Alternative Dispute Resolution Act of 1998: Implementing a New Paradigm of Justice, 76 N.Y.U. L. Rev. 1768 (2001).

Eric R. Galton, Representing Clients in Mediation (1994).

Trina Grillo, The Mediation Alternative: Process Dangers for Women, 100 Yale L. J. 1545 (1991).

Leo Levin, Beyond Techniques of Case Management: The Challenge of the Civil Justice Reform Act of 1990, 67 St. John's L. Rev. 877 (1993).

Andreas Nelle, Making Mediation Mandatory: A Proposed Framework, 7 Ohio St. J. on Disp. Resol. 287 (1992).

Thomas L. Shaffer & Robert Cochran, Lawyers, Clients and Moral Responsibility (1994).

CHAPTER 5

THE OBLIGATION TO MEDIATE

As the use of mediation has increased, additional factors and issues concerning the process have emerged. In particular, one thorny issue surrounds mandatory mediation and specifically what it means to "mediate."

This issue can be significant in court-ordered mediation, as well as those instances where the parties are contractually bound to mediate. Preliminary questions surround who must attend the mediation and what they must do when present. A critical issue involves making the decision that the parties who are obligated to mediate have actually mediated. The primary question is whether the parties have complied with the court order or with the contractual obligation to mediate.

In the contractual situation, mediation is sometimes considered a condition precedent to taking another action. For example, some contracts require mediation before pursuing another course of action such as arbitration or litigation. (*Weekley Homes, Inc. v. Jennings,* 1996). In order to access another dispute resolution procedure, the parties must have participated in mediation. Consequently, a determination of when and how this participation is accomplished is vital. In the court-annexed arena, the parties may be required to mediate prior to obtaining a trial setting. Alternatively, a court may simply order the parties to mediate and may require notification upon compliance with the order.

Some experts have urged courts and legislatures to enact and enforce a standard for the conduct of mediation participants. Others, however, claim that to do so is inadvisable, and perhaps impossible, as it conflicts with a number of other established principles of mediation. One contention is that courts and legislators should not be interfering in the conduct of a private, consensual process. Some argue that dictating conduct at mediation may undermine the parties' self-determination. Another claim is that interference with the lawyer's ability to conduct a case as he deems appropriate violates litigant autonomy. In spite of these concerns, mediation literature, along with courts and statutes, has begun to require specific conduct for those participating in mediation. More generally, the question of what it means to mediate is a topic being examined in a variety of settings ranging from court decisions to law review articles.

One current view is that "mediating" is likely to involve a variety of behaviors. These include but are not limited to: attendance at the mediation; preparation for the process; possession of adequate settlement authority; participation at mediation; and even participation in good faith. A corollary issue involves methods to determine whether the parties have actually mediated, and are therefore entitled to pursue the next step or process. As mediation use increases, no doubt additional attention will be directed to these matters.

A. ATTENDANCE AND AUTHORITY ISSUES

One aspect of compliance and an obviously necessary element of participation is presence. A party cannot participate in mediation without being present. Although some exceptions to physical presence exist, such as when mediation takes place by telephone or video conferencing, most experts, cases, and statutes contend that the parties should be present at the mediation, in addition to their lawyer representatives.

1. PARTIES/PRINCIPALS

In order to fully discuss the dispute as well as options for settlement, it is generally necessary that the parties themselves—those individuals who are to be the final decision makers in the matter—be present at the mediation. Much of the mediation process involves communication: direct, subtle, verbal, and non-verbal. Decisions regarding resolution are often based on communication. In order to communicate with the others in dispute, physical presence is required. As mediation may involve a re-evaluation of the case for settlement, being able to physically view the parties can be an important factor. In some cases, attempts have been made to delegate the settlement authority to an attorney representing a party. In most cases, that option has not proven to be effective, and such an approach has not been endorsed by courts. The Seventh Circuit was one court that examined this issue more closely. The Court affirmed a district court order requiring that a corporate representative be present for a pretrial settlement conference, and upheld sanctions on the corporation for failure to comply with the order. (*G. Heileman Brewing Co. v. Joseph Oat Corp.*, 1989).

2. ATTORNEYS

In most cases, the presence of the attorney for the party is not required, but because the matter is in litigation, lawyers do attend. Various roles for participation of the lawyer representative in mediation have been identified, and are fairly self-explanatory. These include the lawyer as a non-participant, a silent advisor, a co-participant, or primary participant. (Rau, Sherman, Peppet). Although it is important to make a preliminary determination of which role the lawyer will play, it is also valuable to remain willing to modify the approach. This may be at the discretion of the mediator, by request of the parties, or on the lawyer's own initiative.

3. OTHERS

While not commonly part of the court order, in some cases presence of additional individuals may be critical to the ultimate resolution of the case.

One example is that of experts. Experts involved in mediation may be the expert witnesses employed by each side or alternatively, a neutral expert retained by the mediator. Another possibility, perhaps more common in areas of specialized application of mediation such as family law, is the presence or participation of a counselor or therapist.

The importance of relevant individuals at the mediation has been considered by the courts. In fact, one California court imposed sanctions against defendants for failing to bring their expert witnesses, as required, to a court-ordered mediation. In this instance, however, the order imposing sanctions was vacated since plaintiffs had violated confidentiality statutes when they filed their supporting documentation. (*Foxgate Homeowners' Ass'n v. Bramalea California, Inc.*, 2001). Nevertheless, the significance of expert participation is clear.

Other common non-party participants in mediation are insurance representatives. A recent case examined the court's ability to require the attendance and participation of a representative of a defendant insurance company. The court of appeals overturned the trial court's sanction of an individual who attended the mediation but was without the authority to settle the matter since other representatives with authority to settle were present at the mediation. In this instance, the sanctioned individual was not technically representing the carrier. As a consequence, the court failed to have jurisdiction over him. (Adkins v. Hansen)

4. PROBLEM SITUATIONS

Although there may be general consensus that it is imperative to have the decision makers in the dispute physically present at the mediation session, actual presence in some instances becomes impossible or impractical. This issue arises frequently in disputes involving a governmental entity, a large corporation such a bank or an insurer, or those parties who are in distant locations.

a. Public Governmental Entities

Mediating with local, state, or federal governmental entities creates special challenges for the mediation process itself and for the mediator. One difficulty involves the large number of lawsuits some governmental agencies handle. For that reason, the court in *In re Stone* found that a trial judge had abused his discretion by requiring that the federal government send a representative with full settlement authority to attend settlement conferences in person, stating that availability by telephone was sufficient. However, in a subsequent case, the same court took a different view. The Court, while urging trial courts to first consider options other than physical presence, held that where the government agreed to participate in mediation, a trial court did not abuse its discretion in ordering a representative with full authority to be present at the mediation. (*In re United States of America*, 1998).

Additionally, when government entities are involved, the mediator may have to deal with a number of government representatives and may encounter logistical problems concerning the drafting and signing of any agreement reached. For example, most cities and counties are governed by a council or group of elected officials. The authority to make decisions, such as those concerning the settlement of a lawsuit, particularly where money is to be paid, is a shared responsibility. No one person is given the authority to make a final and binding decision. In a dispute involving a city, the city will typically send a representative from the city council to the mediation. The assumption is that the representative will have a clear idea of what the city council will likely approve. But this individual is without authority to speak unconditionally on behalf of the city council.

A suit against a state or government agency, which is often answered by the government's attorney poses similar challenges. Ultimately, an agreement may need approval from the specific state agency sued and another ranking official such as the governor. In such cases, the representative who attends the mediation is only in a position to make a recommendation. In these situations, any agreement will likely be "subject to final approval" by a governing body or elected official.

b. Corporations

Many large corporations are managed, at least in part, by a board of directors. Having the entire board present at a mediation may be difficult, if not impossible. While the decision for much of litigation related matters may fall within the general counsel's office, most of those decisions relate to the course of litigation. Specific decisions involving the settlement of a lawsuit, particularly where a substantial amount of money is to be paid, will likely need approval from someone other than the general counsel. While a CEO or CFO might be in a position to make a final determination, it is unlikely, unless involved directly in the dispute as a party, that the individual would attend the mediation. Often, it may be that a mid-level manager with specific authority is present but is without final decision making ability. Again in this instance, an agreement would not be binding until approved by the Board of Directors.

c. Insurance Companies

Another problem arises in situations where an insurance carrier for a party is the one to ultimately decide whether or not a matter settles. The insurance industry is hierarchical, with multiple levels of authority and decision making capacity. In any one day, a major insurance company may have hundreds of mediations occurring simultaneously throughout the country, rendering the presence of the ultimate decision maker at every mediation impossible. An insurance company may send a representative to the mediation with a certain predetermined limit of monetary authority. In order to obtain additional authority, the representative may have to telephone the regional or home office, requesting that an individual who has not experienced the mediation grant additional authority. While such situations are not optimum for the purposes of mediation, logistically this may be the only practical method for large insurance carriers to participate and resolve matters in mediation.

d. **Multi–National Disputes**

As the world becomes smaller, it is not uncommon that disputes arise which involve a number of individuals residing reside in different countries. While the best situation for mediation remains to have all of the parties together in person, it simply may not be possible. Although courts have ordered litigants to travel long distances to attend mediation, usually these are situations where the party is named in a lawsuit. While in most cases such an order is and would be upheld, other alternatives show promise. When mediations are conducted pursuant to contract, the issue remains open as to whether a court will order such attendance. In other cases, travel may be cost prohibitive or timing factors make attendance impossible. In those instances, different alternatives for the mediation process should be explored.

5. ALTERNATIVE APPROACHES

Some options have developed over time with regard to the attendance problems at mediation. The following are some of the more common responses to such difficulties. The earlier the mediator is aware of these difficulties, the better the chance for finding workable solutions. Gathering information during the preliminary preparation stage may go a long way in either preventing disappointment regarding attendance or at least having an alternative approach planned in advance.

a. Delegation of Authority

If an individual or group of individuals are entirely unable to attend the mediation, one option would be to delegate a representative to speak and make decisions on behalf of the entity, be it a governmental entity or a business. When authority is delegated to an individual it is important to be specific and detailed with regard to the extent and nature of the authority. Delegation approaches are used in large multi-party class actions, where a spokesperson is frequently appointed to negotiate a tentative agreement or partial agreement with the understanding that a subsequent ratification will be necessary by the class.

b. Telephone and Video Conferencing

Another option utilizes either telephone or video conferencing devices. While the telephone allows the absent party to participate minimally in the mediation, a significant portion of the communication is lost. This presents particular difficulties where the nuances of communication are important to the resolution of the matter. Video conferencing allows the parties to at least see one another, which can be an improvement. On the other hand, in situations where there is merely a need for the decision maker to authorize an increase in the amount of settlement, the use of the telephone may be effective in reaching a final resolution.

c. Subsequent Ratification of Tentative Agreement

Reaching a tentative or conditional agreement at the mediation, even if subject to subsequent approval or ratification, is another means to deal with an absent final decision maker. In some instances, the party may be able to delegate authority to an individual present at the mediation to negotiate within a predetermined range. Should an agreement be reached at mediation, often it must be later ratified by the entity of decision makers. This method should be made clear to the other side and the mediator in advance. The downside to such predetermination is that the flexibility to explore diverse options for resolution may be limited.

B. A REQUIREMENT OF PREPARATION

Preparation on the part of both the parties and their representatives, most often lawyers, is a key element of mediation. Without such preparation, the mediation session may be a waste of time and effort. Adequate preparation may consist of reviewing the case to gain sufficient knowledge and understanding of the dispute, meeting with the parties, and considering potential options for resolution.

Preparation for mediation helps the participants focus on the issues and think about the goals they hope to achieve. In many instances, mediators encourage the parties and their representatives to spend some preparation time in moving away from the win-lose dichotomy and considering an interest-based approach to resolution. Although there is nearly universal agreement that adequate preparation is beneficial to the mediation process, a requirement for such preparation may be a more complicated matter.

One issue is whether courts can realistically order that the parties be adequately prepared for mediation. The meaning of adequate preparation will likely vary depending upon the type of case and parties involved. For example, in an employment case where a lengthy relationship between the parties exists and various options for settlement are present, a number of different issues may need to be considered in advance. Identifying the parties' underlying interests is important. Additional matters might include an initial decision regarding continuation or termination of employment. If employment is maintained, then conditions such as types of assignments, revising policies, or changing supervisors will need to be addressed. Alternatively, where termination is the result, other issues including severance pay and letters of recommendation will need to be resolved.

On the other hand, in a car accident where the parties have not met one another and have no interest in doing so, then the only focus may be a monetary settlement. Preparation may not need to be as intricate. It should be noted, however, that even in those cases which may at first glance appear to be focused on a single issue, there is always potential for additional matters to surface when exploring interests and alternative options for resolution. Although more time consuming, the most thorough approach is to prepare for all aspects of mediation. In pending litigation matters where the parties are represented by counsel, preparation will likely result in an increased amount of attorneys' fees as time passes. Another view, however, is that ultimately money is saved if the case is resolved prior to trial.

It is undoubtedly difficult for a mediator to judge whether the participants are adequately prepared for mediation. Even harder, though, is determining how courts can realistically enforce an order that the parties be prepared to participate. While including enforcement provisions may encourage the parties to prepare for the session, actively monitoring and discovering what the lawyers and clients have done is difficult, if not impossible. Beyond the obvious cases in which a lawyer fails to appear or comes to mediation without any information about the case, an inquiry regarding participation will likely necessitate exceptions to mediation confidentiality and the lawyer work-product privilege.

C. PAYMENT OF THE MEDIATOR'S FEE

Another consideration of participation in mediation involves the payment of the mediation fee. Generally, mediators in private practice charge a fee for their service, which in most instances is divided evenly among the parties. The inability of one party to pay may lead to the other party covering the entire fee. In most instances, this is strongly discouraged due to concerns regarding neutrality.

When a court orders litigants to participate in mediation, in many instances the payment of the fee is an implicit element of that participation. Fee payment is also considered by some as a separate indicator of participation.

D. MANDATORY INFORMATION DISCLOSURE AND EXCHANGE

Another suggested guideline for participation in mediation is the exchange of position papers or other means of mandatory disclosure of information. (Sherman) Individuals often misunderstand each other because they have different perceptions, based on varied and diverse information. An exchange of information would assure that all parties are "reading from the same page." An understanding or acknowledgment of the other party's viewpoint often encourages increased participation and interaction at the mediation.

In addition, making decisions about potential options for resolution may require specific information. For example, in an injury case, review of medical reports is often vital. An exchange of necessary and critical information with the mediator, as well as the other parties, can serve as the foundation for meaningful consideration of settlement alternatives.

Sherman's suggestion of a mandatory information exchange includes four elements. Specifically, he recommends that prior to the mediation the parties exchange a plain and concise statement of: (1) the legal and factual issues in dispute, (2) the party's position on those issues, (3) the relief sought (including a particularized itemization of all elements of damage claimed), and (4) any offers and counter-offers previously made. (Sherman)

A few concerns have been raised regarding this mandatory exchange of information. In court cases, it is likely that much of this information has already been disclosed through the normal discovery channels. Moreover, to limit the information from the outset seems to refocus on the legal aspect of the dispute, rather than help the parties move away from the right-wrong paradigm. Finally, even with an information exchange, there is no guarantee that the participants will actually provide the details necessary for resolution.

E.   MEANINGFUL PARTICIPATION

Meaningful participation in mediation is another standard that has been suggested to assist in determining what it means to mediate. Dean Ed Sherman, noting that a good faith requirement is unworkable and encroaches upon the litigant's rights to control litigation, calls for minimal meaningful participation instead.

1. DEFINITION

Minimum meaningful participation, as urged by Sherman is participation beyond merely minimal, in that it is meaningful. The specific type of meaningfulness essentially depends upon the particular ADR process. In a more facilitative process, this would entail making a statement of position, listening to the other parties, and providing a response to the other party's statements. One court found that participation was satisfied by attendance and a statement of position by the party. (See *Graham v. Baker*, 1989). Because of mediation's unique focus on interests, other experts urge that discussion of underlying interests and options might also be a necessary element of meaningful participation.

2. DETERMINATION

Unlike more objective requirements such as attendance, payment of a fee, or information exchange, participatory standards of conduct for parties and representatives in mediation present more difficulty in determining compliance. Should a meaningful participation standard be established, the subsequent issue would be how to decide whether the parties and lawyers have meaningfully participated. Because such standard is dependant upon the particular process, it seems that the neutral, in this case the mediator, would need to make the decision.

F. GOOD FAITH PARTICIPATION

Discussions regarding mediating in good faith and enacting a standard which would require such conduct have increased in recent years. Authors have urged that such a standard be enacted, and some state statutes actually provide for such a standard, although enforcement of the standard is an issue which has rarely been addressed.

1. DEFINITIONS

One difficulty in enacting a good faith standard is reaching an acceptable and workable definition of good faith. While a good faith standard has been used in collective bargaining and commercial matters, no consensus has been reached on a specific definition of the phrase. Although most individuals including legislators, judges, lawyers and parties assume they already know what good faith means, a detailed definition does not exist.

In an effort toward clarification, discussions of these definitional issues have increased. Definitions which have been urged include specific elements which comprise good faith (Kovach) and a totality of the circumstances (Weston). In the few reported cases addressing the topic of good faith, none actually provide a working definition. For the most part, the courts say what good faith is not, rather than provide terms of proscriptive conduct or behavior. (See *Halaby v. Hoffman*, 1992). Even in the absence of a clear definition, good faith in mediation is an element seen with increasing frequency.

2. POLICY CONSIDERATIONS

In considering a requirement of good faith participation in mediation, one critical aspect includes
policy issues. While some commentators advocate
such a standard (Kovach, Weston), others warn of
its problematic nature (Lande, Sherman). No doubt
courts, legislators and drafters of agreements to
mediate will consider the policy as well as practical
implications of such a standard.

An argument in favor of a good faith standard is
the need for a process where the participants can be
assured that all are treated equally, and more importantly, that mediation is not misused to disadvantage a party. Examples include situations where
a mediation is scheduled to increase expense for the
less affluent party or to gain information. When
participants in mediation take an adversarial or
belligerent approach, the process is often derailed
and impasse results. An obligation of good faith
would likely deter this type of inefficient conduct.
Most analysts agree that mediation will be productive and fruitful only if all participants take an
active role in the process. A good faith standard can
aid in such efforts. Good faith also assists in guar-
anteeing honesty in the process.

In those instances where concerns about good
faith are voiced, several matters are discussed. Definitional difficulties and conflicts with the confidential nature of mediation are raised. Making a determination about good faith may impact and even
conflict with mediator neutrality. Additional objec-

tions include allegations that a good faith requirement would violate party autonomy and work-product privilege and negatively impact trial strategy. Finally, because of the need to make determinations with regard to the absence of good faith, increased satellite litigation is another concern.

3.   CURRENT LEGAL PARAMETERS

At the time of publication, several states have enacted statutes providing a requirement that mediation be conducted in good faith. Courts as well as legislators have begun to address these issues, with diverse results. Over seventy-five statutes, court roles and orders exist which call for good faith in mediation.

a.   Statutes

In a number of states, statutes which mandate or merely suggest mediation also include a good faith provision. For example, one of the first reported cases involved the farmer-lender arena where a Minnesota statute obligated the parties to mediate in good faith and specifically defined that obligation. In Maine and Texas, statutes require mediation in family law cases and further state that the process be conducted in good faith, although a specific definition of the term is absent. Delaware and Hawaii statutes direct the mediator in adult guardianships and probate matters to terminate the mediation if a party is not mediating in good faith. A Florida statute provides that in nursing home cases all parties must mediate in good faith. Even more comprehensive, an Indiana rule clearly imposes a general requirement of good faith in mediation on the parties as well as the lawyers.

b. Case Law

Although legislation has established the good faith requirement, in many cases it will be in the purview of the courts to enforce it. Early cases which confronted the issue assumed that a good faith requirement was feasible, as the decisions focused on the determination of whether good faith was demonstrated in the settlement conferences. For example, in a Colorado case where the defendant refused to change his maximum settlement offer, the court found he was not acting in bad faith. (*Halaby*, 1992). In most instances, this holding is consistent with those who propose good faith, making it clear that compliance is not dependant upon the offers or "movement" of position during the mediation.

As court-annexed mediation became active in Texas, the first case to address the good faith issue was *Decker v. Lindsay*. In this case, a Houston appellate court determined that the state statute providing for court referrals allowed courts to mandate that the parties attend mediation, but not that they demonstrate good faith. Later Texas cases have split regarding whether good faith can be required in mediation, although none address what exactly is contemplated with such requirement. (*Texas Dep't of Transp. v. Pirtle*, 1998; *Texas Parks & Wildlife Dep't v. Davis*, 1999). Instead, most opinions focus on the trial courts ability to sanction a party.

In a somewhat controversial case, a federal court in Missouri held that an employer violated an order referring the matter to mediation by failing to submit the required mediation memorandum and failing to send a corporate representative with authority to settle the case. Calling these actions a violation of good faith, the sanctions were upheld by the Court of Appeals. (*Nick v. Morgan's Foods, Inc.*, 2000).

A California court of appeals viewed a good faith participation requirement as vital to the mediation process as confidentiality, although the California Supreme Court overturned the decision, recognizing a compelling necessity for confidentiality and refusing to create an exception. (*Foxgate Homeowners' Ass'n v. Bramalea California, Inc.*, 2001). It is likely that additional cases will address similar issues.

Once a court or statute establishes some type of good faith requirement, the next issue is deciding whether the parties complied with such a requirement. Exactly who makes that decision is a critical and controversial issue. And after a determination has been made, the next issue to be addressed involves establishing the consequences for failure to comply with good faith requirements.

4. RELATION OF MEDIATION PARTICIPATION TO ETHICAL CONSIDERATIONS FOR ATTORNEY REPRESENTATIVES

Most, if not all of the ethical rules and regulations set out in Attorney Codes of Professional

Responsibility address the lawyer's work in an adversarial setting. Yet, the concept of lawyering has expanded and encompasses general problem solving activities as well as representation in non-adversarial situations such as transactions, mediation and negotiations. Most of the rules have failed to maintain or embrace such actions and remain entrenched in the adversarial practice.

A recognition that different types of lawyering may require distinct standards and ethics has been expressed (See Kovach, Rapoport, Alfini). Separate standards have been advocated in a number of practice areas, including representation in mediation (Kovach). Specific ethical guidelines for lawyers who represent clients in a mediation or problem solving (non-adversarial negotiation) may include duties not generally found in the adversarial sphere. These may embrace conduct such as good faith, empathy, honesty, and communication. While such an approach has not been adopted by any formal group, advancement is being made in this regard.

G.   SANCTIONS AND OTHER CONSEQUENCES FOR NONCOMPLIANCE WITH GUIDELINES

Once a standard is established or required, whether by statute, court order, or contract, the next logical consequence is the consideration of sanctions or penalties for noncompliance. Several of the difficulties in determining compliance with such a requirement have been previously discussed.

Nonetheless, as courts continue to superintend court-annexed mediation, they increasingly confront these issues. Thus, courts and the mediator community have begun to address matters surrounding the enforcement of good faith directives.

1.   NECESSITY

While aspirational standards can be of some benefit, particularly in serving an educational function, only with real enforcement of standards will the parties be assured of conduct which is compliant. Often an enforcement process is necessary to assure that requirements or guidelines of particular conduct are taken seriously. Strict enforcement of a level of participation in mediation will also assist in deterring some of the conduct that commentators have claimed to be examples of bad faith, and perhaps it will provide an increase in positive expectations of the process as well. Enforcement mechanisms also provide the opportunity for a party harmed or disadvantaged by some misuse of mediation to be compensated or otherwise provided a remedy.

2.   DETERMINATION OF NON–COMPLIANCE

Several difficulties exist regarding the determination of compliance or violation of any participation guideline or rule. Most, if not all, available methods to determine whether the parties have complied with a court's order or contract provision, pose thorny issues. The first issue concerns who will be making the determinations.

Two possibilities exist concerning who will decide whether mediation participants have complied with a directive regarding their conduct. In most instances, the mediator will be in the best position to know whether the parties attended and what they did or didn't do when there. Some early statutes and cases seemed to direct the mediator to make the decision. (See *Obermoller v. Federal Land Bank of St. Paul*, 1987). On the other hand, more recent sanctions have come from the courts. If mediators do not make the decision regarding the standard of participation, the decision is then left up to the court. That decision maker, usually the judge, will need additional information. In fact, an Indiana court failed to find bad faith, citing a lack of evidence as all that was before the court was the mediator's report noting compliance with ADR rules. Plaintiff offered no evidence of a lack of good faith. (*State v. Carter*, 1995). While each side may report to the court (if exceptions to confidentiality are recognized), there will obviously be bias in their testimony. A more impartial perspective would come from the mediator.

Yet, mediators for a variety of reasons are quite reluctant to make disclosures. For one, any disclosures are likely viewed as a violation of the sacrosanct confidential nature of the session. (See Chapter Seven for an in-depth examination of confidentiality.) Mediators, both those in private practice as well as volunteers, strongly resist any breach of confidentiality. Another difficulty of reporting is the possible destructive impact on mediator neutrality. Mediators do not want to be in a position to make decisions regarding the parties' conduct. In the event however, that mediators are required or ordered to disclose such information, the use of objective data can be helpful in making a straightforward determination.

3. RANGE OF POSSIBLE CONSEQUENCES

Appropriate consequences for failing to conform to guidelines set forth for mediation participation may include a variety of remedies. Generally, the most common penalty imposed in civil cases is a monetary sanction. For example, where parties fail to appear at mediation (without filing an objection or informing the others involved in the matter), reimbursement of costs incurred by the other side is likely proper. Often the amount of the sanction will be proportionate to the costs incurred by the failure to comply with the order. This may include the lawyer's fees incurred in preparing for the mediation as well as time spent at the session. It may also include reimbursement for the other portion of the mediator's fee.

While striking pleadings is usually a severe sanction, there is a situation where it may be a more common occurrence. This measure is frequently used in courts where the obligation to mediate is necessary to avoid a dismissal for want of prosecution. Inactive cases are given the opportunity to stay on the docket if they participate in mediation. However, the failure of a plaintiff to appear generally results in the case being dismissed.

In many cases, striking pleadings and entering a default judgement is considered a "death penalty" sanction, and should only be imposed after less severe sanctions have been undertaken. (*Wal–Mart Stores, Inc. v. Butler*, 2001). But other courts have a contrasting view. When a party refused to appear for mediation, striking the answer and entering a default judgment was found to be within the trial court's discretion. (*Triad Mack Sales v. Clement Bros.*, 1994).

Other possible sanctions that exist include fee penalties, reduced time to prepare for trial, or a remedial sanction matched to the specific abuse. For example, where a party secretly brought a jury consultant to the mediation, that individual was then prohibited from participating in the subsequent trial.

4.   WHO IS SANCTIONED?

One consideration not discussed a great deal in the cases or the literature, relates to determining the appropriate party to levy sanctions against. In most legal circumstances, such as discovery abuse, the sanctions are issued against the party although exceptions exist. Where no one appears for mediation, for example, then both the attorney as well as the client may be sanctioned. Several statutes calling for good faith require such conduct on the part of the attorney as well as the client. Courts also appear to be considering the relative fault of the parties in handing out sanctions. (*Roberts v. Rose,* 2002). In most cases, however, the court is without the authority to sanction someone who is not a party to the lawsuit. (*See Adkins v. Hansen,* 2002).

a. Attorney

Where the attorney is responsible for the action or inaction, then some sanction or fine may be levied against the attorney. If the attorney is responsible for the clients' non attendance, then the sanction may be issued only against the attorney. (*Roberts*).

b. Client

In other situations, courts have made clear that the client can also be sanctioned for conduct that violates a court order. One instance where the sanction would likely be only against the client is where the lawyer has little client control. In most cases, however, the sanction will be issued against both the attorney and client.

c. Both

In many cases, courts have held that sanctioning both the lawyer and client is proper. This consideration also has bearing on appellate issues. Should an appeal be necessary, the individual having standing to raise issues will be only the one against whom the sanctions were issued. In general, trial courts have wide discretion with regard to sanctions.

References

James Alfini, Settlement Ethics and Lawyering in ADR Proceedings: A Proposal to Revise Rule 4.1, 19 N. Ill. U.L. Rev. 255 (1999).

Kimberlee K. Kovach, Good Faith in Mediation—Requested, Recommended or Required? A New Ethic, 38 S. Tex. L. Rev. 575, (1997).

Kimberlee K. Kovach, New Wine Skins Requires New Wine: Transforming Lawyer Ethics for Competent Participation in Non–Adversarial Problem Solving: Mediation, 28 Fordham Urban L. J. 935 (2001).

John M. Lande, Using Dispute System Design Methods to Promote Good–Faith Participation in Court–Connected Mediation Programs, 50 UCLA L. Rev. 69 (2002).

Nancy B. Rapoport, Our House, Our Rules: The Need for a Uniform Code of Bankruptcy Ethics, 6 Am. Bank Inst. L. Rev. 45 (1998).

Alan Scott Rau, Edward F. Sherman & Scott R. Peppet, Mediation and Other Non–Binding ADR Processes (2d Ed. 2002).

Edward F. Sherman, Court–Mandated Alternative Dispute Resolution: What Form of Participation Should be Required? 46 SMU L. Rev. 2079 (1993).

Maureen Weston, Checks on Participant Conduct in Compulsory ADR: Reconciling the Tension in the Need for Good–Faith Participation, Autonomy, and Confidentiality, 76 Ind. L.J. 591 (2001).

Primary Cases

Contractual Mediation:

DeValk Lincoln Mercury, Inc. v. Ford Motor Co., 811 F.2d 326 (7th Cir.1987).

Weekley Homes, Inc. v. Jennings, 936 S.W.2d 16 (Tex. App., San Antonio, 1996).

Court–Annexed Mediation:

G. Heileman Brewing Co. v. Joseph Oat Corp., 871 F.2d 648 (7th Cir.1989).

Keene v. Gardner, 837 S.W.2d 224, (Tex.App.1992).

Attendance Issues

Adkins v. Hansen, 2002 WL 1070693 (Ohio App. 5th Dist.)

Graham v. Baker, 447 N.W.2d 397 (Iowa 1989).

In re Stone, 986 F.2d 898 (5th Cir.1993).

In re United States of America 149 F.3d 332. (5th Cir. 1998).

Roberts v. Rose, 37 S.W.3d 31 (Tex.App.2000).

Triad Mack Sales & Service Inc. v. Clement Brothers Company, 438 S.E.2d 485 (N.C.App.1994).

Wal–Mart Stores, Inc. v. Butler, 41 S.W.3d 816 (Tex.App. 2001).

Good Faith

Avril v. Civilmar, 605 So.2d 988 (Fla.Dist.Ct.App.1992).

Bennett v. Bennett, 587 A.2d 463 (Me.1991).

Bulkmatic Transport Company, Inc. v. Pappas, 2002 WL 975625 (S.D.N.Y.2002).

Decker v. Lindsay, 824 S.W.2d 247 (Tex.App.1992).

Foxgate Homeowners' Ass'n v. Bramalea California, Inc., 25 P.3d 1117 (Cal.2001).

Halaby, McCrea & Cross v. Hoffman 831 P.2d 902 (Colo. 1992).

Nick v. Morgan's Foods, Inc., 99 F.Supp.2d 1056 (E.D.Mo. 2000); aff'd 270 F. 3rd 590 (8th Cir.2001).

Obermoller v. Federal Land Bank of St. Paul, 409 N.W.2d 229 (Minn.Ct.App.1987).

State v. Carter, 658 N.E.2d 618 (Ind.App.1995).

Stoehr v. Yost, 765 N.E.2d 684 (Ind.App.2002).

Texas Dep't of Transp. v. Pirtle, 977 S.W.2d 657 (Tex. App.1998).

Texas Parks & Wildlife Dep't v. Davis, 988 S.W.2d 370 (Tex.App.1999).

Bibliography

Wayne D. Brazil, Continuing the Conversation about the Current Status and the Future of ADR: A View from the Courts, 2000 J. Disp. Resol. 11 (2000).

Roger L. Carter, Oh, Ye of Little (Good) Faith: Questions, Concerns and Commentary on Efforts to Regulate Participant Conduct in Mediations, 2002 J. Disp. Resol. 367 (2002).

Steven Hartwell, Understanding and Dealing with Deception in Legal Negotiation, 6 Ohio St. J. on Disp. Resol. 171 (1991).

Lucy V. Katz, Compulsory Alternative Dispute Resolution and Volunteerism: Two Headed Monster or Two Sides of the Coin, 1993 J. Disp. Resol. (1993).

Kovach, Kimberlee, Lawyer Ethics in Mediation: Time for a requirement of good faith, 4 Disp. Resol. Mag. 9 (Winter 1997).

Charles J. McPheeters, Note, Leading Horses to Water: May Courts Which Have the Power to Order Attendance at Mediation Also Require Good Faith Negotiation?, 1992 J. Disp. Resol. 377 (1992).

Edward Sherman, Good Faith Participation in Mediation: Aspirational, Not Mandatory, 4 Disp. Resol. Mag. 14 (Winter 1997).

David S. Winston, Participation Standards in Mandatory Mediation Statutes: "You Can Lead a Horse to Water . . .", 11 Ohio St. J. on Disp. Resol. 187 (1996).

Alexandria Zylstra, The Road from Voluntary Mediation to Mandatory Good Faith Requirements: A Road Best Left Untraveled, 17 J. Am. Acad. Matrim. Law. 69 (2001).

CHAPTER 6

ISSUES SURROUNDING MEDIATOR NEUTRALITY AND IMPARTIALITY

In mediation literature, the terms neutrality and impartiality are often used interchangeably. Yet attempts have been made to define neutrality and impartiality in different ways. For example, the Standards of Practice for Family and Divorce Mediation promulgated by the Academy of Family Mediators, now a division of the Association of Conflict Resolution, provide separate, distinct definitions for the terms. According to the standards, impartiality refers to the specific conduct of the mediator with regard to the participants. This means that the mediator will not act with favoritism or bias toward either party. On the other hand, neutrality is used to describe the nature of the relationship between the mediator and the parties, particularly the mediator's freedom from prejudice in conducting the process. Essentially, neutrality demands that the mediator withdraw if she is unable to remain neutral throughout the process.

Upon close examination, the terms seem nearly identical. In most situations, they are used interchangeably, as both describe basic principles of the mediation process. Matters of neutrality and impartiality are also quite frequently included as integral elements of codes of ethics for mediators. (See Chapter Nine for further discussion on Ethics.)

It may seem that a requirement or standard of neutrality is implicit in the practice of mediation and should not cause many difficulties; yet in some instances, problems arise. Certain mediation situations can be troublesome and present significant neutrality issues. One critical issue involves an imbalance of power between the parties. It is possible that one party may attempt to use the process to take advantage of the other party, by increasing costs, attempting to gather information, or using newly acquired information to achieve an advantageous agreement. The proper mediator's response to this type of situation is subject to some debate. Some argue that the moment the mediator attempts to correct an imbalance, he becomes an advocate for the weaker or less capable party, essentially compromising his own neutrality.

Although this topic has been the subject of much consideration, mediators are often left without specific guidance to govern their conduct. Often mediators must make immediate decisions on an individual, case-by-case basis. This chapter first examines the more traditional view of the mediator's role, one which aims for near absolute neutrality. The discussion then turns to situations that call for intervention and further considers the level and type of mediator involvement which might be appropriate. Consequences of the failure to maintain neutrality are also mentioned.

A. TRADITIONAL CONCEPTIONS OF THE MEDIATORS ROLE

It may be helpful to examine the concepts of neutrality and impartiality by isolating the mediator's primary tasks. Looking closely at the various responsibilities and objectives of the mediator's actions provides a window through which impressions or perceptions of neutrality can be examined. One important area concerns the mediation process and its implementation. Another focus is on the content or subject matter of the dispute. A third topic involves more personal matters, such as the identity or background of the parties and potential sensitive or underlying issues involved. Evidence of prior relationships with the mediator, either personal or professional, may also impact neutrality directly or indirectly, depending on how the parties perceive the relationship. Similarly, the potential for future relationships may also present a threat to neutrality.

1.   PROCESS MATTERS

Most experts would agree that ideally the mediator begins and remains neutral at all times throughout the session. Difficulties may arise, however, when one party is more educated, knowledgeable or articulate than the other. Such disparities may threaten the boundaries of the mediator's impartiality.

Most experts agree that the mediator should maintain a neutral process and provide the parties an equal opportunity to participate in the process. Mediators commonly face the situation where some parties are more verbose and willing to participate than others. This can be especially disconcerting during the presentation of opening remarks. As such, neutral behavior may require that the mediator allows the parties adequate time to speak and express themselves during the process. Although providing specific limits of time may be logistically difficult, mediators generally provide each party ample opportunity not only to be heard, but also to ask questions, while maintaining a fair and neutral process.

Time spent in caucus or private sessions is another area which can impact mediator neutrality. While mediators do not meet with each party for identical periods of time, they do attempt to balance the time spent with each side. This illustrates that the mediator exhibits no favoritism or partiality toward one side.

An additional aspect of a neutral and fair process includes allowing each party to obtain the information necessary for informed decision making. This may occur prior to the mediation, or a need for information could arise during the process. As a result, permitting the disputing parties to be accompanied by counsel or other representatives is often considered an element of a fair and neutral process.

2. ISSUES OF DISPUTE

The subject matter of the dispute is another aspect of mediation neutrality. It is imperative that mediators not be biased or opinionated about the substance or content of the dispute, as there is a potential danger that such biases might affect potential resolutions. While it may be impossible to be completely neutral about some matters, as all individuals are human and sometimes have involuntary reactions to certain issues, it is important that opinions, experiences and preferences do not impede the mediator's ability to conduct the mediation in an impartial manner. Furthermore, mediators are expected to refrain from offering judgments or opinions concerning possible resolutions. Exceptions to this rule are limited to the occasions where a highly evaluative model of mediation is used. Such evaluative models may permit the mediator to evaluate or provide a judgment regarding the potential outcome of the case. However, this approach is controversial and is viewed by some as a serious threat to neutrality.

In most instances, mediators are able to maintain impartiality with regard to matters discussed in the mediation. There may be, however, a particular subject or issue about which the mediator feels he cannot remain totally neutral. This is particularly difficult in some specific types of disputes, such as family law. Many mediators acknowledge that some issues exist which test the bounds of their neutrality. In these cases, whenever possible, mediators identify as part of preparations those subjects which present potential challenges to neutrality and determine whether such challenges might impact their ability to serve in a neutral capacity. Upon a recognition of strong bias, most mediators decline to take the case.

In rare cases, discussion of an illegal or immoral matter may occur at mediation. With regard to moral matters, the decision to continue or alternatively, to terminate the mediation is within the discretion of the mediator. Most experts and practitioners contend that should an illegal matter surface during mediation, such as the option of paying past due rent with cocaine, then the mediator should immediately terminate the session. Exceptions, of course, are in the mediation of criminal matters and victim-offender mediations. Even in those instances, however, mediators do not condone illegal agreements.

3. RELATIONAL CONCERNS

The relationships a mediator may have with the parties is another aspect which impacts neutrality of the process. The existence of a prior relationship or promise of a future one can effect both neutrality and impartiality. Mainly, the danger is that one party may believe any previous dealings between the mediator and the other party may create a bias. The intensity, frequency, and duration of such prior relationships are factors which may impact such perceptions. Usually, the longer the relationship has lasted or the closer in time to the present mediation, the more difficult the problem becomes.

Nevertheless, instances of prior professional relationships are not uncommon. It is possible that mediators may have had previous dealings with one of the parties at the mediation. Mediators who are also lawyers may have represented one of the parties in the past. Similar situations present themselves for mediators who are simultaneously engaged in mediation and another professional practice such as accounting, social work or psychotherapy. A mediator who is a therapist may have had a prior professional relationship with one of the parties. In the same manner, prior relationships with the representatives of the parties can present challenges to neutrality. For example, a mediator's prior law partner may be representing a party at mediation. Although it is necessary to acknowledge and disclose such prior relationships, to enact an absolute prohibition would be extremely difficult as well as unfair. As a practical matter, these kinds of relationships assist with business development. Currently, most situations involving prior relationships are resolved or determined on a case-by-case basis.

Potential relationships with participants after the mediation may not be as obvious a threat to neutrality, but these future relationships can be problematic nonetheless. One concern raised in ADR literature involves repeat players—those individuals who use the mediator's services on a regular basis. For example, consider one party, perhaps a plaintiff in a personal injury lawsuit, who is a one-time user of mediation. Imagine the defendant is an insurance company that has hundreds, possibly thousands of cases it will be taking to mediation. Although most mediators contend they could remain neutral and completely impartial regardless of potential future business, a significant amount of repeat business could jeopardize neutrality. Such a situation raises issues for the disputants, and such relationships may impact the public's perception of the mediation profession.

When confronting neutrality issues, often the mediator's first hurdle is self-analysis. A mediator must determine whether neutrality is an issue, given the relationship that exists. If so, then most experts contend that next step is to disclose the particular relationship to all participants. Once the relationship is exposed and only if all parties agree, then the mediation can proceed. However, some relationships are so close that it would not be proper for the mediator to handle a case, even after disclosure and acceptance by the parties.

Maintenance of neutrality is also consistent with the mediator avoiding conflicts of interest. Conflict of interest issues are generally addressed within the ethical considerations for mediators, which are examined in greater detail in Chapter Nine.

4.   OUTCOMES OR RESOLUTION

A mediator also has the potential to confront difficulties with maintaining impartiality when considering the final agreement or outcome of the mediation. In some instances, mediators may perceive, accurately or not, that the outcome is unfair to one of the disputants. One problem is that the mediator may not have all of the information to properly view the outcome. In that case, the mediator's belief that the resolution is unfair is flawed. Additionally, when a mediator makes a judgment regarding the fairness of a final resolution, she is in essence substituting her judgment for that of the parties. This is specifically prohibited by statutes or rules in a number of jurisdictions.

Even if such judgments are not prohibited, it can be very difficult for a mediator to determine, after a very short period of time, what is fair or acceptable to another individual. Individual values differ; what is one person's trash is another's treasure. Mediation emphasizes tailor-made and innovative solutions. In mediation, creativity is valued, and to judge the outcome for disputing parties may likely stifle that creativity.

Another difficulty lies in the fact that often the parties have not shared with the mediator all of the information they considered in making their decision. Thus, what may seem unfair to the mediator at first, may, after the discovery of additional information, not be so one-sided.

Another problem arises when the mediator becomes so concerned with the outcome that the agreement is no longer that of the parties. If the parties are satisfied with the final resolution, most mediators do not wish to be in a position to second-guess the parties' decision. Of course, exceptions exist where the resolution violates the law or is so grossly unfair that nearly any objective person would protest.

Defining the mediator's role in cases in which an obvious injustice has occurred is difficult. Generally, most experts say that the mediator should not do anything, especially where the parties are represented by counsel. They argue that it is not the mediator's job to intervene when the parties have their own advocates or representatives.

One safeguard used by mediators is reality testing the feasibility of the agreement. By asking the parties direct questions about potential outcomes throughout the process, the mediator can assist the parties in making informed and consensual decisions.

5.   PARTY PERSPECTIVES

Mediation historically has focused on party participation, empowerment and satisfaction with the process. Thus, in the beginning, even if no reason existed to question neutrality, the issue was presented to the parties. Originally, as part of the mediator's introduction, the parties were asked if they believed that the mediator was neutral and not biased. This was done so that if the participants had concerns, even if unfounded and groundless, they might be alleviated. The mediators did not want to begin the process with the parties having negative ideas that could potentially impact their participation or undermine any agreement reached.

Although that particular practice is no longer commonplace, in the unlikely event that a party perceives the mediator as biased, two responses usually exist. One option is for the mediator to withdraw and for the parties to find another mediator. The second option is for the mediator to ask questions and delve into the reasoning behind the feelings of bias, to see whether such concerns can be alleviated.

Party perception of a lack of neutrality may also occur during the mediation. For example, a party may perceive that the mediator is spending more time in caucus with the other party or may believe that a mediator's reality testing suggests a lack of neutrality.

B. CONSIDERATIONS OF FAIRNESS: MEDIATING WHEN PARTIES LACK KNOWLEDGE OR INFORMATION

At first glance, it seems easy to require the mediator to remain impartial with regard to the process and content of the mediation, as neutrality is a foundation of the process. Yet many cases present circumstances where it may be necessary for the mediator to intervene to prevent one party from taking advantage of the other. One such instance is where a substantial imbalance exists between the parties during negotiations and most likely if an agreement is reached in mediation, it would not be upheld. For example, parties may agree to resolving a claim for an amount of money which is unusually low. Another situation where there is potential for this problem is within the arena of family law. Some recent literature calls for the mediator to take a more active role in family and divorce cases, especially refraining from approaches that disadvantage women. (Bryan)

Other difficult situations involve the mediation of lawsuits. Some experts believe that the law which would control the legal outcome of the dispute should have a role in the mediation process. If the parties lack knowledge or understanding of such legal parameters, they should not be disadvantaged by their participation in mediation. This idea, as well as the extent of the mediator's role is subject to some debate.

Another way of looking at this issue is through a lens of informed consent. This view contends that in order for the parties to actually reach an agreement, they must have knowledge of the mediation process, as well as an understanding of the potential outcomes that may be reached. (Nolan–Haley). This approach recognizes that party empowerment and self-determination are foundations of the mediation process. Concern arises where the parties lack necessary information, and therefore are unable to make decisions that are informed.

1. THE ROLE OF LAW IN MEDIATION

Theoretically, because mediation is a move away from the legal win-lose, right-wrong paradigm, many feel the law has no role or a very minor one in the mediation process. On the other hand, because in many cases litigation is one of the most viable options should the case not settle in mediation, parties must be aware of the potential consequences and the probable court outcome. Another perspective considers whether the final resolution is, or should be, needs or interest-based or alternatively, dependent upon the relative rights of the parties. These issues present many challenges for the mediator's role.

If the mediator is a lawyer, it is more likely that she may be familiar with the law, but there is a possibility that she will be engaged in the practice of law or found to be representing one or both of the parties if she discusses legal consequences. And if a party relies on the information which turns out to be incorrect, the mediator has increased his potential liability. Mediation has not traditionally been viewed as the practice of law. However, when non-lawyer mediators begin to provide legal information, analysis, or advice they run the risk of being charged with the unauthorized practice of law. If the mediator is not legally trained, then it is doubtful that he will know all of the legal implications. Most ethical guidelines or practice standards currently attempt to limit the amount of legal information that the mediator may provide to the parties.

If parties are represented by counsel, most mediators and experts agree that the responsibility for legal advice and information rests with the lawyers. In these cases, difficulties arise when the lawyers are uninformed or misunderstand some of the issues. Nevertheless, the majority view is that the mediator should refrain from intervening and should not inform the lawyer of his mistake. Providing such assistance to one side could profoundly and negatively impact neutrality. In some cases, if the mediator fears that an injustice will result, most experts recommend that the mediator terminate the mediation session. The party will still have recourse against his own lawyer. Usually, these types of situations become even more problematic when the parties are not represented by counsel.

2.   UNREPRESENTED PARTIES

When the parties do not have legal or other expert representation, several situations may present challenges to the mediator's neutrality. For example, consider a case pending in court. It is not uncommon for the parties involved to have some expectation of "justice through law." Nolan–Haley contends that if litigants are mandated to mediate, then justice requires that the bargaining which occurs during mediation be influenced by legal knowledge. As the parties are the decision makers, they may need assistance at least in understanding the legal basis for decisions. Reliance on legal norms, however, is also seen as directly conflicting with the notion that parties in mediation should act creatively and pursue their personal sense of fairness based on nonlegal values such as culture, morals and individual ethics.

Imbalances of power between unrepresented parties also present difficult situations for the mediator. For example, one party may be much more knowledgeable, sophisticated, or experienced than the other. These parties might use their assets to try to gain advantage over the other party. Consider a landlord who owns properties and has had twenty years of experience in lease matters. Generally, one would expect that the landlord knows much more about landlord-tenant law than a tenant who is renting his first apartment. There is a very real possibility that in mediation the landlord may attempt to take advantage of the tenant's lack of knowledge, perhaps by claiming a justification for the security deposit even though he knows that he is legally not entitled to keep it.

In these situations, mediators face difficult dilemmas, which at this time, are resolved on an individual, case by case basis. In mediation, parties may also want to know what may happen if case is pursued in court. Yet many cannot afford a lawyer. The difficulty then, is in assigning the responsibility for assuring that the parties have sufficient information.

3. THE NEED FOR INFORMED CONSENT

A basic foundation of mediation, self-determination essentially provides that through the mediation process individuals are able to make their own decisions and not be coerced into agreements. (Welch). In order to make decisions which are truly informed, the parties must have the requisite information. Once a determination is made that additional information may need to be provided to the parties, there is a range of advice that might be provided.

4.   TYPES OF INFORMATION OR ADVICE

To say that a mediator may or may not give legal information or advice is a simple, basic statement which may appear uncomplicated. A closer examination of the issue, however, reveals that there are more intricacies involved.

Some experts draw a line between information and advice. Information, whether legal, financial or other is considered more factual and general. Such information would be applicable in all types of cases. In fact, information may often be provided by another source, such as a mediation program administrator or a brochure, rather than the mediator herself. Advice, on the other hand, refers to the specific application of information to the facts or situation at hand. The mediator is usually the only one in a position to provide advice, but doing so may directly conflict with the mediator's maintenance of neutrality.

Many experts have examined the types of information or advice a mediator may provide. Four models of mediator-party relationships have been identified, which demonstrate a range of methods utilized by mediators to provide information to the parties. The models are as follows: paternalistic, instrumentalist, informative, and deliberative. (Nolan–Haley).

In a paternalistic approach, the mediator acts primarily as the parties' surrogate in assessing what outcome might be best, whereas in an instrumentalist model, the parties' objective is simply to reach settlement. The third model is an informative model, where the mediator acts as an information conduit. Finally, in the deliberative model, the mediator provides parties with the same factual and legal information described in the informative model, but also helps the parties understand, articulate, and finally, choose the values that should govern their ultimate choices. (Nolan–Haley).

Other authors demand that mediators balance power by assuring that all interests are represented and taking a more active role with the parties. In examining this issue, Professor Ellen Waldman categorizes mediation into three types: norm-generating, norm-educating and norm-advocating. The last two types have the potential to directly collide with impartiality. (Waldman).

Finally, the appropriate time to provide such information or advice is another important consideration. In most instances, mediators would prefer that the parties have all of the necessary information in advance of the mediation. However, in many cases difficulties concerning information arise during the mediation itself.

C. CAPACITY ISSUES

In some types of mediations, concerns may surface about the capacity of the individuals to reach or make a knowledgeable decision about an agreement. Not only would reaching an agreement without capacity be unfair, it would also be a defense to the enforceability of the agreement. In some instances, affirmative duties to be certain that the parties possess capacity have been established. For example, such a duty exists in the mediation of cases that involve claims of violations of the American with Disabilities Act (ADA). ADA Mediation Guidelines specifically state that the mediator is obliged to be sure that the parties are able to understand the process and the options under consideration, as well as be able to give voluntary, informed consent to any resolution. The guidelines also provide that in making an assessment, consideration includes medical diagnosis as well as individual case evaluation.

D. A NORMATIVE ROLE FOR MEDIATION

Some cases by their very nature imply or bring an imbalance of power or knowledge. In very difficult cases, including matters involving domestic violence or discrimination, normative standards exist, which some allege should never be violated. Included are both legal norms, those standards encoded in the law, as well as societal norms, principles and standards that have attained consensus status in society. Party and societal interests may need to be protected by adherence to these norms. Professor Waldman's first view of mediation as a norm-generating process allows the parties themselves to determine the values and fairness of the outcome. This approach is closest to a purest or traditional view of the process. The two other approaches describe a more active role for the mediator. Norm-educating refers to a process where a mediator informs the parties about the prevailing norms which apply to their dispute, but stops short of insisting that the resolution adhere to these norms. Norm-advocating goes a step further and after educating the parties about relevant norms, insists that they be incorporated into any mediated agreement. (Waldman).

Therefore in some types of matters, the mediator may assume a role that does not appear on the surface to be completely neutral. Rather than allow the parties to arrive at their own conclusions, the mediator will commonly provide some guidance regarding what legal and societal standards may exist and in some instances, insist that any agreement reached adhere to such standards or norms.

E. CONSEQUENCES OF THE LACK OF NEUTRALITY

A variety of consequences may result from the lack of neutrality on the part of the mediator. Some of these are dependent upon whether the lack of neutrality is discovered or known prior to the mediation. In some of the cases mentioned above, the mediator takes on a normative role, providing information and even strong recommendations for resolution. In doing so, the mediator may no longer appear or be entirely neutral. If it is known in advance that the mediator will take on a normative role, the parties should be informed. Educating or discussing this approach with the parties in advance is important so that they understand their role in the process. If unknown to the parties, this conduct may not be expected, and the parties may be uncomfortable with the approach.

1. DURING THE MEDIATION

If information arises during the session which appears patently unfair, if one party hides information from the other, or if a party deliberately misrepresents information in his statements to the other side, most mediators would terminate the session. First, however, the mediator might try to allow the party an opportunity to correct their behavior, although it is possible that one side can later claim he was coerced into settlement, rendering the agreement invalid. Claims of mediator malpractice may also be a consequence of a violation of neutrality.

2. SUBSEQUENT CONFLICTS

In some cases, challenges to neutrality may arise after the mediation. While this type of situation will not directly effect the outcome since the mediation has ended, it can have an impact on the parties' perception of the mediation process. For example, if the mediator and one of the parties continue a business relationship, whether in the context of the mediation or in subsequent representation, this may cause the other party to be concerned about the neutrality of the mediator during the session. Although there are ethical standards in place for mediators, few specific rules or guidelines that govern how mediators should behave when faced with these situations exist. Most often it remains an issue that mediators must answer for themselves.

References

Penelope E. Bryan, Killing Us Softly: Divorce Mediation and the Politics of Power, 40 Buff. L. Rev. 441 (1992).

Jacqueline M. Nolan–Haley, Court Mediation and the Search for Justice Through the Law, 74 Wash. U. L.Q. 47 (1996).

Jacqueline M. Nolan–Haley, Informed Consent in Mediation: A Guiding Principle for Truly Educated Decisionmaking, 74 Notre Dame L. Rev. 775 (1999).

Ellen A. Waldman, Identifying the Role of Social Norms in Mediation: A Multiple Model Approach, 48 Hastings L. J. 703 (1997).

Nancy A. Welsh, The Thinning Vision of Self–Determination in Court–Connected Mediation: The Inevitable Price of Institutionalization?, 6 Harv. Negot. L. Rev. 1 (2001).

Cases

No reported cases dealing directly with neutrality, however, some tangentially, for example, Allen v. Leal others.

Bibliography

Allison Balc, Making it Work at Work: Mediation's Impact on Employee/Employer Relationships and Mediator Neutrality, 2 Pepp. Disp. Resol. L.J. 241 (2002).

Dwight Golann, Is Legal Mediation a Process of Repair—or Separation? An Empirical Study and its Implications, 7 Harv. Negot. L. Rev. 301 (2002).

Trina Grillo, The Mediation Alternative: Process Dangers for Women, 100 Yale L.J. 1545 (1991).

Joel Kurtzberg & Jamie Henikoff, Freeing the Parties From the Law: Designing an Interest and Rights Focused Model of Landlord/Tenant Mediation, 1997 J. Disp. Resol. 53 (1997).

Judith L. Maute, Public Values and Private Justice: A Case for Mediator Accountability, 4 Geo. J. Legal Ethics, 503 (1991).

Jacqueline M. Nolan–Haley, Lawyers, Clients, and Mediation, 73 Notre Dame L. Rev. 1369 (1998).

Kimberly A. Smoron, Role, Conflicting Roles in Child Custody Mediation: Impartiality/Neutrality and the Best Interests of the Child, 36 Fam. & Conciliation Courts Rev. 258 (1998).

Ellen Waldman, The Role of Legal Norms in Divorce Mediation: An Argument for Inclusion, 1 Va. J. Soc. Pol'y & L. 87 (1993).

Ellen Waldman, Substituting Needs for Rights in Mediation: Therapeutic or Disabling? 5 Psych. Pub. Pol'y & Law 1103 (1999).

CHAPTER 7

CONFIDENTIALITY IN MEDIATION

Over the last twenty-five years, a basic assumption of mediation practice has been that everything occurring within the mediation room was absolutely confidential. In most instances, mediators and participants both viewed the entire proceeding as one cloaked in secrecy. Yet, as experience with the process has expanded, and in particular, as mediation has merged with the litigation system, a number of difficult issues relating to confidentiality have surfaced. Some of the more critical matters concern the duty to disclose and the court's need for evidence or additional information.

The modern mediation field has entered a phase of regulation, as statutes and case law continue to evolve. Because of the great diversity in mediation confidentiality provisions throughout the United States, the American Bar Association (ABA), through its Dispute Resolution Section, and the National Conference of Commissioners on Uniform State Laws (NCCUSL) have spent the last four years examining in great detail matters surrounding confidentiality in mediation. The result has been the drafting of a Uniform Mediation Act, which provides for confidentiality in mediation, but also explicitly carves out exceptions.

173

In 1997, NCCUSL determined that time was ripe for drafting a Uniform Mediation Act. The organization also decided that the act would focus primarily on issues of confidentiality. At the time NCCUSL initiated its work, there were over two thousand statutes, rules and regulations across the nation dealing with mediation confidentiality, many of which were inconsistent with one another. In an attempt to establish uniformity, national experts worked with NCCUSL and the ABA Section of Dispute Resolution to draft the Act. During the course of this effort, a variety of critical issues were raised and debated.

One result is an explicit recognition that the time of absolute confidentiality in mediation has likely passed. During the last few years, the realization has emerged that circumstances and situations exist which necessitate an exception to the private nature of mediation. Examples are included in this chapter.

Several states already have extensive confidentiality provisions in place and may not consider the UMA. Other jurisdictions may readily benefit from its provisions. While this effort has been enormous and is laudable, critics of the UMA have also been vocal. Undoubtedly, many issues remain and various matters that will need to be decided on a case-by-case basis.

A. IMPORTANCE OF OVERARCHING GENERAL POLICY CONSIDERATIONS

A number of policy arguments exist for supporting confidentiality in mediation. Yet competing policy issues also demonstrate the need to disclose information learned at mediation or provide evidence regarding what occurred during the process. Even with statutes in place, occasions will continue to arise that require the courts or individuals to make immediate decisions concerning the issues presented during the mediation process. Thus, it is quite helpful to understand the general policy arguments concerning confidentiality.

1. IN FAVOR OF CONFIDENTIALITY

The arguments for maintaining confidentiality are numerous, and many date back to the early work done in the mediation field. In fact, one primary assertion is that confidentiality has always been part of the mediation process. This premise of confidentiality forms the foundation of the assumption that disclosures made by the parties are maintained in confidence by the mediator. Another consideration relates to the trust element of mediation. In many ways, establishing trust between the participants and the mediator is at the core of the process. Parties are more likely disclose important information and personal needs if they feel that they can trust the mediator. Because of the nature of a dispute, participants in a mediation may inherently distrust one another and may be unwilling to share information. One way that the mediator establishes a trusting and comfortable environment is to assure the participants of confidentiality.

From a legal perspective, the longstanding exclusionary rules surrounding negotiation discussions provide another policy consideration for the establishment of confidentiality in mediation. Arguments for confidentiality in mediation are similar to those underlying Federal Rule of Evidence (FRE) 408. Rule 408 and its state counterparts essentially prohibit the use of settlement offers as evidence of liability in a trial of a lawsuit. The purpose of these rules is to encourage settlement discussions.

Parties probably would resist actively participating in settlement negotiations if during the discussions could be used against them in a subsequent trial. With the assurance of confidentiality, however, parties and lawyers are more willing to openly discuss all matters and propose settlements. Settlement agreements, as well as offers to compromise in disputed claims, have traditionally been inadmissible at trial in order to prove liability. It follows logically that the same treatment, for the same reasons, should be afforded to mediation participants. Mediators and lawyer representatives in mediation often rely on these grounds to assure parties of a confidential setting in mediation.

Another policy favoring confidentiality is tied to the concept of mediator neutrality. In mediation, the mediator facilitates a negotiation as a neutral third party. If the mediator is either able or required to convey information to a decision maker of any kind, the mediator may compromise the neutrality of the process. If testimony were required, it is likely that both sides would urge the mediator to testify on their behalf, making impartiality impossible.

If disclosure were permitted or required in the course of conducting the mediation, a mediator might be distracted by concerns about what information could or should be included in subsequent testimony. If the participants are concerned about post-mediation disclosures, it is likely that the information they choose to share with the mediator would be limited. Furthermore, if mediation participants are aware that the mediator may make a report to another entity at a later date, the mediator may be perceived as affiliated with that entity, which affects his impartiality. As a result, most participants would be reluctant to disclose all information pertaining to the dispute.

While confidentiality is generally considered to be a protection afforded to the mediation participants, confidentiality requirements also protect the mediator. Most mediators work to facilitate a resolution or agreement of a dispute and are not further involved with the case. Establishing and upholding confidentiality helps limit the potential for later involvement, as most mediators do not wish to have to testify in court.

Confidentiality is also extremely important for effective use of caucusing during the mediation process. In many cases, the mediator meets separately with the parties. In these private meetings or caucuses, the parties are usually more willing to share additional information with the mediator, often due to the confidential nature of the meetings. This allows the mediator to facilitate a resolution based upon the parties' true interests or to understand the parties' limits of compromise. Many individuals are willing to make disclosures and openly discuss their underlying interests, needs, wants and desires only if the process is confidential. Without a guarantee of confidentiality, many mediators contend that the process would not be very productive.

2. VIEWS IN OPPOSITION TO CONFIDENTIALITY IN MEDIATION

Despite all of the benefits that confidentiality affords mediation, problems with a secret process can arise. A few years ago, a review of ADR literature would have revealed nearly universal agreement among academics and professionals that confidentiality was necessary to the survival of mediation. Although the considerations in favor of confidentiality remain strong, today an increasing number of situations provide arguments for exceptions.

For instance, if a mediator is prohibited from disclosing anything that happened at mediation other than the fact that the parties were present (and some would contend even the fact of attendance is confidential), then parties might misuse the mediation session to accomplish other tasks. One example would be scheduling mediation for the sole purpose of delaying litigation or to postpone a trial setting. Another tactic is for a party to voluntarily attend mediation and, once present, refuse to negotiate. Misrepresentations of information during the mediation have also been reported, and the confidential aspect of mediation could encourage some participants to be less than honest in their negotiations. If a party relies on misrepresentations made by the other side during mediation, it would be nearly impossible to prove a contract defense of fraud if the mediation is strictly confidential. These problems demonstrate a few rising concerns over the misuse of the process.

In many jurisdictions, the mediated agreement is considered a contract. (Chapter Seven explores the mediation agreement in greater detail.) In these jurisdictions, generally, if a party fails to comply with the agreement, then the other side must bring an enforcement action to achieve compliance. Without evidence of what happened at the mediation, proving the validity or invalidity of the agreement may be quite difficult. Mutual mistake offers another reason for setting aside a contract. To prove such an allegation, the evidence of what happened at the mediation is necessary.

In some types of sensitive matters, or with very emotional parties, it is possible that one party may threaten the other during the mediation. Threats of harm to a party or to those outside the session provide another compelling reason for creating limits to any confidentiality protection. Criminal activity should not be given confidential treatment solely because of mediation participation. Other types of troublesome situations may also be disclosed in mediation. For example, consider the circumstances of an admission of sexual harassment or product defects. Many contend that an individual or company should not be able to use participation in mediation to conceal discoverable or admissible evidence—particularly of the sort that will likely harm others. (Hughes).

In addition, strict confidentiality also conflicts with a general need for evidence, which litigants are entitled to in court proceedings. However, most courts adhere to the general rule that statements made during mediation sessions are considered for evidentiary purposes as having been made in the context of settlement negotiations. Therefore, they are inadmissible in court. Nevertheless, a few courts have ruled otherwise.

With absolute confidentiality, it is also difficult to monitor mediators' conduct. As the profession becomes more regulated and quality control issues become more prominent, the need to obtain information about the mediator's conduct will likely increase. If a mediator's actions would violate a standard, individuals would be unable to obtain recourse if all activity during the session remains completely confidential.

Finally, some commentators contend that the relationship between the mediator and the parties does not rise to a level that calls for a privilege of confidentiality. In particular, other privileged relationships such as those between a lawyer and client, doctor and patient, or priest and penitent are non-adversarial, whereas the parties in a mediation are in a relationship contrary to those traditionally protected by privilege. (Reich).

B. PROTECTIONS AFFORDED BY CONFIDENTIALITY

When confidentiality is discussed, it is usually in very broad terms, often suggesting that everything in the room remains strictly confidential. In reality, confidentiality provisions include a variety of sub-issues. These may include terms or context of the disclosure, the level of protection afforded, the persons prohibited from disclosing, and exceptions to any general rule.

1. WHO IS PROTECTED?

Mediation presents the first situation where the relationship between the participants may be adversarial, yet where confidentiality protections afforded to other more synchronized relationships such as lawyer-client and doctor-patient may be extended. This raises questions about exactly who confidentiality provisions are designed or intended to protect. Corollary issues have surfaced addressing who may assert a privilege of confidentiality, how far these protections extend, and how such provisions may be defeated or waived.

a. The Parties and Representatives

In mediation, the parties to the dispute are generally interested in knowing that any information disclosed will be kept in confidence. The private nature of the process is usually one of its enumerated benefits. Parties are more willing to disclose information if they are comfortable with the mediator and the process. Representatives of the parties, usually lawyers, are also keenly interested in the notion that matters discussed in mediation will not be disclosed later in trial should the matter not be settled. If this protection did not exist, then frank discussions may not occur during mediation. If the parties are protected, then they are comfortable to disclose information without the fear of reprisal. Assurance of confidentiality is also a component of trust building between the mediator and the parties.

b. The Mediator

Mediators contend they must assure parties of confidentiality for a number of reasons. First, the mediator does not want to testify or otherwise report on the session. Such disclosures interfere with neutrality and implementation of the process. Thus to prohibit or limit what the mediator can disclose or testify to provides protection and precludes the mediator from having to become a referee if the parties have subsequent disputes. Maintaining neutrality is also enhanced by a mediator's confidentiality.

Even in those instances where both parties agree or stipulate to the mediator's disclosure and testimony, most mediators will refuse. While no cases analyze the issue specifically, one often cited case involves a similar situation, where a therapist was not compelled to testify even though both parties had consented. (*Fenton v. Howard*, 1978). If the privilege of confidentiality is a protection for the mediator, then even in those instances where the parties stipulate or request the mediator to testify, the mediator can assert the privilege.

c.   The Process

Many proponents of mediation confidentiality urge that this protection is such a critical aspect of the process that without it, the process would not work. In that regard, it might be argued that the mediation process itself is protected by confidentiality and that administrators and others could claim such protection.

d.   Others

Other outside parties who are involved or tangentially related to the dispute may also be entitled to a confidentiality protection. For example, children in divorce mediation, while technically not parties, are greatly affected by the discussions during mediation, as well as the ultimate resolution. In mediations where criminal acts are an issue, such as in victim-offender mediations, parties may not feel comfortable discussing matters of a personal nature unless they are assured that the information will not be used at a later proceeding. Broad grants of confidentiality also work to keep courts from overinvolvement in the mediation process.

2.   WHAT IS PROTECTED?

In terms of the substantive aspects of confidentiality, another consideration involves the exact nature of the material that is protected. A number of different components of evidence can sometimes be excluded. These include verbal and nonverbal communications, such as how a party behaved or the demeanor of the participants. Additionally, documents which are made for mediation are thought to be protected. Yet in a Texas case, the court allowed the parties to discover a videotape made solely for the purposes of the mediation. (*In re Learjet*, 2001).

In many instances, provisions exist stating that if evidence or information is discoverable then it remains so even if it was used in mediation. This rule is designed to prevent a party from hiding information through the mediation process. Thus, determining specifically what information is protected, as well as the extent of the protection can be a daunting task.

3.   SCOPE OF CONFIDENTIALITY

The degree to which confidentiality affects information varies. In some instances, a mediator may be prohibited from disclosing information to a court, but can reveal it to the rest of the world. In other cases, the mediator is viewed as possessing a privilege or duty of secrecy and cannot disclose information learned through the mediation process to anyone. Therefore, it is imperative that when confidentiality is considered, mediation participants know the range and limitations of the confidentiality provisions.

a. Evidentiary Exclusion

The term evidentiary exclusion is used to describe information, that for some reason, will be excluded or kept out of a trial other adjudicatory procedure. Evidentiary exclusions set forth in rules of evidence are generally designed to keep unreliable information from a trier of fact. Specific rules are enacted for circumstances when a variety of reasons may dictate that certain evidence, (here the information in mediation) is not reliable or competent as evidence. If asserting an exclusion, it is necessary to make an objection when the evidence is requested or proffered in court. Establishing an evidentiary exclusion for information discussed in mediations assures the participants that what they disclose to the mediator and to each other will not be used in a later proceeding.

Consistent with Rule of Evidence 408, which limits the admissibility of discussions of compromise and settlement, an evidentiary exclusion for mediation provides that testimony about what happened or information disclosed in mediation, is not admissible in court. While many of the state statutes are not precisely drafted, most do appear to prohibit testimony of the parties as well as the mediator. Evidentiary exclusions can also offer protection for the mediator, since if determined not to be admissible, then any testimony or information which the mediator may provide would not be permitted. A number of issues must be determined when considering the evidentiary exclusion including who can claim the exclusion, whether exceptions or waivers exist, and in what proceeding(s) it can be asserted.

While an evidentiary exclusion is a form of protection that disallows testimony in a court, arbitration or administrative hearing, it does not prohibit general disclosures. When the only form of confidentiality is through an exclusion of evidence, the parties and the mediator remain free to discuss all matters concerning the mediation outside of a court proceeding unless other protections are in place. Because rules of evidence do not apply in mediations, it is also quite likely that evidence not allowed in court due to an exclusion would be open for discussion in a subsequent mediation.

b.   Testimonial Privilege

Claiming a testimonial privilege is another way that evidence can be blocked at a court hearing or other adjudicatory procedure. A privilege has a similar effect as the exclusion but is of a different origin. Privileges have often been construed to recognize that the evidence may be credible, but that a confidential relationship exists which must be protected. Privileges from testimony are created by statute as well as common law.

In court proceedings, differences may exist, depending in part upon whether the case is pending in state or federal court. Federal Rule of Evidence 501 provides that courts recognize state laws of privilege in a number of instances. A variety of privileges have been recognized by the courts.

One analysis helpful in demonstrating whether a privilege should be recognized by the courts is the Wigmore test. This test provides four conditions that may demonstrate the need for the privilege at common law. Arguably, these conditions are present in mediation, although at least one commentator disagrees. (Reich). However, as courts are often reluctant to create new privileges, new claims of privilege solely based upon common law can be problematic.

A privilege from testimony assures that the information is not brought forth in an evidentiary hearing, but still allows the mediator or participants to make disclosures to the general public. Most mediators, however, are of the opinion that disclosure of the discussions that occurred during mediation should be made to no one.

c.   Existence of a Privileged and Confidential Relationship

Special types of relationships, such as those that exist between a doctor and her patient or lawyer and his client are considered to be privileged. Most of the provisions creating such a confidential relationship are found in the codes of ethics or standards of a profession.

Whether a broad, all encompassing mediator-disputant privilege has been, or should be established is a matter of substantial debate. On one hand, many believe that such a privilege has already been established. For example, a Texas statute dictates that unless parties agree, all matters in mediation are confidential and may never be disclosed to anyone. These privileges appear to prohibit the mediator from disclosing any information to anyone. However, exceptions usually exist in the event that the parties consent.

Alternatively, others claim that the mediator-disputant relationship is not one which rises to the level that necessitates such confidentiality. (Hughes, Reich) Those opposed to a mediator's privilege contend that while the need for trust exists and the importance of the relationship between the mediator and the parties is recognized, such confidences are not the same as what might exist between lawyer and client or clergy and parishioner. Should this view gain wide acceptance, then mediators are likely free to disclose what they learn in mediation to anyone outside of a court or other adjudicatory proceeding, unless other protections, such as contractual provisions exist. Currently, the mediation profession operates with an assumption that a broad mediator-disputant privileged relationship exists.

d. Impacts Upon Discovery

Another consideration which has not been discussed or examined in detail concerns the impact that confidentiality provisions could have on discovery in litigation. Several statutes provide that if information discussed at mediation is otherwise discoverable or admissible, it remains so. Therefore, as discovery is quite broad, it would seem that most anything revealed at mediation could potentially be the subject of discovery. In one case where this issue was examined, a videotape had been prepared for a mediation. The trial court enforced the subpoena to produce the entire unedited video, rejecting both the mediation protection as well as attorney-work product privilege. (*In re Learjet*).

It is conceivable that even if the mediator's testimony would not be admissible in a court, he could be still be compelled to attend a deposition to provide information about the mediation. Such information might involve documents presented to the mediator, as well as the communications which occurred during the mediation process. On the other hand, if a broad privileged relationship is recognized, then it is doubtful that the mediator will be compelled to testify or disclose such information.

Another view concerns the parties or representatives who may also be subject to subsequent discovery. This may occur in the same case or subsequent proceedings and related or unrelated matters. For example, in a suit against a contractor in Illinois, during a court-ordered mediation, the defendant made disclosures regarding illegal billing practices.

Later, similar difficulties surfaced in structures built in Georgia. If the defendant is subpoenaed for his deposition, the claims he makes may depend upon which state law applies as well as the extent or limit of protection provided, issues recently addressed by the UMA.

C. TYPES OF DISCLOSURE

1. DISCLOSURE TO OTHERS

One type of disclosure is a general discussion or communication that is made to another individual. This may occur in a private situation where a mediator tells friends about a case he has mediated. Alternatively, the disclosures may be public if one of the parties, upset over the fact that the case did not settle, contacts local media and makes allegations about the other side's refusal to bargain.

2. REPORTING TO PUBLIC AGENCIES

Public agencies to which mediators may need to report include police departments and children's protective services. In most, if not all states, a statutory obligation to report any allegations of child abuse exists. Many mediation confidentiality statutes provide explicit exceptions for this type of reporting. This duty to report should be distinguished from a separate obligation or ability to testify. In those instances where a mediator may be legally obligated to report an act or accusation, later testimony could nonetheless be prohibited.

3. NEED OR DUTY TO WARN

In some cases, a mediator may learn during the session of an individual's intent to harm someone or commit a criminal act. In most states, even where a confidential relationship is recognized, exceptions exist where there is a need to warn others of potential harm or an individual's intent to commit a future crime. The drafters of the UMA clearly recognize this exception to confidentiality, explicitly providing an exception to confidentiality where there is an intent to commit a crime. However, an affirmative duty to warn established under Tarasoff, has not been established for mediators. In most instances, mediators make judgment calls on a case by case basis.

4. TESTIMONY IN ADJUDICATORY PROCEEDINGS

One of the most common types of mediator disclosures discussed involves a mediator's testimony in a court or other adjudicatory proceeding. While most of the methods calling for confidentiality provide occasional exceptions for special situations where information is needed, most contend that other available alternative methods to obtain this information should first be exhausted before confidentiality is compromised. Only in rare instances have mediators been compelled to testify. (*Olam v. Congress Mortg. Co.*, 1999).

5.   GENERAL PUBLIC

Two instances exist where disclosures to the general public may occur. One is in the situation where the dispute itself or the parties are newsworthy. In some instances, parties may try to use the media as leverage in the dispute. Attempts to then determine what occurred in mediation will be common, as the matter or individuals are thought to be public figures.

The other situation involves disputes and controversies where the government is a party. Local, state and federal agencies and governing entities are subject to disputes and the mediation process. Yet, resolutions which may be reached, along with the information which may be disclosed in the mediation are often considered to be in the realm of public knowledge and not a matter to be kept private. Open records acts and open meetings provisions add to the demand that exceptions to confidentiality exist when a public entity is involved. Local, state and federal agencies have dealt with this concern in a variety of ways.

6.   EDUCATIONAL AND RESEARCH NEEDS FOR INFORMATION

Another type of disclosure involves educational or research efforts. Some contend that purposes of research and education are reasons for exceptions to confidentiality. Many mediation programs are subject to research for purposes of continued funding or general evaluation. In order to assess the quality of mediation, researchers need to be able to obtain information from the participants about conduct in the session. In many instances, researchers code the data so that the parties remain protected. Other times, however, they may need to determine the identity of the parties, the mediator or the matter in dispute.

Another situation involves programs, such as in mediation clinics, where law and graduate students serve as mediators in actual cases. Class work may include discussions of the mediations which have taken place. Although no specific guidelines have been carved out, both educational efforts and research have proceeded on the implicit assumption that such exceptions to confidentiality exist.

D. METHODS OF PROVIDING FOR CONFIDENTIALITY

Issues surrounding confidentiality are complex, and providing for confidentiality is a matter that is considered to be very important by the parties and their representatives, as well as mediators. A number of options exist and have been utilized. A few are discussed below.

1. STATUTE

A primary method of confidentiality protection in mediation is through statutes or other regulatory provisions. Although many statutes providing for confidentiality are in existence, the available case law provides little consistency in terms of clarification, construction, or interpretation. Until recently, however, this had not been an issue as the cases which came before courts were few. The variation in the multitude of state statutes was a primary impetus behind the drafting of the Uniform Mediation Act.

Federal statutes setting out the mandate for mediation also include provisions for confidentiality. These include the Administrative Dispute Resolution Act, which contains confidentiality provisions for agency mediation programs, and the Alternative Dispute Resolution Act of 1998, which requires federal district courts to protect confidentiality in their ADR programs by local rule.

2. CASE LAW

Courts, through the establishment of precedent, also provide for confidentiality in mediation. Many courts, however, are hesitant to do so, particularly where they would be creating new law rather than interpreting an existing statutory provision. Relying on the division of interpreting and applying the law, as opposed to creating new law, courts have looked to legislative mandates. For example, in an older Florida case, the court noted that because no statute establishing confidentiality existed, they would not create such a provision. (*State v. Castellano*, 1984). In the labor arena, however, one case set out the longstanding policy considerations for confidentiality and revoked a subpoena to a mediator. (*NLRB v. Macaluso*, 1980).

Many state and federal statutes that possess some type of confidentiality protection exist. Local court rules and contracts also provide for confidentiality. As a result, courts are more likely to find their primary role as one of interpreting and enforcing confidentiality provisions rather than creating them.

3. COURT RULE

In many jurisdictions, both state and federal courts have established a scheme of mediation referrals through the use of local rules. In many of these rules, provisions regarding the confidential aspect of the mediation proceeding are also included. In a few other jurisdictions, however, specific provisions may not be included. Therefore, it is often important to review local rules, as well as any local case law regarding construction and interpretation with regard to specific application of the rules.

4. COURT ORDER

A court order in this context refers to an individual, independent court's directive to mediate a specific case. Orders mandating mediation may often include a statement about the parameters of confidentiality. However, these orders are usually individualized and address the highly specific needs that may arise in a particular matter.

5.   CONTRACT

Contracts provide another means of ensuring for confidentiality. A variety of contractual relationships can be created when parties participate in mediation. These may include contracts between the parties themselves, the parties and the mediator or between the parties and mediator organizations. In each of these instances, it is possible to include a provision which addresses confidentiality, although some question regarding enforceability of such agreements exists. In the unlikely event such a provision is not upheld, it may still serve a deterrent function for the parties.

a.   Between the Parties Themselves

Parties in a dispute have several occasions to contract, and including a specific provision is another method to assure confidentiality. One concern, however, surrounds enforcement. Even though confidentiality is agreed to in some instances, the consequences for a violation of such an agreement are not always clear.

i.   Predispute Clause

Parties might establish confidentiality by including a provision in their predispute mediation agreement. When parties agree in advance to use mediation in a dispute, many times the parameters of that use, such as selection of the mediator, location, and costs are noted. If confidentiality is critical or even desirable, then including such a provision early on will likely be beneficial to setting these conditions for the mediation session.

ii.   Post-dispute, Pre-mediation agreement

Individuals may also agree to go to mediation after a conflict has arisen. After the recognition of a dispute or conflict, the parties contract for mediation. Many, if not most of the facets of the mediation are considered at this juncture, including the parameters of confidentiality.

iii.   Integrated in the Mediated Agreement

In some instances, the parties in conflict may not initially recognize or realize that maintaining confidentiality about the conflict and/or its resolution is a paramount concern. In these cases, confidentiality concerns arise only once the case is in mediation. Many times, a confidentiality provision is negotiated as part of the final resolution. The agreement may provide that the discussions is confidential, the agreement remains confidential, or both.

b.   Contract with the Mediator

Some mediators enter into agreements with the participants about the terms and conditions of mediation services. Frequently included are provisions setting forth boundaries of the mediator's role. For example, there may be statements that the mediator does not represent the parties and that she will not provide legal advice. An obligation that the parties not subpoena the mediator may be included. Some mediators contend that such contracts are necessary for a more confidential process—particularly where the case law or statutory provisions are unclear. These agreements may also serve a deterrent function, as mediators occasionally include a provision that a party must pay the mediator's attorneys' fees if the party subpoenas the mediator and the testimony is not compelled.

E.   CURRENT LEGAL PARAMETERS

Although many statutes, perhaps several thousand, provide some sort of confidentiality protection, most have not been construed by the courts. In fact, comparatively little case law has actually addressed statutes involving confidentiality in mediation. Despite all of the debate and discussion in the legal literature, most mediations proceed with an assumption that all is confidential.

With the increase of mediation use, particularly in litigation matters, case law is beginning to clarify in greater detail the issues surrounding confidentiality in mediation. When confidentiality issues have been presented to a trial court, most have been resolved in favor of protecting confidentiality. No appeals were taken and hence, no case law has developed. Few cases have made their way to the appellate level. One of the first cases addressing confidentiality and included a policy discussion was Macaluso. Although set in the labor arena, the courts' discussion in this case of the importance of confidentiality to the mediation process has general applicability. Overall, cases seem to uphold confidentiality when it is addressed directly and where a provision had been enacted.

Of the newer cases, some barely address the issue and proceed directly, with little explanation, to admit evidence of what happened at mediation into the courts record. A few cases provide thoughtful, detailed analysis of the issues. For example, there have been cases where the courts engaged in a balancing of sorts, discussing the importance of confidentiality but holding that another concern has priority. (*Folb v. Motion Picture Industry Pension & Health Plans*, 1998; *Olam v. Congress Mortgage Co.*, 1999).

As mediation continues to take place within the court-annexed arena and the need for evidence arises, it is likely cases will come before the courts which will require additional interpretation of statutory provisions.

F. UNIFORM MEDIATION ACT (UMA)

1. BACKGROUND

In 1997 both the ABA Section of Dispute Resolution and the NCCUSL recognized that the time was ripe to investigate whether a need existed for a uniform law with regard to mediation. One focal point was confidentiality, since at that time, thousands of statutes, rules, and regulations regarding mediation confidentiality had been enacted. Parallel efforts soon were combined, and for the first time a collaborative effort to enact a uniform law was commenced. Over several years, many meetings and discussions took place, during which time contentious debate occurred. The end result is an Act which has the endorsement of both organizations, as well as several dispute resolution groups. While the provisions address several areas of mediation practice, the primary focus remains on confidentiality.

2.   CONTENT OVERVIEW

In addition to the provisions on confidentiality, the UMA includes several other sections. It begins with definitional provisions,and recognizes that certain types of mediation, such as peer mediation and collective bargaining, are not intended to be covered by the Act. Additionally, the Act sets out some affirmative duties for mediators, such as an investigation and disclosure of potential conflicts of interest, disclosure of the mediator's qualifications, and a general statement of neutrality. Parties are also permitted to have representation, whether through a lawyer or other representative in the mediation.

The bulk of the Act contains several sections on confidentiality. While the first several drafts contained provisions that would have established a broad privilege for mediators, similar to the lawyer-client privilege and an overall confidential relationship, the exceptions began to be too difficult for the drafters to include. Consequently, they opted to delete that segment. There is, however, one broad statement that the mediation process is confidential to the extent agreed upon by the parties or provided by other law. Some experts contend such provision still will grant the all-encompassing protection to mediators.

With regard to the specific confidentiality provisions, it was determined to opt for a testimonial privilege rather than an evidentiary exclusion, and the privilege appears to be held by all mediation participants, including the mediator and nonparty participants. A section details consideration of waivers, and specific exceptions are set out along with a balancing test which courts will likely utilize. The entire UMA is included in this book's Appendix, and a version with extensive reporter notes can be found at 22 N. Ill. U. L. Rev. 165 (2002).

3.   FUTURE

Despite some criticism, the UMA has a great deal of support. Most emphasize the need for uniformity among the states. As with uniform laws generally, the next step is to urge state legislatures to enact the act. In that regard, a few states have introduced the act, but it has yet to get out of the legislative committees. While enactment of the UMA in many states will assist in maintaining consistency, but just how each court will interpret provisions leaves many open questions.

References

Administrative Dispute Resolution Act, 5 U.S.C. § 574 (2000).

Alternative Dispute Resolution Act of 1998, 28 U.S.C. § 652(d) (Supp. V 1999).

Scott H. Hughes, The Uniform Mediation Act: To the Spoiled Go the Privileges, 85 Marq. L. Rev. 9 (2001).

National Conference of Commissioners on Uniform State Laws, The Uniform Mediation Act, 22 N. Ill. U. L. Rev. 165 (2002).

J. Brad Reich, A Call for Intellectual Honesty: A Response to the Uniform Mediation Act's Privilege Against Disclosure, 2001 J. Disp. Resol. 197.

Primary Cases

Fenton v. Howard, 575 P.2d 318 (Ariz.1978).

Folb v. Motion Picture Industry Pension & Health Plans, 16 F. Supp. 2d 1164 (C.D.Cal.1998).

In re Grand Jury Subpoena Dated December 17, 1996, 148 F.3d 487 (5th Cir.1998).

In re Learjet, 59 S.W.3d 842 (Tex.App.2001).

NLRB v. Joseph Macaluso, Inc., 618 F.2d 51 (9th Cir. 1980).

Olam v. Congress Mortgage Co., 68 F.Supp.2d 1110 (N.D.Cal.1999).

Randle v. Mid Gulf, Inc., 1996 WL 447954 (Tex.App. 1996).

Rinaker v. Superior Court, 74 Cal.Rptr.2d 464 (Ct.App. 1998).

State ex rel. Schneider v. Kreiner, 83 Ohio St.3d 203, 699 N.E.2d 83 (1998).

Smith v. Smith, 154 F.R.D. 661 (N.D.Tex.1994).

State v. Castellano, 460 So.2d 480 (Fla.Dist.Ct.App.1984).

United States v. Gullo, 672 F.Supp. 99 (W.D.N.Y.1987).

Bibliography

Phyllis E. Bernard, Only Nixon Could Go to China: Third Thoughts on the Uniform Mediation Act, 85 Marq. L. Rev. 113 (2001).

Ellen E. Deason, Enforcing Mediated Settlement Agreements: Contract Law Collides with Confidentiality, 35 U.C. Davis L. Rev. (2001).

Ellen E. Deason Predictable Mediation Confidentiality in the U.S. Federal System, 19 Ohio St J. Dipst Resol. 240 (2002).

Ellen E. Deason, The Quest for Uniformity in Mediation Confidentiality: Foolish Consistency or Crucial Predictability?, 85 Marq. L. Rev. 79 (2001).

Charles W. Ehrhardt, Confidentiality, Privilege and Rule 408: The Protection of mediation Proceedings in Federal Court, 60 La. L. Rev. 91 (1999).

Michael B. Getty, Thomas J. Moyer & Roberta Cooper Ramo, Preface to Symposium on Drafting a Uniform Model Mediation Act, 13 Ohio St. J. on Disp. Resol. 787 (1998).

Eric D. Green, A Heretical View of the Mediation Privilege, 2 Ohio St. J. on Disp. Resol. 1 (1986).

Scott H. Hughes, A Closer Look—The Case for a Mediation Confidentiality Privilege Still Has Not Been Made, Disp. Resol. Mag., Winter 1998, at 14.

Pamela A, Kentra, Hear No Evil, See No Evil, Speak No Evil: The Intolerable Conflict for Attorney–Mediators Between the Duty to Maintain Mediation Confidentiality and the Duty to Report Fellow Attorney Misconduct, 1997 BYU L. Rev. 715 (1997).

Allen Kirtley, The Mediation Privileges' Transformation from Theory to Implementation: Designing a Mediation Privilege Standard to Protect Mediation Participants, the Process and the Public Interest, 1995 J. Disp. Resol. 1.

James L. Knoll, Protecting Participants in the Mediation Process: The Role of Privilege and Immunity, 34 Tort & Ins. L.J. 115, 115 (1998).

Gregory A. Litt, Note, No Confidence: The Problem of Confidentiality by Local Rule in the ADR Act of 1998, 78 Tex. L. Rev. 1015 (2000).

Nancy H. Rogers & Craig A. McEwen, Mediation Law, Policy & Practice (2d ed. 1994) (Sarah R. Cole, ed., Supp. 1998).

Joshua P. Rosenberg, Keeping the Lid on Confidentiality: Mediation Privilege and Conflict of Laws, 10 Ohio St. J. on Disp. Res. 157 (1994).

Andrea K. Schneider, Which Means to an End Under the Uniform Mediation Act?, 13 Ohio St. J. on Disp. Resol. 787 (1998).

Brian D. Shannon, Confidentiality of Texas Mediations: Ruminations on Some Thorny Problems, 32 Tex. Tech. L. Rev. 77 (2000).

CHAPTER 8

ISSUES SURROUNDING THE MEDIATION AGREEMENT

A. GENERALLY

Once the mediation process reaches a point where an agreement is likely, the mediator begins to narrow the focus of discussion in order to sort out the details of the resolution. This is followed by drafting the agreement or in some cases, the memorandum of agreement. In many, if not most, instances, responsibility for drafting the agreement rests with the mediator. In some cases, however, for a variety of reasons, parties or their representatives (usually lawyers) assume the task of preparing the agreement.

Drafting an agreement is an important part of the mediation process. The implicit objective is that the agreement does not become the source of additional conflicts or disputes. Therefore, wording and substance are critical, and details are extremely important. In fact, some jurisdictions have created specific rules to address mediated agreements, and in many jurisdictions, statutes and regulations provide that any mediated agreement must be in writing in order to be enforced.

B. DRAFTING CONSIDERATIONS

Once a mediator recognizes the existence of an agreement, she frequently makes detailed notes about the substantive content and other significant elements to be included. In most instances, the mediator is in the best position to know and record the material aspects of the agreement. In those situations where the mediation was conducted in a caucus format, the mediator is sometimes the only individual acutely aware of each and every detail of the agreement. When the parties have communicated directly with each other, they may understand the basics of their agreement; however, they may also perceive or recall certain points differently. As a result, it becomes the mediator's task to keep detailed notes and clarify the content of the agreement. Although the mediator commonly takes charge of the drafting process, in some instances, due to a variety of reasons, the parties or their lawyers or representatives may assume a more active role.

1. MEDIATOR'S RESPONSIBILITY

One of the mediator's responsibilities is to make sure that any agreement reached during the mediation process is put into writing. While in some instances a simple oral agreement may be desired, few exceptions to having a written agreement exist. Most of the statutes addressing the mediated agreement require that it be in writing to be enforceable. As such, most mediators take notes during the entirety of the process, and these are used as a basis for drafting the agreement.

Some mediators will ask the parties, or their lawyers, to participate in the drafting process, but ultimately it remains the mediator's duty to be sure that the participants do not leave the mediation without a complete understanding of the details of their agreement.

When mediating pending lawsuits, the mediator does not draft any of the pleadings or other official legal documents. That task is left to the lawyers or other representatives for the parties. The mediator may, however, create a record of those responsible for drafting such documents or note any timelines that have been agreed to by the parties. In court-annexed programs, the timelines can be very critical, as judges, court administrators and clerks anticipate knowing relatively promptly whether the case settled or alternatively needs to be placed back on the court's docket. In many cases, there will be a scheduling order that may set out some deadlines as well.

2. ROLE OF THE PARTIES AND LAWYERS

While the primary responsibility for drafting the agreement commonly rests with the mediator, the mediation participants may be in a position to provide assistance. Particularly, lawyers for the parties may draft more complex documents, such as releases or other matters which may serve as attachments to the agreement. The lawyer representatives also tend to consider issues surrounding enforceability and durability of the agreement. It is not uncommon to have legal or practical constraints not considered during the mediation arise during the drafting stages. Thus, it is critical to proceed through the drafting stages while all parties and their representatives remain at the session. In some more complex cases, the agreement drafting phases of the process last nearly as long as the mediation itself.

On one hand, a short, simple accounting of the main points of agreement may be all that is necessary at the conclusion of the mediation; the lawyers will be able to draft the more complex and detailed documents. On the other hand, it may be advantageous and more efficient to verify all of the details of the agreement while everyone is still at the table. As time passes, memories fade, and recalling the details with specificity may be more challenging. Another advantage to completing the majority of the agreement while at the mediation is to have the use of the mediator's notes. Most mediators destroy any notes they take at the conclusion of the mediation. The mediator is usually in the best position to have written details with regard to the agreement. Thus use of her notes can be quite valuable.

The parties themselves may also take an active role in drafting the mediated agreement, particularly in those cases where they are not represented at mediation. While the general consensus is that the mediator drafts the agreement, variations may occur. Some mediators believe that the parties themselves will be more committed to and thus, more apt to comply with a mediated agreement if they have been active in the drafting process. Party participation can take on a number of forms ranging from merely reviewing the substance as the mediator drafts the agreement to actually doing the primary drafting themselves.

3. OTHERS

In rare situations, someone other than the mediator or lawyers may be involved in the drafting of the agreement. In highly complex or technical cases, where an expert is utilized, there may be occasions that necessitate the expert's involvement in the drafting process. For example, in a complicated construction dispute, where the agreement incorporates a redesign of the building, it may be valuable to include the architect and general contractor in drafting the agreement or its attachments.

C. CONTENT ISSUES

The content of the agreement refers to the substance of resolution. In most instances, the agreement will conform quite accurately to what the parties decided in their discussions and negotiations. In some instances, particular content matters, for example in personal injury cases, the conditions of release may be referred to as the standard release. However, as discussed below, such reference can also present later problems should a disagreement arise. Additionally, some items not raised during the mediation session may need to be included in the final agreement, particularly if such details are necessary to avoid confusion or disagreement during execution of the agreement.

1.   DETAIL

The extent of specificity in the mediated agreement is a matter subject to some debate. On one hand, providing a complete and detailed account of each and every item that was discussed, as well as explaining additional contingencies can be a daunting task. Excessive particulars may extend far beyond what is desired or needed by the parties. Furthermore, the amount of time necessary to consider each and every detail often requires more time than what the parties care to spend. On the other hand, a minimum level of comprehensiveness is imperative. Omitting matters critical to the final resolution can negatively impact both the parties' satisfaction with the agreement, as well as its durability and enforceability.

In a simple debt matter, for instance, Party B agrees to pay A a sum certain, $10,000 in 20 monthly installments of $500 each. They also agree to no interest. The question becomes just how detailed the mediator must be with regard to the manner of payment. Most mediators would agree that factors such as dates, times, place and manner (check, money order) of payment are necessary elements of the agreement. The difficulty surrounds whether the mediator should raise issues such as contingencies should a payment be missed or not made pursuant to the agreement, and if he does, how far to go into detail.

Detail issues commonly arise in employment cases. Many times, one item agreed to by the participants may involve providing a letter of recommendation or a neutral reference. In these cases, it may be necessary to determine the content of the letter and allow opportunity for its review while all parties are present at the mediation. Simply agreeing on a summary of the information to be included and assuming that the parties implicitly have the same understanding often presents additional difficulties after the mediation has been concluded. In some cases the result is further need for mediation.

A recent North Carolina case addressed such a situation. In *Chappell v. Roth,* a personal injury case, the parties reached an agreement regarding the amount of payment to be made, and included language in the written agreement that the release would be "mutually agreeable to both parties." The trouble arose when the parties were unable and unwilling to agree on the language of the release, and plaintiff filed a motion with the court to enforce the agreement. (Ma'luf) Although the court of appeals emphasized the strong presumption in upholding mediated agreements, the North Carolina Supreme Court concluded that since the agreement was missing an essential term, it was not an enforceable contract. Cases such as this illustrate the need for detail in concluding the mediation and in drafting the agreement.

2.   PARTIAL AGREEMENTS

In some instances, the parties will not be able to reach a complete full and final agreement concerning every item or point in disagreement. In some of these instances, mediators find that it is valuable to ascertain whether a partial or limited agreement is feasible. Partial agreements may involve an agreement on a few of the substantive issues. Alternatively, partial agreements may consider information that is lacking and provide options for the parties to continue their negotiations, either by participating in another mediation or negotiating directly with one another. In most instances, mediators put any partial agreement in writing, and have it signed by all of the participants.

3.   TENTATIVE AND CONDITIONAL AGREEMENTS

In some particular types of cases, most commonly family and public policy matters, the need arises for a draft or tentative agreement which may be reviewed by others. The parties may take the provisional agreement to lawyers or other experts for consultation and advice before it is finalized. In matters of absent decision makers, the agreement is often conditional upon a subsequent ratification. In some cases, the agreement can be modified before finalization as well. Most mediators draft the agreement, in detail, and include specific language pointing out that it is conditional or tentative, subject to later endorsement before it is finalized.

Another possibility is that of an interim agreement. In some matters, immediate action may be necessary, for example to stop a foreclosure. An interim agreement to refrain from some official action for instance, can provide the parties with a temporary solution, allow additional time to gather information, and continue the mediation in attempt to reach a final solution.

D. ISSUES OF ENFORCEABILITY

1. Generally

One of the benefits of mediation voiced early on was that parties who participate in reaching their own agreement are generally more satisfied with the content. In contrast, in situations where a decision is imposed on the parties, they are less likely to be pleased with the outcome. With the initial success of mediation, a general expectation developed that parties satisfied with their agreement would naturally comply with its terms. This led to the belief that technical or legal enforcement mechanisms were rarely necessary. Yet, reality has demonstrated that in some cases, parties fail to uphold their agreements. This seems to be more common in court-annexed matters. In some cases, it is inevitable—buyer's remorse occurs, or parties simply change their minds. In other cases, conduct during the mediation may be at the root of noncompliance, especially if the party believes he may have been coerced, pressured or forced to reach an agreement.

As a result, the party then refuses to comply with the terms of the agreement.

These instances have come before courts on numerous occasions. When courts consider issues surrounding enforcement of the mediated agreement, a number of other factors come into play. The most dominant element involved is the confidential nature of the process. Generally, the ability of a court to enforce, or alternatively, set aside the mediation agreement involves the submission of evidence. This directly conflicts with confidentiality. In many circumstances, one or both of the parties want the mediator to testify about the agreement. Doing so however, would also directly challenge the mediator's impartiality.

Although it is possible that parties can support their claim or denial that an agreement was reached without disclosing the communications of the mediation, it is unusual. Most of the time, some discussion of what transpired during the mediation comes before a court or other decision-maker. Recognizing the wide variations in the handling of mediated settlement agreements, many legislatures have allowed the courts to make enforceability decisions on an individual case-by-case basis.

2. Key Considerations of Enforceability Issues

A number of issues arise when considering matters surrounding the mediation agreement, its existence, validity and enforcement. The primary issues can be broken down into three major considerations: the existence; the content; and the enforceability of the agreement.

The first question is whether an agreement has been reached at all. In other words, one party disputes the very existence of an agreement. This is most common in situations where an oral agreement is reached. And while some statutes provide that a mediated agreement must be in writing, some courts have, in fact enforced oral agreements. (Silkey). The problem is that when no writing exists, it is quite difficult to prove or disprove the agreement's existence without a significant inquiry into the details of what transpired during the mediation.

Another concern relating to existence involves the content of the agreement. (Deason). Determining the substance of the agreement when no writing exists is a challenging assignment. Even in those instances where a writing does exist, sometimes disputes arise concerning the specificity of certain terms. If details were omitted, they then become extremely difficult to prove, especially because of confidentiality limitations. Consequently, without a clear-cut and detailed document, the content of the agreement is often a matter subject to disagreement among the mediation participants.

The other, somewhat related aspect of mediated agreements concerns the ability of the court to enforce it. In these cases, a party usually acknowledges that a written agreement exists, but, for a variety of reasons, questions its validity. In many states, mediated agreements are recognized as contracts and as such, they are subject to the general contractual defenses. In fact, several states explicitly provide that the mediation agreement is a contract. Generally, courts use the basic rules of contract law to govern mediated settlement agreements. Defenses that have been raised to challenge the enforceability of a mediated agreement include claims of fraud, duress, coercion and lack of authority. However, in order to determine whether such claims are valid, courts must investigate what took place at the mediation. A central concern is that such an investigation directly conflicts with provisions of confidentiality. Moreover, because of the adversarial nature of the disagreement, even if the parties themselves decide to testify, their testimony will differ. Mediators are then called in to be the "tie breaker," a task most mediators would rather avoid. Primary concerns are the breach of confidentiality provisions which such testimony would necessitate, and a resulting destruction of mediator neutrality.

3.   Legal Analysis

When examining the parameters of agreement enforceability, from a legal view point, one usually first looks to any existing statutory provisions which govern the mediated agreement. Over the last decade, there have also been a steadily rising number of cases addressing issues surrounding the validity and enforceability of mediated agreements.

a. Statutory Provisions

A number of states have provisions which address the mediated agreement. Some merely state that it should be in writing; others provide more detailed requirements for enforcement. For instance, some states require that the document clearly state it is meant to be enforceable, and others require the signature of the parties, the attorneys, and the mediator. Yet, the majority of state laws remain silent on the issue of detail. In these circumstances, often the parties look to contract law or other general rules of court procedures as a basis for their arguments. However, mediated settlement provisions do not always fare well when they are inconsistent with traditional court rule or contract law.

b. Case Law

Courts have begun to develop procedures to address mediated settlement agreements when statutory provisions are silent. Enforceability has been addressed in a number of cases, with wide variation in results. Several courts have been able to avoid issues regarding mediated settlement agreements by strictly enforcing rules of attendance and good faith requirements. Some courts have been able to resolve disputes by examining the pleadings and supporting documentation, such as affidavits, without having to probe into the mediation discussions. Unfortunately, these techniques are not always sufficient.

For some situations, it is necessary to delve into the specifics of the mediation to reach a decision about the validity or enforceability of an agreement. In these cases, judges must decide whether confidentiality or conversely disclosure is paramount. Some judges have "released" the parties from their pledges of confidentiality to determine what occurred at mediation, and provided little or no discussion of the importance of confidentiality. (Allen v. Leal) In other instances, the court has engaged in a balancing test, weighing the need for the evidence and the importance of confidentiality. (Olam; State ex rel. Schneider v. Kreiner). Other judges have allowed testimony in camera or refused to breach confidentiality provisions. With the lack of clear rules in place to guide the courts, these situations will likely increase in number and diversity in outcome.

4.   CHOICE OF LAW PROVISIONS

While many cases addressing the enforceability of issues are reported, very few if any have dealt with parties who reside in different jurisdictions or who attempt to enforce state law privileges in federal courts. It has been suggested that the parties determine in advance, what state law may control in the event of a disagreement. In most federal diversity cases, if the state confidentiality privilege provides an answer, federal courts are required under Federal Rule of Evidence 501 to apply state law privileges.

Although it is not uncommon for federal courts to adopt state law in certain situations, some disputes regarding enforceability are considered to be procedural issues, and federal law controls. At any rate, determining the applicable law for enforcing mediated settlement agreements is not a settled matter. As mediation use continues to grow, these issues will increasingly arise in the future.

References

Ellen E. Deason, Enforcing Mediated Settlement Agreements: Contract Law Collides with Confidentiality, 35 U.C. Davis L. Rev. 33 (2001).

Allison Ma'luf, A Mediation Nightmare?: The Effect of the North Carolina Supreme Court's Decision in Chappell v. Roth on the Enforceability and Integrity of Mediated Settlement Agreements, 37 Wake Forest L.Rev. 643 (2002).

Cases

Allen v. Leal, 27 F.Supp.2d 945, 947 (S.D.Tex.1998).

Barnett v. Sea Land Serv., Inc. 875 F.2d 741, 743–44 (9th Cir.1989).

Carr v. Runyan, 89 F.3d 327, 330 (7th Cir.1996).

Chappell v. Roth, 548 S.E.2d 499 (N.C.2001).

Cohen v. Cohen, 609 So.2d 785 (Fla.Dist.Ct.App.1992).

Gordon v. Royal Caribbean Cruises Ltd., 641 So.2d 515, 517 (Fla.Dist.Ct.App.1994).

Haghighi v. Russian–American Broad. Co., 577 N.W.2d 927 (Minn.1998).

In the Matter of the Marriage of Ames, 860 S.W.2d 590 (Tex.App.1993).

Olam v. Cong. Mortgage Co., 68 F.Supp.2d 1110, 1133, 1139 (N.D.Cal.1999).

Patel v. Ashco Enterprises, Inc., 711 So.2d 239 (Fla.App. 5th Dist.1998).

Randle v. Mid Gulf, Inc., 1996 WL 447954 (Tex.App. 1996).

Ryan v. Garcia, 33 Cal.Rptr.2d 158 (Cal.Ct.App.1994).

Silkey v. Investors Diversified Services, Inc., 690 N.E.2d 329 (Ind.App.1997).

Spencer v. Spencer, 752 N.E.2d 661, 663–64 (Ind.Ct.App. 2001).

State ex rel. Schneider v. Kreiner, 699 N.E.2d 83 (1998).

George B. Murr, In the Matter of Marriage of Ames and the Enforceability of Alternative Dispute Resolution Agreements: A Case for Reform, 28 Tex. Tech. L. Rev. 31 (1997).

R. Wayne Thorpe & Jennifer Boyens, Mediation Settlement Agreements: Legal, Ethical, and Practical Issues, in 16 Alternatives to the High Cost of Litig. 93, 107 (1998).

West Beach Marina, Ltd. v. Erdeljac, 2002 WL 31718136 (Tex. App.—Aus. 2002).

Bibliography

James R. Coben & Peter N. Thompson, Minnesota's Phantom Menace: The Civil Mediation Act, Vol LVI Bench and Bar of Minnesota Sept. 1999.

Leslie C. Levin, The Emperor's Clothes and Other Tales About the Standards for Imposing Lawyer Discipline Sanctions, 48 Am. Univ. L. Rev. 1 (1998).

George B. Murr, In the Matter of Marriage of Ames and the Enforceability of Alternative Dispute Resolution Agreements: A Case for Reform 28 Tex. Tech. L. Rev. 31 (1997).

CHAPTER 9

ETHICAL CONSIDERATIONS

A. GENERAL AND DEFINITIONAL CONSIDERATIONS

An overview of the meaning of "ethics" may be helpful in understanding the nature of many of the regulatory issues surrounding mediation. Much controversy exists concerning the concept of ethics in the mediation profession. A cursory glance at defining "ethics" is illustrative of the many considerations that are discussed and debated. One definition of *ethics* is "[t]he discipline of dealing with what is good and bad and with moral duty and obligation." Ethical is also defined as "conforming to accepted professional standards of conduct." (*See Websters New Collegiate Dictionary.*) A legal definition from Black's Law Dictionary provides that ethics are "of or relating to moral action, conduct, motive or characteristics conforming to professional standards of conduct."

Ethics in mediation can be viewed from differing perspectives and persons involved in mediation. Mediation participants for whom ethics may be enacted include mediators, parties, lawyers and other representatives in mediation, private service providers, public agencies, trainers, referring entities such as courts, or private persons or groups. Most often discussed and frequently examined are those ethical considerations for mediators.

The existence of ethical guidelines is often considered a hallmark of becoming a profession. Implementing and enforcing these guidelines are also important ways to regulate a profession. Most self-regulating professions typically require their members to adhere to a common set of ethical rules and have enacted disciplinary procedures for those who fail to comply with such standards.

A discussion of ethics in mediation practice necessarily includes a variety of other considerations. As demonstrated by the definitions above, overlap between ethics and standards of practice or a best practices scheme exists. Distinguishing ethical behavior from a particular recommended conduct in mediation can be difficult. For example, the issues surrounding confidentiality and neutrality are often considered ethical in nature. Yet confidentiality is guided by statute and case law. Mediator qualifications may also include ethical considerations, although attempts have been made to distinguish ethics from practice, quality and competency matters. Nevertheless, some cross-over discussion is inevitable, as other professions have mixed or combined these issues. Another influencing factor springs from the fact that the mediation profession is currently at a point where many issues are in a developmental stage and therefore ripe for examination. As these matters evolve and mature, the lines between them will likely become more defined.

B. ETHICS FOR MEDIATORS

Instituting ethical standards for mediators has been contemplated for some time. Although several ethical codes have been created by both public and private mediator organizations, discussions continue. A large emphasis continues to be placed on the idea of creating a professional code of ethics for the mediator profession as a whole. A number of reasons for this heightened interest exist, including but not limited to, the increase in the volume of mediation; the numerous jurisdictions in which individuals may mediate; the number of variations in the approaches to the process taken by mediators; the diversity of specialized contexts in which mediation takes place; and the variety of backgrounds and educational levels of mediators.

Participant expectation is another important factor impacting the creation and enactment of ethical guidelines for mediators. This is particularly critical in those instances, which remain the majority of situations, where mediation is still viewed as a new and different process for dispute resolution. As with any new or unfamiliar process that is introduced to the public, there is often hesitancy in widespread adoption of the new method. It is important that new users of mediation have confidence and trust in the process if they are to support the process and participate in it repeatedly. The existence of ethical standards for the process can assist in the effort. The enactment, and just as importantly, the enforcement mechanisms, for ethical codes and provisions are the most valuable methods of creating, building and continuing trust and confidence in the innovative and evolving process of mediation.

A number of different efforts have taken place with regard to mediator ethics. Some of these attempts have been very localized to particular mediation programs, while others attempt to cast a very broad approach, designed to encompass all mediators. As a result, in both the United States, as well as throughout the world, a large number of ethical codes and guidelines for mediators are in existence. While variations in these codes exist, a number of similarities can be found throughout many, if not most, of the schemes.

1.   BACKGROUND OF MEDIATOR ETHICS

Despite the need for and attention placed upon mediator ethics, there are many difficulties regarding the implementation of a code of ethics for mediators. These include the interdisciplinary nature of the field, the inherent flexibility of the process, the absence of one governing body or entity, the lack of an enforcement authority, and the lack of uniform definitions concerning the process to be regulated.

Although divergent views concerning mediation exist, there is likely universal agreement that mediation is a flexible process. Flexibility is advantageous in allowing mediation wide applicability and effectiveness in the resolution of an extremely varied array of disputes. Adaptations have been made, creating many different or specialized applications of the process. However, this flexibility makes it difficult to provide a simple definition of the process. The difficulty in defining mediation specifically and precisely contributes to the complications in determining appropriate ethics and standards of practice, especially those with detailed provisions.

In most settings, mediators are a diverse group, coming from all walks of life. Until the profession as a whole is subject to some form of licensure or regulation, the ability to impact all mediators may be impossible. Many mediators are volunteers and arguably should not be overburdened by regulation. On the other hand, adopting a standard of ethics that excludes volunteers might send a message of a two-tiered approach to competency in mediation services.

A number of entities have enacted ethical codes. At least two primary codes have been on a national level. The *Model Standards of Conduct for Mediators (Joint Standards)*, was developed and adopted by the American Arbitration Association, the American Bar Association Section of Dispute Resolution, and the Society of Professionals in Dispute Resolution (now the Association for Conflict Resolution (ACR)) in 1994. Due in part to the numerous developments in mediation practice, these three national organizations are currently working on revisions to the standards.

The other is the *Model Standards of Practice for Family and Divorce Mediation,* an update of the 1984 ABA Model Standards of Practice for Family and Divorce Mediation. The Family and Divorce Standards were approved by the ABA and as their name indicates, apply only to family cases. Other standards have been adopted for statewide application in a number of jurisdictions, for example by a state's highest court and are mandatory for mediators in court-sponsored programs. Several other states provide standards of conduct for all neutrals, rather than singling out mediators. Other ethical guidelines have been created by the dispute resolution committees or sections of state and local bar associations, and most community mediation programs have ethical guidelines in place as well.

2. CONTENT OF ETHICAL CODES FOR MEDIATORS

The numerous ethical codes in existence often show specific themes or principal areas of concern throughout the provisions. A survey of the mediation literature and current drafts of proposed codes reveals that some fundamental ethical concerns for mediators exist. These areas include: Competency, Neutrality, Confidentiality, Self–Determination, Quality, Advertising and Fees.

a. Matters of Competency of the Mediator

Universal agreement seems to exist within the mediation community that a mediator must be competent in her role within the mediation process. Most agree that the mediator must possess "process expertise." She must be comfortable with her position as the mediator and as a neutral, knowledgeable about the structure of the process, capable of leading and facilitating the mediation, and able to deal with any problems that arise. However, there are wide differences of opinion concerning the appropriate level of "subject matter expertise," often viewed as the other component of competency. On one hand, some say that the mediator need not be an expert in the subject area. One strong argument supporting this contention is that a mediator with less knowledge is less likely to be biased. In other cases, particularly more complex and technical matters, a mediator may be required to have more expertise. Generally, the consensus is that the mediator must possess sufficient knowledge about the subject matter of the dispute so to be able to talk intelligently with the participants in mediation.

b. Neutrality and Impartiality

Neutrality and Impartiality are essential to the mediation process. In her role as an impartial neutral, the mediator does not take sides in the dispute. She must be neutral with regard to the all participants involved in the mediation, as well as unbiased about the subject matter of the controversy. Nevertheless, the debate concerning how detached a mediator should be continues.

While some argue that mediators should at all times remain distanced and unbiased, others suggest that mediators may sometimes need to utilize power balancing techniques in order to promote fairness and reduce inequalities in the process, as well as the result. Admittedly these variations make drafting a specific rule for conduct problematic, especially since many neutrals approach mediating with flexibility and tailor the process to match individual case-by-case needs. Yet, much of the same individuality is required with regard to conduct in other professions that have ethical codes of conduct, so it would seem regulation is not wholly impossible. Neutrality and impartiality and the problems surrounding practice were addressed in detail in Chapter Six.

c. Avoidance of Conflicts of Interest

An extension of neutrality considerations centers on matters of conflicts of interest. Here, issues arise concerning how neutral the mediator must be with regard to relationships with the participants and their advocates or representatives. Ethical dilemmas include whether a mediator may serve in a case where one of the parties is a former partner or a former client, even if the matter is totally unrelated to prior representation. Additional issues surround subsequent relationships. Once a mediator serves in a neutral capacity, concerns may arise if she provides additional services (legal, accounting, therapy etc.) to one of the individuals. Certainly in smaller communities, where mediators are likely to know or at least be familiar with the participants, such a restriction would impede the development of mediation practice.

Most ethical provisions merely state that a mediator must avoid conflicts of interest. Problems have arisen in cases where lawsuits were filed subsequent to a mediation, and the neutral or his law firm was requested to serve in a representational capacity. The primary result has been the disqualification of the law firms. (Poly Software International, Inc. v. Su, 1995.)

Additional substantive situations have produced even more debate over the necessity for a mediator to be impartial and free from bias. For example, should a mediator who is divorced be prohibited from mediating divorce cases? Should the prohibition be for a specific period of time or forever? Likewise, if a mediator has been in a car accident, should he, for any period of time, refrain from mediating automobile accident cases? While these issues have been debated and the possibility for personal bias exists, clear guidelines for these circumstances do not.

Impartiality and neutrality are often defined as "having no interest in the outcome." Yet, if a mediator is an advocate for settlement, some argue that he does have an interest in the outcome. This is especially troublesome in those cases where a settlement may result in future business for the mediator. Balancing ethical standards with these types of practical considerations presents many challenges for the mediation profession.

d. Provisions of Confidentiality

For many years, it has been thought that everything in mediation should be absolutely confidential. Yet, as the use of mediation has increased, a number of situations have surfaced, emphasizing the need for a new examination of mediation confidentiality provisions. In many instances, confidentiality is established through legal channels such as statutes or court rules. In addition, ethical provisions for mediators include confidentiality constraints.

In most codes of ethics, confidentiality is painted with a rather broad brush, with little detail as to exceptions. Some however, believe this is not the best approach. For greater detail on issues of confidentiality, see Chapter Seven.

e. Preservation of Party or Participant Self–Determination

Self-determination by the parties is another element at the very core of the mediation process. Self-determination can be considered in two separate, but related component parts. One component deals with the process itself while the other is focused on the outcome. These matters have been the subject of debate regarding evaluative and facilitative mediation methods. Most experts appear to agree the mediator should disclose the primary approach that will be taken, although the difficulty with disclosure is that sometimes what is necessary to assist parties in overcoming barriers in their negotiation is not apparent until long into the mediation process.

In addition, the degree of mediator directiveness can clearly impact the level of self-determination of the parties. Mediator directiveness refers to the extent that a mediator will push the parties toward an agreement. Several different elements of directiveness may be observed in mediation. One is with regard to the process, and concerns how far the mediator presses the parties to continue with the process. Moreover, in some types of mediation, the process is highly structured and the mediator is the one with agenda control. Alternatively, in a more transformative approach (Bush & Folger), the parties are in more control of the process. They may determine matters such as when to call a caucus or how the communication among the parties occurs.

Another issue of directiveness and self-determination concerns the outcome or reaching a settlement. In some instances, mediators forcefully push the parties to an agreement, but stop short of dictating what the settlement should be. In other cases, mediators will also try and dictate the final resolution of a matter. Regardless of the type of approach used by the mediator, the parties must possess some level of informed consent in order to effectuate a valid and enforceable agreement. Difficult issues arise when the parties are not represented by counsel or other informed representative. The existence and extent of a mediator's duty to ensure that parties have sufficient information regarding available options and the consequences of those options can be difficult to determine.

At least two competing ethical considerations drive this issue: the mediator's duty to be neutral and the obligation to achieve a fair, fully informed settlement. If the mediator is to empower the parties to exercise self-determination, it is reasonable to assume the mediator should ensure decisions are being made with complete information and under-standing. Frequently, this information and under-standing is of a legal nature. A related question is whether or not the mediator should provide this information. Ethical questions arise regarding whether the mediator is or should be obligated to provide missing information or advice, whether it be legal, financial, technical or therapeutic in na-ture. Furthermore, concerns exist about how com-petent or knowledgeable in the given area the medi-ator must be in order to provide information.

Many purport that once a mediator provides ad-vice or information to a party, his role becomes that of an advocate. Yet, some mediators do provide legal information. Others view the mediator's duty not as one who directly provides the information, but rath-er one who advocates that the parties obtain inde-pendent legal counsel. Some believe providing any advice is unethical, and while the issue has yet to be resolved, at the very least, it is likely that the mediator should not continue with the process if any of the parties lack sufficient knowledge about the options for final resolution.

f. Quality of Process

Considerations of party self-determination, medi-ator neutrality, and professional advice are linked to the quality of the mediation process. These fac-tors interact and together, affect the role of the mediator. In instances where a party is uninformed or uneducated about a particular matter, the con-siderations may be quite significant.

Another aspect of process quality relates to how the mediation is conducted. Often included in this provision is the directive that mediators be diligent in managing the process. According procedural fairness in the process is another element to quality mediation. Standards attempt to define boundaries for mediators and dictate that expectations of participants with regard to the process are clarified. While some critics suggest there is no assurance of quality in mediation, enacting ethical regulations can help standardize procedures and practices and thereby provide acceptable safeguards to the process.

g. The Mediators Ability to Provide Professional Advice

The mediator's ability to provide professional advice is an aspect of practice that is closely related to the type of approach a mediator uses. Depending on whether the mediator engages in a facilitative or evaluative method (See Chapter Two), her tactics and strategies may be very different. Regardless of style, however, most commentators and practitioners suggest that clear lines be drawn in order to protect mediation as a separate and distinct dispute resolution process. Mediation activities must be delineated from those of arbitration and other alternative dispute resolution methods.

In some instances, mediators may "change hats" during the session in order to assist the parties in their negotiations. Most experts contend that should this occur, a need for some level of public disclosure arises. In fact, a requirement of disclosure of information to the mediation participants about a variety of matters, such as the mediator's qualifications and particular approach to mediation, prior to the mediation session is an ethical provision which has been included in codes with increased frequency. For example the Family Standards specifically require that mediators clearly distinguish mediation from any other professional service that divorcing individuals might encounter such as therapy or legal representation.

h. Protection of the Process and its Attributes

It is critically important that the mediation process be conducted fairly and professionally, and that the parties' self-determination be preserved. On an individual level, this is considered in quality of process issues. On a broader scale, mediators may be obligated to protect and encourage mediation more generally.

The mediator may have a duty to assure that those involved share a common understanding about the nature of the process in which they are participating. As such, it is important that each party be informed about the process, be knowledgeable about its boundaries, and have has the right or opportunity to have counsel or other representative present at mediation. The existence of ethical standards assists to promote mediator accountability and prevent process abuse.

Additionally, protection of the process may address matters concerning the mediator's behavior or conduct aside from mediation. For example, there may be ethical provisions requiring that the mediator not be convicted of any criminal activity. As mediation use continues to increase, quality control issues and accountability of mediators will be a central focus of the public's attention.

i. Advertising and Solicitation of Matters

Mediator advertising and solicitation of cases is another topic found in several codes of ethics. Basically, while no prohibition has been placed upon the solicitation of cases, it is suggested that mediators be honest and truthful in advertising, and refrain from misleading the consumer. Often these standards are similar in purpose to those regulations that govern an attorney's conduct in advertising and solicitation, although they are usually more general and not as detailed. Nevertheless, as regulations for mediators increase, there are likely to be additional rules in this area.

j. Disclosure and Appropriateness of Mediator Fees

Fee schedules and fee disclosures have also caused some concern in the field. The general consensus is that the only guidance which should be provided to mediators is that fees be reasonable. There is also a common prohibition against contingency fees. This ban is based upon the premise that a mediator cannot have an interest in the outcome of the case. Yet, a few people subscribe to the minority view, and a handful of practicing mediators are compensated on a contingency basis.

3. ISSUES SURROUNDING THE ENACTMENT OF ETHICAL CODES

Despite the work in the area, there has also been some criticism of the current codes of ethics, in particular calling for greater detail and direction. (Henifkoff & Moffit).

As the mediation profession evolves and ethical codes are enacted and enforced, new and more detailed rules will emerge to govern the process. It is important, however, to decide what level of ethical regulation is necessary and desired, in order to formulate appropriate guidelines for the profession. At the same time, it is critical to determine whether these rules are to become part of other governing ethical considerations. For example, they may be part of the standards that govern the practice of law. Alternatively mediator rules can be an independent set of guidelines, with a separate governing body and enforcement organization for the mediation profession alone.

The variety of ethical issues facing mediators is considerable. The difficulty in determining which issues to address in a code of ethics is evidenced by the sheer number and wide variety of codes in existence. In addition to content issues, the additional aspects of enactment and enforcement must be confronted.

One important issue concerns the mediator's background prior to joining the mediation profession. Many mediators were or still are engaged in another professional practice. Dilemmas arise when the mediator is bound to comply with other professional ethical standards as well as those governing mediators. The problem is exacerbated when the ethical regulations conflict. Thus, a determination about what code has precedence must be made to address the issue of when codes that regulate a mediator whose primary professional role is doctor, lawyer, accountant or therapist conflict. In most situations there will likely be much greater consistency than conflict. In the event of conflict, however, one suggested option is that the activity in which the individual is engaged at the time the ethical question arises should be the paramount factor in choosing which code governs.

Just as troublesome, and equally critical in the creation of ethical guidelines is the determination of enforcement. Some argue that the mere existence of ethical standards is sufficient and suggest that individual mediators will voluntarily abide by them. Others, however, stress that there must be specific procedures in place to enforce the ethical guidelines. These commentators would hold mediators responsible for more than voluntary compliance with guidelines; they would dictate strict consequences for any violations of ethical standards.

The majority of the current codes of ethics were established as guidelines for mediators. In these instances, no real sanctions exist for violations by mediators. Thus, even mediators who knowingly breach ethical guidelines usually go unpunished, since there is no enforcement entity to provide appropriate sanctions. Few mediators are prohibited from practicing mediation by the entity which enacted the standards they violated. In addition to the lack of enforcement authority is the lack of defined penalties appropriate to various ethical violations. The type of disciplinary process, the structure of the process, and the consequences of violations must be determined. Whatever codes are to govern a mediator's conduct, it is imperative that the rules and ramifications be known in advance so that the mediators will be informed.

Another issue, viewed by many to be the most important, is how to introduce ethical codes to new mediators and even more important, experienced mediators. In many jurisdictions and programs, there is only a minimal, one-time training requirement for mediators. Training and educating of mediators are far from standardized. There is no consistency regarding course content and it is difficult to ascertain whether trainings actually include an ethical component. Although some mediator membership organizations provide ethical guidelines for their members, it is practically impossible to determine whether the mediators are familiar with them. Since, there is no standard testing of mediators, many may not even be aware of the existence of ethical guidelines or standards for their profession. Furthermore, in the majority of cases, when mediators are provided the Ethical Codes and are trained with regard to the considerations, very little has been done to assure continued familiarity with the guidelines and subsequent changes or amendments. Assurance of incorporation of ethics into practice is another concern.

4.   ENFORCEMENT ISSUES

Enacting a specific and detailed code of ethics for mediators is a good foundation upon which to foster trust and build confidence in the mediation process. Consumers of mediation services, however, want to be assured that the mediators are being held accountable to such standards on a regular and continuing basis. While codes that are aspirational can be valuable in improving the profession of mediation, it is only with strict enforcement mechanisms that parties can be assured of consistent high standards for the mediation process.

Professions that are self-regulating, such as law, have in place internal enforcement procedures for addressing violations of ethical provisions. Those who must comply with the code must be aware not only of the actual contents and provisions of the ethical code, but also the consequences of failing to comply with them. In the event that violations occur, procedures are in place to investigate a report or grievance, as well as determine appropriate consequences. In the case of mediation, only a few jurisdictions such as Florida, have established specific procedures which address allegations of mediator misconduct. For the most part, ethics remain aspirational.

One difficulty has been in determining who will or can make disciplinary decisions. As very little real regulation is in place, there are very few, if any, entities which have assumed that role. In recent years, however, considerations of the establishment of disciplinary organizations have become more common. Many experts consider such oversight to be a necessary component of regulating the profession.

Theoretically, two primary methods exist by which violations might be reported to a governing board. The first is through a grievance process, where a complaint may be placed by a consumer of mediation services. This might be the party at the mediation or that party's lawyer or other representative. The other means of learning about violations may be through the observation by other mediators or a program's staff members.

Historically, the means of investigating an ethics violation or complaint made against lawyers, accountants and other professionals, has been through the use of an investigatory type of procedure. In some instances, an evidentiary hearing is conducted and findings are made. From those findings, consequences are then derived. Interestingly, however, in the mediation profession, some of the programs and centers in the United States have decided to first employ a more facilitative approach before progressing to a full evidentiary hearing. Any process that is used to determine violations of ethical rules however, most likely necessitates an exception to confidentiality.

As is the case in a number of other professions, it is also essential that those making the decisions regarding mediator conduct are knowledgeable and have experience in the field.

With regard to the action taken or consequences imposed upon the mediator in the event of a finding of misconduct, a number of possibilities exist. Potential options may include a series of sanctions, progressive in order, with a final ultimate sanction being the suspension from the program. There is also the possibility that immediate suspension would be appropriate for some egregious violations.

A monetary sanction against the mediator is another option. Alternative consequences include, but are not limited to: a remedial education program; shadowing another experienced mediator; being permitted to only co-mediate; requiring a number of observations of other mediators; a payment of fees, should any damages be established, and suspension from the practice for a specific period of time or permanent suspension, if appropriate under the circumstances.

C. PARTICULAR PROBLEMS FOR ATTORNEY MEDIATORS

While there are general difficulties in establishing mediator ethics, additional problems must be confronted when dealing with attorney-mediators. Difficulties arise when there is no acknowledgement that the responsibilities of an attorney and the role of a mediator are distinctly different. Unfortunately, neither the Model Rules of Professional Conduct nor the Model Code of Professional Responsibility have provided sufficient guidance concerning their conduct in the dispute resolution process for attorneys who are also mediators. (Menkel–Meadow). And the ABA's Commission, Ethics 2000 decided to take a minimalist approach, and consequently has addressed very few issues for attorney neutrals. (Yarn).

Several specific concerns have been voiced. One somewhat problematic situation may occur when the mediator is a lawyer and observes the blatant misconduct of another lawyer in the mediation. Rules of Professional Responsibility for Lawyers in most jurisdictions require that lawyers report the unethical conduct of other lawyers. Not only does this cause problems and usually result in a ineffective mediation, it also directly impacts the confidentiality of the mediation. When the lawyer-mediator discloses attorney wrongdoing, she potentially breaches the obligation of confidentiality that is critical to the mediation process.

Issues become even more problematic where the same individual is engaged in both law and mediation practice simultaneously. Often attorney mediators are forced to straddle the two professions.

Another difficulty arises as a result of mediation's development within the litigation system. Although the nature of mediation is very unlike the adversarial process, some lawyers tend to bring the adversarial character with them into the mediation process. These lawyers have had difficulties in conducting a truly facilitative process. (Guthrie)

Attorney ethical provisions have not yet clarified or explained when the attorney-mediator might be subject to legal malpractice or professional sanctions for his conduct. The question regarding whether bar association grievance committees and procedures have jurisdiction over a lawyer who is acting solely as a mediator has not yet been definitively decided. Currently, there is no requirement that a mediator be licensed in a specific jurisdiction in order to mediate cases. Some commentators urge the creation of rules narrowly targeted to the particular dilemmas faced by lawyer-mediators. (Laflin).

D. ETHICS FOR PROVIDER GROUPS

While ethics for individual mediators have received a great deal of attention, increased consideration is also being given to private organizations of mediators or service provider groups. Work in this area is being done by the CPR–Georgetown Commission on Ethics and Standards of Practice in ADR. The Commission defines an ADR provider organization as "any entity or individual which holds itself out as managing or administering dispute resolution or conflict management services." While addressing dispute resolution broadly, some considerations may be limited to mediation. Other research and reports have recognized that courts are considered providers of dispute resolution, and therefore may be responsible for ensuring competence and quality in dispute resolution. Finally some organizations may maintain rosters of approved mediators; in doing so, such entities may also be considered provider groups.

Specifically, many feel that private providers of dispute resolution services may need to adopt ethical guidelines that set parameters for appropriate conduct in both soliciting and administering mediation. These ethical rules might address the following: disclosure requirements for any and all conflicts of interest for both the organization and the individual mediator; provisions of confidentiality; prohibitions against false or misleading information or advertising; and the establishment of grievance and complaint mechanisms. An organization or mediation firm may also have a duty to provide information about the mediation process to the participants or possibly even the public. Furthermore, the organization, if responsible for its members or mediator rosters, may be responsible for assuring a competent process and additionally, that their neutrals adhere to a code of ethics.

E. ETHICS FOR REFERRING ENTITIES

Ethics are continuing to develop for another area in mediation: the referring entity. Those that refer cases to mediation may include courts, attorneys, business organizations, schools and other public entities. These groups may face certain ethical considerations in the course of their referrals, including conflicts of interest, impartiality and bias, future business potential, and issues concerning mediator fees. Similar considerations may apply to private organizations as well.

1. COURTS AND OTHER PUBLIC ENTITIES

Courts have been particularly active in referring cases to mediation. In doing so, it is extremely important that neutrality is preserved. There must not be any impropriety or favoritism exhibited. When a judge refers cases to a particular individual mediator or group of mediators, there is a danger of ethical violations and an opportunity for conflict of interest. Importantly, if the parties and the public perceive the referral process as unfair, it will likely undermine the mediation process as whole and possibly destroy the chance for resolution. As a result, ethical standards should be in place for courts to ensure that the mediator referral process is fair, that the mediator to whom the case has been referred is competent, and that the court does not receive any confidential information from the mediator.

2. PRIVATE REFERRALS

Those engaging in private mediation referral face similar challenges. Ensuring that neutrality and impartiality are maintained and that no conflicts of interest exist are important matters. Additionally, a prime consideration for private entities concerns the issue of fees. The questions of whether a mediator may provide a referral fee or whether fees may be split by the mediator and the referring individual or entity are complicated ones. Although it may seem to be an acceptable business practice to some, others believe that fee splitting directly conflicts with a mediator's impartiality. As referrals become more common, ethical standards are needed to address these issues and provide guidelines regarding acceptable practices for the mediation profession.

F.　ETHICS FOR PARTICIPANTS IN MEDIATION

Finally, a critical ethical consideration involves the enactment of ethical standards for all of those participating in mediation: the parties and their representatives, including attorneys acting as advocates. One such suggested ethical requirement mandates that all lawyers inform their clients about mediation at the initial interview or other early opportunity. (See Chapter Four). Other ethical requirements are more concerned with activity once parties and the lawyers have agreed or been mandated to participate in the mediation process. In particular, a debate exists over what is considered to be adequate participation. Many court orders require that a decision maker be present at mediation but nothing more. Others have begun to advocate a much stronger good faith requirement. Of course, a number of very controversial and difficult issues are then presented, including the additional burden on the mediator and the courts, finding exceptions to confidentiality, and the difficulty in defining good faith. (Chapter Five addresses these matters in detail).

The parties also may be bound by certain ethical guidelines associated with their primary profession. For example, professionals such as accountants and physicians often participate in mediation as parties negotiating past due accounts in small claims courts. These professionals may also find their way to the mediation table in response to a claim of malpractice. Ethical concerns may arise in the course of the mediation and could even be the subject of the dispute. For instance, doctors have specific ethical guidelines which must be adhered to when dealing with a patient. It is likely that these guidelines will continue to be operable in a mediation session between the physician and her patient.

With regard to ethical matters, we are likely at a time in the evolution of mediation that more questions than answers exist. While a number of codes and rules attempt to provide guidance, most mediators and mediation participants alike will need to make immediate and independent decisions with regard to their conduct. This then illustrates the growing need to examine additional methods of regulation, such as certification, training and general quality control.

References

Joseph P. Folger & Robert A. Baruch Bush, Transformative Mediation and Third Party Intervention: Ten Hallmarks of a Transformative Approach to Practice, 13 Mediation Quarterly 263 (1996).

Chris Guthrie, The Lawyer's Philosophical Map and the Disputant's Perceptual Map: Impediments to Facilitative Mediation and Lawyering, Harv. Negotiation L. Rev. 145 (2001).

Jamie Henifkoff & Michael Moffit, Remodeling the Model Standards of Conduct for Mediators, 2 Harv. Negotiation L. Rev. 87 (1997).

Maureen E. Laflin, Preserving the Integrity of Mediation Through the Adoption of Ethical Rules for Lawyer–Mediators, 14 Notre Dame J.L Ethics & Pub. Pol'y 479 (2000).

Carrie Menkel–Meadow, Ethics in Alternative Dispute Resolution: New Issues, No Answers from the Adversary

Conception of Lawyers Responsibilities, 38 S. Tex. L. Rev. 407 (1997).

Douglas H. Yarn, Lawyer Ethics in ADR and the Recommendations of Ethics 2000 to Revise the Model Rules of Professional Conduct: Considerations for Adoption and State Application, 54 Ark. L. Rev. 207 (2001).

Primary Cases

Fields–D'Arpino v. Restaurant Associates, Inc., 39 F.Supp.2d 412 (S.D.N.Y.1999).

Lange v. Marshall, 622 S.W.2d 237 (Mo.Ct.App.1981).

McKenzie Construction v. St. Croix Storage Corporation, 961 F.Supp. 857 (V.I., St.Croix Div.1997).

Poly Software International, Inc. v. Su, 880 F.Supp. 1487 (D.Utah 1995).

Bibliography

James J. Alfini, Chapter VII, Mediator Ethics in Dispute Resolution Ethics—A Comprehensive Guide, Edited by Phyllis Bernard and Bryant Garth, ABA Section of Dispute Resolution, 2002.

James J. Alfini, Settlement Ethics and Lawyering in ADR Proceedings: A Proposal to Revise Rule 4.1 19 N. Ill. U. L. Rev. 255 (1999).

Robert A. Baruch Bush, *The Dilemmas of Mediation Practice: A Study of Ethical Dilemmas and Policy Implications*, A report on a study for the National Institute of Dispute Resolution (1992).

Robert P. Burns, Some Ethical Issues Surrounding Mediaiton, 70 Fordham L.Rev. 691 (2001).

Dispute Resolution Ethics—A Comprehensive Guide, Edited by Phyllis Bernard and Bryant Garth, ABA Section of Dispute Resolution, 2002.

John D. Feerick, Toward Uniform Standards of Conduct for Mediators, 38 S. Tex. L. Rev. 455 (1997).

Scott H. Hughes, The Uniform Mediation Act: To the Spoiled Go the Privileges, 85 Marq. L. Rev. 9 (2001).

Kimberlee K. Kovach, Mediation: Principles and Practice (2d ed. 2000).

Kimberlee K. Kovach, New Wine Requires New Wineskins: Transforming Lawyer Ethics for Effective Representation in a Non–Adversarial Approach to Problem–Solving: Mediation, 28 Fordham Urb. L.J. 935 (2001).

Judith L. Maute, Public Values and Private Justice: A Case for Mediator Accountability, 4 Geo. J. Legal Ethics, 503 (1991).

Robert B. Moberly, Ethical Standards for Court–Appointed Mediators and Florida's Mandatory Mediation Experiment, 21 Fla. St. U. L. Rev. 701, 719 (1994).

Robert B. Moberly, Mediator Gag Rules: Is It Ethical for Mediators to Evaluate or Advise?, 38 S. Tex. L. Rev. 669 (1997).

Jacqueline M. Nolan–Haley, Court Mediation and the Search for Justice Through the Law, 74 Wash. U. L.Q. 47 (1996).

Jacqueline M. Nolan–Haley, Lawyers, Clients, and Mediation, 73 Notre Dame L. Rev. 1369 (1998).

Nancy H. Rogers & Craig A. McEwen, Mediation Law, Policy & Practice (2d ed. 1994) (Sarah R. Cole, ed., Supp. 1998).

Andrea K. Schneider, Which Means to an End Under the Uniform Mediation Act?, 13 Ohio St. J on Disp. Resol. 787 (1998).

Harry M. Webne–Behrman, The Emergence of Ethical Codes and Standards of Practice in Mediation: The Current State of Affairs, 1998 Wis. L. Rev. 1289 (1998).

CHAPTER 10

REGULATION OF MEDIATORS: DEVELOPMENT OF THE PROFESSION

A. OVERVIEW

Regulatory matters in mediation involve a variety of issues ranging from case referral to confidentiality to mediator qualifications. The most common consideration and that which this chapter addresses is the regulation of mediation practice. Another way of looking at the issue is to consider the quality control of mediation. Although quality control and regulation may not be completely synonymous, in this chapter the terms are used interchangeably to indicate efforts to ensure that mediators are competent and qualified, and that consequences exist for those failing to meet appropriate or established standards. If, in fact, as many mediators contend, a new profession has evolved, then regulatory aspects of practice such as credentialing and establishing a complaint process is likely inevitable.

An assurance of quality control for mediators may seem, at first glance, a very simple endeavor—perhaps even unnecessary. After all, mediation is a voluntary process and the mediator doesn't impose decisions upon the participants. But issues of quality control are widely discussed and debated among mediators as well as program administrators and mediation teachers and trainers. As mediation evolves into a wholly separate and distinct profession, these matters have become more critical.

A number of factors work together to define a "profession". These include a specialized knowledge and skill from training or education; independent membership organizations; charging a fee for service; and the opportunity for full time employment. Mediation practice is clearly embracing these facets of "professionalism" and seems to be moving toward the establishment of an independent profession. Yet, many complex matters surrounding professionalism are open for consideration, beginning with whether any regulation is even necessary.

B. POLICY CONSIDERATIONS

Although it appears that the mediation practice is headed toward the formation of a distinct profession and consequently regulation, a number of policy issues remain open. Practitioners, academics and consumers often disagree about whether any type of regulation is necessary for mediators, as well as the particular types of approaches to regulatory efforts.

1. ADVANTAGES AND BENEFITS OF REGULATION

Those who urge regulation do so for a variety of reasons. One primary justification is the establishment of the profession. To be a "profession" necessitates some regulatory procedures. In addition, by enacting a regulatory scheme, whether through a licensing or certification process, the general public will be assured that all mediators possess similar educational backgrounds in mediation. Although strict regulatory procedures may limit the number of individuals who can become mediators, this may be viewed as beneficial in providing increased competency as well as demand for services.

A certification or licensing process would also assist in assuring that all mediators are competent with regard to basic skills. The establishment of a separate and distinct mediation profession can also assure that another more recognized profession such as law or psychology will not subsume mediation. Regulation can also provide a method of "policing the mediators" by offering the general public methods through which they would be able to voice complaints.

The implementation of quality control or regulatory measures can also assure that all those individuals who hold themselves out to the general public as mediators have similar training and education and possess similar skills. And as with other professions, once a baseline competency is established, individuals may choose to specialize.

2.   DRAWBACKS TO REGULATION

Despite benefits of regulation, many mediators do not favor current efforts toward regulation. These attempts at regulation are viewed by some as a method to limit entry to the field. By increasing standards and making it more difficult to become a mediator, the number of individuals who can do so will likely decrease. Concerns are expressed that diversity will likely be limited. Cost presents another obstacle to regulation. Most professionals pay licensing fees, and mediators who are not full-time practitioners may have difficulty with such a payment.

Another major concern involves determining the methodologies through which regulation is established. Mediation is a more subjective practice, perhaps more of an art than a science. Defining the regulations with specificity may be quite challenging. Within the mediation community, there is a great divergence just in terms of defining what mediation is, and in particular, the approaches to the process. Finally, great disparity exists with regard to just how to design a regulatory scheme as well as the specific components it should include.

C. METHODS OF REGULATION

Matters of "quality" in mediation encompass many aspects of the mediator's work. As pointed out in the preceding chapter, standards of conduct are related to, and overlap with, ethical considerations. The topic of quality control is even more expansive and is similarly problematic due in part to the variety of forms, functions and definitions of mediation.

Mediation practitioners may be regulated in a number of ways. The prior chapter examined the use of ethical guidelines, standards or rules to regulate conduct. A variety of other methods may be used to standardize or regulate mediators. Although the articulated goal is public protection through quality control, some methods may be more effective in achieving quality than others. Some of the following approaches have not only been mentioned as possibilities for regulatory schemes, but are in place in several jurisdictions. Little similarity can be observed among the states, so it is imperative that individuals planning to mediate check each jurisdiction to determine what specific requirements may be in place.

Quality control efforts have been undertaken by a number of public, private, local and national organizations. With such a variety of entities attempting to assure quality control, there has been little consistency. In order to have uniform requirements for all mediators, one option may be to have each state to create a board of licensure or regulation for mediators similar to the state boards of other professions.

1.   QUALIFICATIONS

Some organizations and court programs have established a set of qualifications for those individuals who wish to be mediators. These range from only a prerequisite of a willingness to mediate to a requirement of extensive training, and even evaluation.

a. General Reputation or Experience

Some individuals are mediators solely based upon their personal reputation, and prior work experience. Factors examined may include the individual's educational background and any other acquired skills or training. Qualifications also include general innate tendencies, such as personality, communication abilities, and conflict management style. For instance, mediators may be appointed or selected based upon political or diplomatic experience. Another common example is the use of retired or former judges as mediators.

Some programs, courts, and statutory schemes provide that only a college or graduate degree is required to become a mediator, as the degree itself establishes sufficient competency. In some states, you must first be a lawyer in order to mediate specific types of cases. Obtaining a master's degree in some states will allow individuals to mediate family cases. Qualification by a formal degree however, is currently one of the more heavily criticized methods of regulation.

Although the degree itself served as the sole basis of qualification in early mediation use, in other instances today, whether in the private sector or in court programs, some additional experience is required. For example, experience in the practice of law is one factor a judge may substitute for training in appointing mediators in Texas.

The rationale behind this approach is the opinion that due to the individuals' past experience, they are instantly qualified to mediate. What is often overlooked in this approach is the question of whether the skills and knowledge demonstrated is transferable or appropriate in the context of mediation. This method of qualifying individuals as mediators has received criticism, and most experts urge that some type of training or education in the process is necessary.

b. Pre–Mediation

The term *qualification*, in this context, refers to the characteristics of an individual prior to participating in mediation training or education. Mediation trainers, educators and administrators have not reached consensus on what characteristics may constitute necessary qualifications. Many assert that it is a combination of factors which indicate the individual's appropriateness for mediation training. Some research has indicated that innate qualities, such as one's predisposition for conflict management, are more important in determining a mediator's effectiveness than training or prior education or experience.

Most professions, however, have initial qualification requirements which must be met before a student can enter a professional school. If mediation is to be established as a "profession," pre-training qualifications may need to be defined and implemented. If it is determined that pre-training qualifications are necessary regardless of subsequent training or education, another concern relates to the assessment of these qualifications. In the case of the requirement of a degree only, it is simple. In other instances, assessment of appropriate characteristics can be difficult. Several programs hold initial screening interviews before accepting individuals into training. Others require potential mediators to "audition" by conducting mock mediations. Some trainers require a number of years experience in a given field, for example, law. Pre-training appraisal via psychological inventories, such as the Meyers–Briggs type indicator, may also be used. On the other hand, the competing view is that if mediation skills can be taught, there should be no necessity for initial screening.

c. Mediation Education and Training

Several states and court programs that have established specific qualifications for mediators. These include requirements such as participation in designated number of hours of mediation training and attending mediations in an observer capacity. When the community mediation movement began, mediators were volunteers, and it was necessary that they were trained in the process. Early training programs focused primarily on skill development, as the theory and law surrounding mediation had not matured. Some of the earlier trainings, such as those conducted by the Neighborhood Justice Centers in Atlanta and Kansas City, consisted of forty hours of instruction. As mediation grew and branched out in other areas, many mediators took the same training. In other instances, separate training programs were created.

Some programs and courts require nothing more than a three to four hour orientation to the mediation process. This is particularly true where a graduate degree such as a law degree, is used as the indicator of mediator competency. Other programs and projects recognize that specific training and education in the mediation process is necessary. These range from a minimum of sixteen hours to forty hour trainings. Currently, very few mediation trainings exceed more than forty or fifty hours. Yet rarely are other professionals trained for such a short period of time. As the mediation profession matures and evolves, an increase in the training requirements will likely be established.

In most other professions at least one year of schooling or education is necessary in order to be licensed or certified. Currently, the most training or education required to "become a mediator" is forty hours. Additional hours are sometimes required for specialty areas, such as in family matters. Some colleges offer both undergraduate and graduate degree programs in conflict resolution that require a minimum of a year of study. If a mediation *profession* is established, it seems likely that the forty hour requirement will increase.

Even in the instances where there is agreement as to the number of hours of required mediation training or teaching, there is no regulation as to the form of that education. Diversity exists in both the method and content of training. Some mediation training programs consist of no more than viewing videotapes of mediations. Others consist primarily of lectures. Some trainers encourage continuous active participation by the trainees. Educators recognize that it is a combination of activities that provides the best learning experience. Most of the ongoing forty hour training programs do, as a rule, have a combination of these activities, although variation exists in the proportion devoted to each component.

Although some instructors and trainers voluntarily share information and methodologies, currently no standards exist for those who train mediators. This lack of a standard curriculum allows mediators to emerge from training programs with very different ideas as to what their "profession" requires. They may share no "core competencies" with other mediators. Here again, movement is toward more coordinated efforts. In Texas, for example, a Texas Mediation Trainers Roundtable was created and approved a curriculum for the forty hour training course.

An even greater difficulty for the mediation trainer is the determination of whether a trainee has "passed" the course. Most training programs merely provide the trainee with a certificate signifying course completion. The certificate itself, however, has no bearing on the individual's competency as a mediator. It merely signifies that the individual completed the requisite number of hours of instruction.

2. TESTING AND EVALUATION

In most professional training or educational schemes, a corollary testing or evaluation component is present. Most mediation training programs do not have a testing element which is mandatory. It is problematic to determine whether a trainee has "passed" the course. Difficulties arise in attempting to design an evaluative component, which would encompass knowledge of the theory and law of mediation and simultaneously the practical skills and elements of practice.

Some mediation courses and trainings, particularly those in law schools or other educational institutions, administer tests to the students. These range from traditional written examinations to performance-based assessments. Court-based programs have experimented with performance-based testing, but have found the time and effort involved is overwhelming. Others continue to experiment with the evaluation process.

Yet, many training programs, whether at the volunteer-community or the private provider mediator level, do not provide a formal evaluation of the trainee at the conclusion of the session. Trainers often evaluate the trainees during the course and provide direct feedback. Such assessment may consist only of informal conversation, or it may involve the use of more sophisticated tools, including forms and charts for evaluation.

There may be several occasions where testing or evaluating new mediators may be appropriate. Most common in professions that time is upon completion of the education. A number of mediation trainers, however, test mediators within a year of training, since it has been noted that experience increases the mediator's skills. These programs include an apprenticeship requirement. Other methods of evaluation which have been used include settlement rates, opinions of judges, attorneys and peers, and user perceptions including their satisfaction with the process.

3.   DEVELOPMENT OF CERTIFICATION AND LICENSING FOR MEDIATORS

While a number of current options exist with regard to the regulatory approaches, little has been done with regard to genuine certification or licensing requirements. Without such a process for mediators, it may be that no real profession will be established. Other professionals are required to become licensed before they are able to hold themselves out to the general public as offering a service. The term licensing and certification is used to connote that some oversight board or organization has taken the responsibility to credential or state that the individual is competent, in this instance in mediation.

A number of concerns arise when an entity establishes a scheme for certification or licensing. Most of the prior issues discussed, such as initial qualifications, training and testing, must be decided with certainty.

Only a few states have certification procedures currently in place. Examples include Florida and Virginia. Procedures in both states are structured through the state supreme court. As a result, only attorney mediators and those mediators who handle court cases are regulated. No state has yet established a comprehensive, mandatory, state-wide licensing procedure.

One of the most elaborate schemes of credentialing has been put forth by Family Mediation Canada (http://www.fmc.ca/). These standards apply to all family mediators and require initial applications which much demonstrate a minimum of eighty hours of training, one hundred hours of related education, videotaped skill demonstration, a written exam and self-evaluation.

4.   CODES AND STANDARDS OF CONDUCT

Numerous codes or standards of conduct exist which prescribe how a mediator is to conduct herself. While there is overlap to a large extent with ethical considerations and regulations, standards of conduct deal more with the behavior or competency issues involved within mediation practice. They may be able to set standards which are advisory or others which are more directive. In rare instances, standards alone provide guidance and the only control or monitoring of mediator conduct.

In most jurisdictions, the standards may also include a minimal training requirement, after which the only other guidance regarding a mediator's behavior is provided through the standards of conduct. The primary difficulty with this approach is that no method exists to enforce or assure that the mediators in practice are complying with the standards. Determining how to teach or train mediators to abide by the standards is another inherent problem. Much of the mediator's work is on a case-by-case basis and immediate responses to dilemmas and difficulties are necessary. Merely reading written standards does not often provide the type of guidance needed in many situations.

5.   MEMBERSHIP ORGANIZATIONS

Another method of establishing qualifications for mediators is the existence of a membership organization which demands certain conditions for membership. For example, one might require a minimum level of experience in mediation. Others organizations may require some training or continuing education. Consequently by virtue of one's membership in the organization, the public can be assured of at least a minimum level of competency. Some organizations attempt to oversee the membership. Those organizations which do monitor qualifications for mediators may terminate membership if the individual is unable to meet the requirements. The mediator may still hold themselves out to the general public, however.

6.   CONTINUING EDUCATION

Another element in the regulation of numerous professions is a continuing education requirement.

Most professionals are obligated to attend a specific number of hours of continuing education each year or biannually, in order to maintain licensure. Several court programs and certification procedures for mediators require attendance at a continuing education program. For example, in Idaho, to maintain certification, a mediator must attend 20 hours of continuing education each year. While much debate surrounds the establishment of licensing or other requirements as set forth earlier, there is little disagreement that continuing education is valuable and advisable for all mediators. Consequently implementation of a continuing education requirement is very likely, and may occur before specific guidelines or procedures for the initial training or qualifications are established or implemented.

D. OBSTACLES IN REGULATORY EFFORTS

As previously noted, until an entity is established at the local or state level that can and will exercise jurisdiction over mediators, then formulating a regulatory scheme is very difficult. Currently only a few states have set regulations for mediation practice; such efforts are through the supreme court or state office of dispute resolution. The regulation only pertains therefore to mediators who mediate pending lawsuits.

Another difficulty is in the specific content of the standards of mediator conduct. While strict standards would impose unnecessary restrictions on the mediator's activities, lack of standards results in little regulation. What has occurred in some jurisdiction is that a number of dispute resolution techniques and procedures are conducted, and all are termed mediation. Mediators must decide which approach to the process to follow. Implementation is also problematic. Usually no one is present to monitor the mediator's actions.

E.   MALPRACTICE AND IMMUNITY CONSIDERATIONS

As professionals practice, the possibility also exists that a dissatisfied consumer may sue the individual for professional negligence. In the instance of other professionals, standards of care or practice have been established. Proving that an individual did not abide by the standard practice will often lead to claims of negligence. This is a method of quality control that occurs "after the fact," as liability is established through malpractice suits. Even though mediation is a new profession with a great number of unanswered questions, there have been a few cases of negligence filed against mediators. Most have been resolved promptly and therefore little case law exists.

In the context of mediation, the initial hurdle is the establishment of a practice standard. Many practitioners and academics contend that it is still too early in the development of the profession to say with certainty what the standards should be. The profession has not reached consensus even on the definition of the process—let alone standards of practice. While a few aspects of the mediator's work, such as neutrality, are fairly definite, others remain far more subjective.

Nonetheless, a number of legal theories exist through which one can allege mediator malpractice. The theory with the broadest ramifications is general negligence. Depending on the nature of mediation practice, others may include violation of a deceptive trade and practices act (DTPA), breach of contract, fraud, false imprisonment, libel, slander, breach of fiduciary duty, and tortious interference with a business relationship. Matters such as libel and slander may fall within a claim of breach of confidentiality. Of course, confidentiality, in the legal sense, varies depending on the jurisdiction, type of mediation and nature of dispute. As time passes, research and practice should determine more specifically what the operable standard of practice is within any mediation organization or entity. Once determined, violations of these standards may result in negligence.

Even where a disputant is able to prove a breach of duty, thereby establishing liability against a mediator, in order to recover, damages must also be proven. In a truly consensual process such as mediation, there may be difficulty in establishing damages.

Likewise, in a case where the mediator provides professional advice, and the advice is incorrect, if the party shows that she relied upon such advice to her detriment, recovery against the mediator is likely. However, in claims against the mediator which turn on the elements of the process, establishing damages will be more difficult. Even if the mediator breached a duty with regard to performance in the mediation, the claimant must also establish that, but for those actions in the mediation, there would have been a better outcome to the case.

There are also a number of situations where a mediator may be immune from liability. One of the older dispute resolution devices, arbitration, has historically provided immunity for the arbitrators. Immunity was initially premised on the fact that the arbitrator was an extension of the court or judge, and as such, should be given immunity. Extension of this immunity to mediators has not been unequivocally established. In fact, some argue that the mediator's role is so dissimilar to that of the court, that a new common law immunity premised along the lines of judicial and arbitral immunity is unlikely. A few courts have begun to address this issue directly, and a number of states have enacted statutes providing immunity for the mediator. These include: Arizona, Colorado, Florida, Iowa, Maine, Minnesota, Oklahoma, Utah, Washington, Wisconsin, and Texas.

Most of these statutes provide for immunity in the volunteer or pro bono setting, often under specific programs or conditions. There has yet to be enacted a statute which provides blanket immunity for all mediators in all actions. Nearly all of the statutes provide a qualified immunity and include an exception for wanton and willful misconduct.

If immunity is absolute, or sufficiently broad, the consumer of mediation services will have no recourse for any damage resulting from participation in mediation. Since mediation is such a new field, essentially without regulations, rules or standardized procedures, there must be a way to guard against abuse of the process and the parties by the mediator. Furthermore, mediators resemble service providers who have not traditionally been protected by immunity. These include lawyers and therapists. Conversely, mediators, particularly those who volunteer, need to do so without fear of having to expend time and money in the defense of malpractice claims. A compromise between these two considerations has resulted in enactment of immunity statutes aimed primarily at protection of the pro bono mediator.

F. A CRITICAL ISSUE: CONSIDERATION OF MEDIATION AS THE PRACTICE OF LAW

One related matter that has also been the subject of much debate surrounds the question of whether mediation is, or can be considered the practice of law. The concern has ramifications for both lawyers as well as other individual mediators.

With regard to lawyers, the question is whether a lawyer who serves as a mediator should be considered to be engaged in the practice of law. Many commentators suggest that the mediator does not represent any of the parties, and hence has no clients. Consequently, the mediator is not engaged in the practice of law. An exception may be when, as at least one individual has suggested, that lawyer mediators who can mediate for and between their clients may be practicing law. A more common situation arises when the mediator, who is also a lawyer, provides legal information or advice to the participants and by such conduct may be engaged in the practice of law.

Similar concerns about whether mediation is considered the practice of law arises for those mediators who do not have a law degree, but for different reasons. In a few instances, state and local bar associations have brought complaints against such individuals for the unauthorized practice of law. In most instances, such behavior is not considered to be the practice of law. One state, taking the lead to assure no further claims of unauthorized law practice, has set out the parameters for nonlawyer mediators with regard to providing information and drafting the mediation agreement.

Cases

Howard v. Drapkin, 271 Cal.Rptr. 893 (Cal.Ct.App.1990).

Smith v. Travelers Indem. Co., 343 F.Supp. 605 (M.D.N.C.1972).

Wagshal v. Foster, 1993 WL 86499 (D.D.C.1993).

Bibliography

Robert C. Barrett, Mediator Certification: Should California Enact Legislation? 30 U.S.F. L. Rev. 617 (1996).

Teresa V. Carey, Credentialing for Mediators—To Be or Not to Be? 30 U.S.F. L. Rev. 635 (1996).

Dorothy J. Della Noce, Mediation Could Be the Practice of Law, But It Doesn't Have to Be, 33 Nat'l Inst. Disp. Resol. F. 16 (1997).

Amanda K. Esquibel, The Case of the Conflicted Mediator: An Argument for Liability and Against Immunity, 31 Rutgers L.J. 131 (1999).

Barbara Filner & Michael Jenkins, Performance–Based Evaluation of Mediators: The San Diego Mediation Center's Experience, 30 U.S.F. L. Rev. 647 (1996).

Jay Folberg, Certification of Mediators in California: An Introduction, 30 U.S.F. L. Rev. 609 (1996).

Bryant Garth, Is Mediation the Practice of Law: The Wrong Question, 33 Nat'l L. Inst. Disp. Resol. F. 34 (1997).

Chris Guthrie, The Lawyer's Philosophical Map and the Disputant's Perceptual Map: Impediments to Facilitative Mediation and Lawyering 6 Harv. Negotiation L. Rev. 145 (2001).

Bobby M. Harges, Mediator Qualifications: The Trend Toward Professionalization, 1997 B.Y.U. L. Rev. 687 (1997).

Stephanie A. Henning, A Framework for Developing Mediator Certification Programs, 4 Harv. Neg. L. Rev. 189 (1999).

Norma Jeane Hill, Qualification Requirements of Mediators, 1998 J. Disp. Resol. 37 (1998) (discussing pros and cons of various state certification programs).

David A. Hoffman, Certifying ADR Providers, 40 B. B.J. 9 (Mar./Apr. 1996).

Brad Honoroff et al., Putting Mediation Skills to the Test, 6 Negotiation J. 37 (1990).

Kimberlee K. Kovach, Mediation the Practice of Law? Not!, 33 Nat'l L. Inst. Disp. Resol. F. 37 (1997).

Kimberlee K. Kovach, What is Real Mediation and Who Should Decide, 3 Disp. Resol. Mag. 5 (1998).

Carrie Menkel–Meadow, Is Mediation the Practice of Law, 14 Alternatives 57 (1995).

Bruce E. Meyerson, Lawyers Who Mediate Are Not Practicing Law, 14 Alternatives 74 (1996).

Bruce Meyerson, Mediation and the Practice of Law, 3 Disp. Resol. Mag. No. 2, at 11 (1996).

Jacqueline M. Nolan–Haley, Lawyers, Non–Lawyers and Mediation: Rethinking the Professional Monopoly from a Problem-solving Perspective 7 Harv. Negotiation L. Rev. 235 (2002).

Nichol M. Schoenfield, Turf Battles and Professional Biases: An Analysis of Mediator Qualifications in Child Custody Disputes, 11 Ohio St. J. on Disp. Resol. 469 (1996).

Joshua R. Schwartz, Laymen Cannot Lawyer, But is Mediation the Practice of Law? 20 Cardozo L. Rev. 1715 (1999).

Dana Shaw, Comment, Mediation Certification: An Analysis of the Aspects of Mediator Certification and an Outlook on the Trend of Formulating Qualifications for Mediators, 29 U. Tol. L. Rev. 527 (1998).

Carole Silver, Models of Quality for Third Parties in Alternative Dispute Resolution, 12 Ohio St. J. on Disp. Resol. 37 (1999).

UPL. Virginia Guidelines on Mediation & the Unauthorized Practice of Law (1999).

CHAPTER 11

SPECIALIZED APPLICATIONS OF MEDIATION

While mediation is an adaptable process, subject to modifications, there are also several defining characteristics which are present in most "generic" mediations. For example, the preservation of neutrality and promise of confidentiality are important in all mediations. There is also an implicit assumption that the mediation session will either result in an agreement or an impasse. Mediation is commonly viewed as a single, one-time intervention, and not a process that takes place over several days, weeks or months. This more generic approach is often adapted in unique ways to assist in the mediation of a particular specialty or specific subject matter. Some of the more specialized applications require mediators to attend additional training for that particular adaptation of the process. Even in situations where further training is not explicitly required such as in employment cases, most programs and consumers may be assured of added quality if such additional and specialized training is completed. A brief overview of some of the more common specialized applications of mediation is set out below.

A. CO–MEDIATION

Used in a number of types of situations, the co-mediation model is highlighted only to distinguish it from the more basic one mediator model. While little specialized training takes place with regard to co-mediation, particular nuances do exist. (Love & Stulberg) For example, in most models of co-mediation there is a shared responsibility for the process. One mediator does not take "the lead" with the other merely following. Instead, the responsibility for the mediation rests equally on each mediator. Although there is never a completely equal division of labor, a benefit underlying co-mediation is that different individuals are able to bring to the process diverse talents and skills.

Benefits of a co-mediation approach are numerous. Included is the ability to blend different expertise in the subject matter of the dispute. In those cases where gender, race, or culture are at the basis of the dispute, having a 'balanced' co-mediation team can assist in the parties' perception that the process will be a neutral one. Moreover, the presence of another individual adds additional eyes, ears and intelligence, which can benefit the process. Each of the mediators may differ in their instinctive approach to mediation. In many instances, a blended approach results. For example, if a very relaxed and casual style is combined with a more directive and structured approach, this may assist in providing the style that is needed at different times during the session. When two mediators are present, their work together also provides an exemplary model of effective communication and cooperation for the parties to follow. Mediators can learn and benefit a great deal from working with each other. Co-mediators are able to provide feedback to each other, whereas someone not present at the mediation would not be in a position to offer such an accurate evaluation.

Despite all of the enumerated benefits of a co-mediation model, mediators acknowledge that difficulties with the approach do arise. For one, conducting the process can be more difficult for the mediators when they are unfamiliar with each other. Mediation may be more time consuming when two mediators are present; questioning may take longer, and the mediators may take breaks to consult with each other between caucuses. In addition, diverse approaches to the mediation process can create conflict and competition between the co-mediators, which if not immediately resolved, can result in disaster for the session. Alternatively, some directive mediators, for fear of stepping on the other's toes, may not be as assertive as they would be if mediating alone.

Nonetheless, co-mediation is commonly used. In particular, it is used in many of the community dispute resolution centers, especially in pairing novice mediators with those more experienced. Family law and divorce mediation is another common category of cases where co-mediation is used, as well as large public policy matters where at least two mediators are often necessary because of the shear number of individuals involved.

Of utmost importance to a co-mediation process is good communication between the co-mediators, before, during and after the mediation. It is also important that they resist the temptation to meet separately with different parties at the same time. In most models of co-mediation, it is considered important that the mediators remain together throughout the process. This assures that each mediator gathers identical information and also avoids the parties' perception that one mediator is more biased toward one party. Although the responsibility for the mediation in totality rests on both mediators, it is not uncommon to decide in advance that each mediator will take on the specific tasks most comfortable for that person in order to promote efficiency in the process. Different seating arrangements are possible, although most often the co-mediators sit side by side. What is imperative, however, is that the co-mediators have established good communication and have planned in advance a "fall-back" approach should any conflicts arise during the mediation.

B. FAMILY MATTERS

When mediation was first used in family law matters, the mediator served a number of roles, ranging from counselor to mediator to legal advisor for the parties. While the mediator was not a representative in a technical sense, the parties were often unrepresented, and the mediator provided information about the divorce process, along with guidelines regarding custody, visitation, child support and property divisions. In many instances, mediators in divorce cases also took on the responsibility for drafting not only the memorandum of agreement at the close of the mediation, but also the final court documents, including the decree of divorce. In a few jurisdictions, this prompted claims of the unauthorized practice of law in cases where the mediator was not a lawyer.

Over time, methods of practice changed, as a number of issues were raised about the lack of representation during the process. (Bryan, Grillo). The process transitioned and it became common practice for family mediators to urge the parties to obtain legal and financial advice after each session. Lawyers served primarily to review only the final agreement upon completion of the mediation. Currently, in an increasing number of instances, lawyers attend each mediation session with their clients. (McEwen, et al.) In limited circumstances, an accountant or a therapist for a party may also attend. Although the children do not normally participate, in occasional instances family mediators confer with them separately and bring their interests into the mediation session.

The family law co-mediation team usually consists of a therapist or other individual from the social and behavioral sciences and a lawyer. An accountant is sometimes included when the focus of the case is on asset division and financial matters.

Most states and court-sponsored programs require specific additional mediation training in family law and family dynamics.

Two distinct methods of mediation may be observed in family cases. The more traditional procedure, modeled somewhat after a therapeutic approach, is that the mediator(s) meet with the spouses once a week for relatively short sessions, for a series of weeks, until all matters have been resolved. In most jurisdictions where this style is practiced, the parties are never separated, and are encouraged to communication directly. In other locales, divorce mediation practice developed with, or subsequent to general civil, legal mediation. Consequently, the process resembles the arduous litigation model of mediation, occurring in just one full day session, with the attorneys very active and the shuttle or caucus method as the prototype.

One very controversial aspect of family and divorce mediation involves cases where domestic violence is present. Many experts contend that cases involving domestic violence should not be mediated at all because a severe, and often irreparable, imbalance of power exists. In some instances, however, the mediator may not be aware of the problem until she is well into the mediation session. Information on recognizing the signs of domestic violence abuse is included in many divorce mediation training programs. Once a mediator suspects that abuse may be present in the relationship, he must proceed with the mediation only with the explicit consent of the victim. Most experts contend that the mediator should have additional specialized training and implement safety and process protection measures as well. (Zylstra). These may include keeping the parties separated, requiring the parties to leave at different times, positioning the victim near a door, or allowing a lawyer, friend or other representative to be present in the session.

Applications of family mediation continue to increase, particularly in situations where families have been redefined. For example, mediation is quite effective in resolving gay and lesbian separation and custody matters. It may also be effective when a grandparent or other relative asserts their desire to have visitation with the child or a hand in making decisions pertaining to the child. In some states, mediation is used in matters concerning the termination of parental rights. At least one state has implemented a statewide program in this area. Mediation is frequently used at an early stage, for instance, when the child is first removed from the home, to assist in determining the possibility of reuniting the family. Mediation is also used in the later stages of the process to finalize the conditions of termination of parental rights or the establishment of adoption.

Most states or court programs require additional training in family mediation. Additionally, a recent focus has been on recognizing and addressing issues of domestic violence in family cases. As more attention is given to this subject, it is likely that domestic abuse training will be included as a component of all family and divorce mediation training in the future.

C. EMPLOYMENT CASES

In the United States, the labor and employment arena is historically seen as the birthplace of modern mediation use. However, mediation was not commonly used in individual complaints, but rather in union or collective bargaining matters. In the traditional labor mediation model, the mediator met with representatives of each group and then was very active in formulating solutions with each representative negotiator. Recently, there has been an increased use of the mediation process to resolve individual complaints concerning employment issues, as well as to resolve intra-organizational disputes. Currently, one of the largest growing areas for mediation practice is with individual claims in the field of labor and employment disputes.

Some major corporations have designed entire dispute resolution systems through which employees may resolve their grievances. Likely the largest public employer in the United States, the United States Postal Service, has designed and implemented a mediation program entitled REDRESS (Resolve Employment Disputes Reach Equitable Solutions Swiftly) to resolve employee grievances. Mediation can also be effective in resolving charges of discrimination in employment. Entities such as the Equal Employment Opportunity Commission (EEOC) have implemented considerable mediation projects in an attempt to resolve charges of discrimination in the work place.

In employment cases, the mediation process used may deviate considerably from one used in more traditional civil cases. One distinction is that there has usually been a lengthy working relationship between the parties, and thus, attachments and emotions are high. In discrimination matters, closely held beliefs and sensitive issues are frequently involved. When these beliefs surface, some matters become more difficult to discuss. Subjects of a personal nature, such as gender, age and race may be involved. Mediators usually allow time for venting from each party. Because the interests are often non-monetary, more creative solutions are likely.

The REDRESS program embraced a particular style of mediation known as the transformative model. In doing so, there was an implicit acknowledgement that these types of cases are often relational in nature. The transformative approach to mediation is based upon the premise that mediation has the potential to transform people. Founded upon principles of party empowerment and recognition, this model of mediation focuses primarily on the relationship between the parties, rather than on outcome. Mediators in the REDRESS program were required to attend additional training in the transformative model prior to acceptance on the roster.

Another deviation from the traditional model involves agenda setting. In employment termination cases, some preliminary matters must be resolved initially, for instance, whether the party will return to employment. In many situations, the remaining agenda items may be shaped by the resolution of an initial issue.

Mediation has successfully resolved wrongful termination claims, age and sexual discrimination issues, claims under the Americans with Disabilities Act, sexual harassment disputes, whistleblower claims, disputes involving retaliation for filing workers compensation claims. As experience with these matters increased, there is a recognition that more specialized training may be necessary. Although currently additional training is not generally required, it is becoming more common.

D. CRIMINAL MATTERS

Mediation of criminal or quasi-criminal matters has been in existence for a long time. Many of the early Dispute Resolution Centers received referrals from prosecutors' or district attorneys' offices. While that continues today, use of mediation is observed in three distinct phases of a criminal matter: before charges are brought; during the pendency of a complaint; and after adjudication, commonly known as victim-offender mediation.

1. PRE–COMPLAINT MEDIATION

Before a formal criminal complaint is filed against an individual, in many jurisdictions a screening process takes place to determine whether charges are in fact appropriate. During that screening, whether the matter or parties might benefit from mediation is considered. The types of complaints are usually misdemeanors; no severe injury or damage to property had occurred. These matters often address neighborhood disputes and other instances where the parties have continuing relationships. Many of the first nonprofit dispute resolution centers obtained their mediation caseload in this manner.

If the mediation resulted in a resolution, then no further action was taken. In the event an agreement was not achieved, then the parties were free to continue to pursue other remedies, including filing a complaint. In most cases, the information gained during the mediation is not available due to confidentiality restrictions.

2. MEDIATION AS A METHOD OF PLEA BARGAINING

Although criminal trials often receive an enormous amount of media attention, many criminal matters are resolved without the necessity of a trial. This usually occurs in what is commonly known as 'plea bargaining,' a negotiation between the prosecutor and the defense counsel regarding the outcome of the case. Usually the defendant will plead to a specific charge, and the corresponding punishment will be negotiated. The use of mediation to assist prosecutors and defense lawyers in the plea bargaining process has not been very common, although the United States Department of Justice, in its general dispute resolution initiatives, has made some effort to educate prosecutors about the potential of mediation.

In some limited cases, where a complaint has been filed and the parties have had a prior relationship, mediation may also be appropriate. On rare occasions, a request for mediation has been voiced by defense counsel, and in other cases, the court makes its own decision based upon a recognition that mediation could be beneficial to the parties. Most often these judges see a larger role for the justice system—that of problem solving.

3. VICTIM–OFFENDER MEDIATION

The foundation for victim-offender mediation is that the offenders, particular first or second time offenders, are often remorseful about having injured someone and could benefit from an opportunity to apologize and make restitution. On the other side, many times the individual involved, a victim, would like the opportunity to ask questions directly of the offender, engage in some personal venting concerning the incident, or achieve closure. Victim-offender mediation or reconciliation (which may connote a more focused attempt on the part of the mediator to reconcile the feelings and the parties) is able to take these needs into consideration. Mediation has developed as an effective process to assist in resolving these types of conflict.

One main difference from the more generic model of mediation is the fact that only one party is compelled to attend the mediation, the offender. The victim's participation is discretionary. Victims in most cases, however, are quite eager to attend. Often victims have several motives for meeting with the offender. In some cases, the individual may want to know why or how they were chosen for the crime, particularly whether it was planned or a random act. Other victims hope for the opportunity to address or confront the offender. Victims may also want to be able to impart to the offender how the incident has affected them and how the lingering effects of victimization have impacted their lives. Frequently, victims hope to bring the matter to closure. Monetary or material restoration is an important component as well.

Philosophies underlying victim-offender mediation are varied. Some are purely efficiency related, as courts and probation officers will no longer need to make decisions concerning restitution. Largely, however, victim-offender mediation (VOM) is based upon notions of restorative justice. The criminal justice system generally is a system of retributive justice where individuals are punished. Restorative justice calls for reconciling matters and relationships and for healing. (Zehr). Some of this is also religiously based, and several religious groups have been quite active in developing VOM, as well as educating mediators and participants of the process.

In most models of VOM, compensation for the victim is but one part of the process. Programs differ, however, in the amount of emphasis placed on reconciliation, which is more attuned to restorative justice principles. Another distinction from generic mediation is that in court-referred VOM cases, there are generally more 'teeth' in the agreement. Often, the VOM is a condition of probation. Any agreement reached is likewise a condition, and probation, or in some instances, parole can be revoked if the offender fails to comply with the agreement.

Another peculiarity in VOM mediation is that the conversations between the parties are often highly structured and focused, whereas in generic mediation, the mediator follows the parties' lead with regard to matters of importance. In most models of VOM, the mediator keeps the parties on task, the goal being to achieve a resolution. Rehashing the incident (the crime), which has already been decided, is generally not permitted.

Early work in the victim-offender cases involved juveniles and less serious matters. Now part of adult criminal justice programs, VOM has also been conducted in serious criminal matters such as rape and murder. Due to the nature of these cases and the dialogue that often occurs, specialized training in neutrality and sensitivity is usually necessary. In fact, many VOM programs are operated through courts or justice system programs and require additional training.

E. CLASS ACTIONS

Class actions, lawsuits usually involving hundreds, even thousands of claimants, can also be resolved through mediation. Certification of a class allows an individual who would not be able to bring a cause of action on their own, to pool resources, such as lawyers and expert costs, for the entire class.

Mediation can be used to assist in the resolution of class action claims in two primary ways. First, mediation may help achieve the global or overall settlement. This is the total amount of compensation or remedies that the defendant(s) agree to provide. Representatives for the class may be present at the mediation, and the process can be rather lengthy. Many of the members of the class may attend the mediation or alternatively, a few representatives may attend on behalf of the class with the lawyers

Once conditions for a global settlement are achieved and the central case settled, there often remains the need to determine how the proceeds will be allocated. Not all claimants are injured to the same degree. Additional mediations may be conducted to determine how the entire settlement will be dispersed. This may occur on a case-by-case basis, where each claimant has the opportunity to participate in a mediation to determine compensation. Alternatively, a more general mediation examining the overall distribution and determining how to divide the compensation may be utilized.

Mediation of class action differs in terms of the amount of time needed in advance of the actual sessions, as well as the time devoted after a settlement has been reached. Like many types of matters where representatives are present, mediators often have an important role in supporting the settlement and persuading all of the class members to agree. The complexity, duration and certainly the number of participants in these cases frequently requires additional planning and preparation.

F. APPELLATE MEDIATION

In many jurisdictions, the mediation of cases on appeal is another aspect of court-annexed programs. In Montana, for example, a statute providing authority to the courts to mandate mediation applies only to appellate matters, and specifically those involving workers compensation claims, domestic relations and money judgments. In appellate mediation, the process often differs because not only are contingencies about the appeal considered, but also if the matter is reversed or remanded, more complex issues must be considered. Concerns arise that resolving too many appellate matters in mediation may harm the lawmaking function of the appellate courts.

In the federal court system, a number of courts have staff mediators who mediate the cases. Some courts have a detailed selection process to identify cases for mediation, while others do not. Settlement rates are often not as high when appellate cases are mediated, as parties have been so committed to the legal system to resolve their dispute. One important consideration is the effect the mediation may have on deadlines for transcripts and briefs. In response, some courts, upon request, will toll the deadlines until the mediation is completed.

G.   PEER MEDIATION

The term *peer mediation* is used to describe a process where the mediator is a peer of those involved in the dispute. Most often, school students have been trained in mediation or conflict management skills. Peer mediation employs trained student mediators to resolve disputes that occur between other students, their peers. When a dispute or conflict arises, instead of resorting to traditional forms of discipline, teachers may refer the disputing students to a peer mediator.

There has been some experimentation with peer mediation, also referred to as school based conflict management, in nearly every state. Peer mediation programs have been implemented in elementary schools, high schools, and colleges. In several states, statutes require that school districts develop teaching outlines in the mediation and dispute resolution area. At the university level, student mediation programs are often administered through offices of student affairs.

H. ENVIRONMENTAL AND PUBLIC POLICY CASES

Disputes involving the environment affect the general public and are some of the more complex public policy cases. (The process of public policy mediation and consensus building is discussed in the following chapter.) Environmental matters are often multifaceted and based largely on scientific principles. Consequently, when these types of disputes are in litigation they may take years, perhaps even decades to resolve. Environmental law is an evolving area of practice, and early on it was recognized that ADR procedures, particularly consensus processes could be effective in reaching resolution in these types of cases. Mediation, or its derivative, consensus building has been used successfully in a number of environmental matters. However, it is important in environmental cases that the mediators have specific expertise and rely on the assistance of engineers and other experts to provide the necessary technical information.

More general public policy matters can take on a number of forms and essentially refer to any matter where at least one of the parties is a governmental entity. Because of the nature of cases involving the government, the various forms and methods of mediation differ from the generic model. In fact, the process has been modified in many instances and currently may be most often referred to as consensus building. Consensus building is generally acknowledged as a separate process with distinctive attributes and is discussed in greater detail in the following chapter.

Several states including California, Oregon, New Hampshire, Texas, Maine, and Vermont have initiated efforts to increase the use of dispute resolution and have created statewide offices for public policy disputes. These statewide offices assist state and local governmental entities in the implementation of mediation, consensus building, and other dispute resolution devices as integral parts of public service. Specialized training for those mediating in public policy matters is strongly advised.

I. INTERNATIONAL AND CULTURAL

Mediation in the international context takes on a number of different forms. International disputes are commonly thought to involve political or security matters between people of different nations. They may also include economic and environmental matters. In these types of mediations, the mediator is not completely neutral but has relations with each country, although he does not favor either side.

What has become known as cross-cultural mediation is the mediation between individuals from different cultures. As the world evolves and globalization increases, many disputes now involve people with differing views and customs. In fact, in many cases, a difference in culture and understanding drives or forms the basis of the dispute in the first place. In what is commonly considered cross-cultural mediation, the parties may be from the same nation or different nations, but have different backgrounds and customs which influence the disputing process. Cross-cultural considerations are necessary as mediation use grows within the United States, as persons in conflict may be from a number of different cultures. Often when disputes arise, they are due to a lack of mutual understanding.

Mediation of cross-cultural disputes is particularly problematic because of the threshold difficulties associated with a lack of understanding and knowledge about the parties, their interests, and cultural directives. It is important that mediators intervening in cross-cultural disputes have a sense of these additional issues. As in many types of specialized applications of the mediation process, specific training is helpful, but rarely required. Basic mediation trainings may include a component on cross-cultural matters, but often more specific information is lacking. While specialized trainings in cross-cultural mediation do exist, difficulties arise surrounding how to balance the impacts culture may have on the mediation without excessively relying on stereotypes remain.

In addition, different cultures have varying concepts of the appropriate role of an intermediary in negotiation. Some cultures favor a more adjudicative model of dispute resolution, based upon individual rights, whereas other cultures are partial to a consensus, community approach. Even within a more facilitative model, mediators can take on a number of different tasks, ranging from providing assistance with the relationships and helping in data collection or exchange to providing advice for decision making. While the first two may be seen as traditional mediation techniques, the last is seen primarily in other ADR processes. Mediators in these matters, before initiating the process, must be sure that the parties are clear about what their role is to be.

J. HEALTH CARE MATTERS

Health care affects everyone. During the period of time that individuals are involved in health care matters, a number of conflicts can arise. Mediation has been used in the health care industry in disputes over provisions and types of treatment, cost and payment, and allegations of medical negligence or malpractice. With the evolution of managed care and all of the accompanying conflict surrounding such an approach to health care, it appears that additional opportunities for mediation exist.

The mediation process can benefit parties during the treatment phase of the patient-health care provider relationship. Due to the circumstances, the time during which individuals are involved in treatment may be a very difficult time, full of emotion and conflict. Reaching an expeditious resolution of these types of disputes in the patient-provider relationship can prevent later conflicts and disputes. Many state legislatures have recognized this potential and have provided statutory authority for mediation in health care disputes.

Additionally, cost and payment disputes can be resolved through mediation. Mediation saves time and money, which are important concerns for the patient, the provider and third-party payors, such as health maintenance organizations. In at least one state, disputes regarding inpatient reimbursement are referred to mediation.

Mediation in health care matters may also assist in life and death decision making, primarily for the patient's family members. In the past, these matters were handled by medical ethicists, many of whom did not have specialized training in facilitation, mediation or communication. In some instances, mediators specifically are being used. In other cases, hospitals are participating in training others, such as ethicists, in the skills needed to assist with difficult decision making. Mediation has been specifically included.

K. RELIGIOUS ORGANIZATIONS

Religious institutions, such as churches and synagogues, experience conflicts which may disrupt the feeling of community or impair the otherwise salient goals of the institution. Such conflicts may take a number of forms. For example, a dispute may arise regarding whether the physical site of a synagogue should move, with half the congregation in favor of the move and half opposed to it. Or, a congregation may become split over the practices and philosophies of a particular priest. A church may become torn over the inclusion and recognition of gay members. Other disputes may arise over the content and efficacy of religious school programs.

If such disputes are not dealt with efficiently and effectively, these matters can be devastating to a religious institution, resulting in destructive feuds between congregants or the splintering of the institution itself. Ironically, conciliation and the peaceful resolution of disputes is an inherent philosophy of all major religions. Mediation or conciliation is clearly etched in both the Old and New Testament.

Some of the early work in mediation was accomplished by religious institutions. While some religious organizations use a more traditional, generic mediation process, others have instituted a unique approach to the process, one based more upon scripture and religious teachings. In a more traditional mediation approach, certain norms, such as potential court outcomes, are often used to guide decision making. (See Chapter Six.) In more religious-based mediation, the norms are set by the religion, most often biblical teachings or passages.

Additionally, religious institutions may be involved as parties in civil litigation. When this is the case, more often the traditional generic model of mediation is used, but many mediators will also acknowledge the more spiritual side of the case.

Based in part upon religious philosophies regarding conciliation and forgiveness, several religious institutions are beginning to create a mediation system to resolve disputes or claims against the church within the church itself. Such systems set out the religious foundation for mediation and conciliation. Training is specialized, and focuses on the mediator's knowledge of and sensitivity to the religious principles of the institution. Religious-based conflict resolution systems emphasize the core foundation of the principles of conciliation and forgiveness as a basis to resolve disputes.

L. DISPUTES BETWEEN LAWYERS AND CLIENTS

In recent decades, lawyers have suffered from a less than stellar reputation among the general public. Many individuals go to lawyers at a crisis time in their lives, and often the final result may not what the client expected. Many disputes between lawyers and clients result simply from lack of communication and understanding. Once the parties are able to better communicate, such disputes are often resolved. Mediation between attorneys and clients can be used in disputes over competency issues, ethics, fees and law firm dissolutions.

In most states, lawyer grievances, whether concerning fee disputes, allegations of misconduct, or violations of disciplinary rules are handled through state and local bar associations. Many times dissatisfaction and claims of attorney malfeasance or malpractice arise out of a disagreement over attorney's fees. Arbitration has often been used to resolve fee disputes. While arbitration can be effective, many clients may want to have more participation in the process and in particular, the final decision making. Currently, some efforts are afoot to utilize mediation in fee matters. State and local bar associations are experimenting with pilot mediation projects to resolve disciplinary matters. Courts have also referred disciplinary cases to mediation, if the matter concerns license suspension. Additionally, courts are active in referring legal malpractice claims to mediation, as they do any professional negligence matter. In some cases, use of mediation to resolve attorney-client disputes early on may prevent subsequent claims of malpractice.

M. INTERNET AND CYBERSPACE

As businesses and consumers ventured into cyberspace, it has only been natural that dispute resolution processes have followed. Online dispute resolution, particularly online mediation, is one of the fastest growing mechanisms to resolve disputes. In this process, the mediator can gather the disputing parties in a "chat room" and conduct the process online. Although most online mediations resemble a form of facilitative rather than evaluative mediation, many different providers and approaches are available. Many sites are connected with consumer transactions, however, almost any type of dispute can be mediated in cyberspace.

While advocates of internet mediation claim time, speed, and convenience are primary benefits, other considerations demonstrate some drawbacks and pitfalls of the process. Many critics cite the loss of direct interpersonal contact as a major disadvantage to online mediation. Verbal and nonverbal communication is extremely important to the mediation process, yet it is very difficult to gauge a party's tone or reaction in an online session. There are no visual clues to guide the participants. Others question whether this electronic distance imposes a psychological distance as well. Some are also troubled by the lack of rules or standards to guide the process. Currently, there is little, if any, regulation of online mediation.

Over the last several years, the use of the Internet for business and consumer transactions has dramatically increased. Not surprisingly, there is a great deal of interest in online dispute resolution processes. In fact, the effects of ecommerce and the growth of online services have been so significant, the ABA Section of Dispute Resolution established a special task force to examine the intricacies of online dispute resolution. Other ABA sections joined the effort, and the project is the ABA Task Force on E-Commerce and ADR. Additional projects involving online mediation have been sponsored by governmental organizations and educational institutions. It is likely the debates over online dispute resolution and online mediation will continue as the processes adapt and evolve.

References

Penelope E. Bryan, Killing Us Softly: Divorce Mediation and the Politics of Power, 40 Buff. L. Rev. 441 (1992).

Trina Grillo, The Mediation Alternative: Process Dangers for Women, 100 Yale L.J. 1545 (1991).

Lela P. Love & Joseph B. Stulberg, Practice Guidelines for Co-Mediation: Making Certain That "Two Heads Are Better Than One," 13 Mediation Q. 179 (1996).

Craig McEwen, et al., Bring in the Lawyers: Challenging the Dominant Approaches to Ensuring Fairness in Divorce Mediation, 79 Minn. L. Rev. 1317 (1995).

Alexandria Zylstra, Mediation and Domestic Violence: A Practical Screening Method for Mediators and Mediation Program Administrators, 2001 J. of Disp. Resol. 253 (2001).

Bibliography

Andrew Ashworth, Some Doubts A bout Restorative Justice, 4 Crim. L. F. 277 (1993).

Lisa B. Bingham, et. al., Exploring the Role of Representation in Employment Mediation at the USPS, 17 Ohio St. J. on Disp. Resol. 341 (2002).

Richard Birke & Louise Ellen Teitz, U.S. Mediation in 2001: The Path that Brought American to Uniform Laws and Mediation in Cyberspace 50 Am. J. Comp. L 181 (2002).

Jennifer Gerarda Brown, The Use of Mediation to Resolve Criminal Cases: A Procedural Critique, 43 Emory L. J. 1247 (1994).

Edward Brunet, Seeking Optimal Dispute Resolution Clauses in High Stakes Employment Contracts, 23 Berkley J. Emp. & Lab. L. 107 (2002).

Jim Consedine, Restorative Justice: Healing the Effects of Crime (1994).

Edward A. Dauer, When the Law Gets in the Way: The Dissonant Link of Deterrence and Compensation in the Law of Medical Malpractice, 28 Cap. U. L. Rev.293 (2000).

Joel B. Eisen, Are We Ready for Mediation in Cyberspace?, 1998 B.Y.U. L. Rev. 1305 (1998).

Karla Fischer, Neil Vidmar & Rene Ellis, The Culture of Battering and the Role of Mediation in Domestic Violence Cases, 46 S.M.U. L. Rev. 2117 (1993).

Timothy L. Fort, Religion in the Workplace: Mediating Religion's Good, Bad and Ugly, Naturally, 12 Notre Dame J. L. Ethics and Pub. Pol'y 121 (1998).

Eric R. Galton, Mediation of Medical Negligence Claims, 28 Cap. U. L. Rev. 321 (2000).

Robert Gatter, Unnecessary Adversaries at the End of Life: Mediating End of Life Treatment Disputes to Prevent Erosion of Patient–Physician Relationships, 79 B.U.L. Rev. 1091 (1999).

Michael Z. Green, Proposing a New Paradigm for EEOC Enforcement After 35 Years: Outsourcing Charge Processing by Mandatory Mediation 105 Dick. L. Rev. 305 (2001).

William S. Haft & Elaine R. Weiss, Note, Peer Mediation in Schools: Expectations and Evaluations, 3 Hav. Neg. L. Rev. 213 (1998).

Gary Richard Hattal & Cynthia Morrow Hattal, Battling School Violence with Mediation Technology, 2 Pepp. Disp. Resol. L. J. 357 (2002).

John M. Haynes, The Fundamentals of Family Mediation (1994).

Camille Hebert, Establishing and Evaluating a Workplace Mediation Pilot Project: An Ohio Case Study, 14 Ohio St. J. on Disp. Resol. 415 (1999).

Diane E. Hoffman, Mediating Life and Death Decisions, 36 Ariz. L. Rev. 821 (1994).

Katherine L. Joseph, Victim–Offender Mediation: What Social and Political Factors will Affect Its Development 11 Ohio St. J. on Disp. Resol. 207 (1996).

Robin M. Kennedy & Jon Michael Gibbs, Cyber–Mediation: Computer–Mediated Communications Medium Massaging the Message, 32 N. M. L. Rev. 27 (2002).

Kimberlee K. Kovach, Neonatology Life and Death Decisions: Can Mediation Help? 28 Cap. U. L. Rev. 251 (2000).

Jeffrey Krivis, Mediating in Cyberspace, 14, Alternatives to High Cost Litig. 117, Nov. 1996.

F. Matthews–Giba, Religious Dimensions of Mediaiton, 27 Fordham U. L. J. 1695 (2000).

Jennifer P. Maxwell, Mandatory Mediation of Custody in the Face of Domestic Violence: Suggestions for Courts and Mediators, 37 Fam. & Conciliation Cts. Rev. (1999).

Mediation In International Relations: Multiple Approaches To Conflict Management (Jacob Bercovitch & Jeffrey Z. Rubin, eds., 1992).

Harry Mika, The Practice and Prospect of Victim–Offender Programs, 46 SMU L. Rev. 2191 (1993).

Rosemary O'Leary & Tracy Yandle, The State of the States in Environmental Dispute Resolution, 14 Ohio St. J. on Disp. Resol. 515 (1999).

Jessica Pearson, Mediating When Domestic Violence is a Factor: Policies and Practices in Court–Based Divorce Mediation Programs, 14 Mediation Q. 319, 332–33 (1997).

Alan Scott Rau, Resolving Disputes Over Attorney's Fees: The Role of ADR, 46 SMU L.Rev. 2005 (1993).

Carrie–Anne Tondo, et. al., Note, Mediation Trends: A Survey of the States 39 Fam. Ct. Rev. 431 (2001).

Mark S. Umbreit & Robert B. Coates, Cross–Site Analysis of Victim–Offender Mediation in Four States, 39 Crime and Delinquency 565 (1993).

Mark Umbreit, et. al., The Impact of Victim–Offender Mediation: Two Decades of Research, 65 Dec. Fed. Probation 29 (2001).

Glenn G. Waddell & Judith M. Keegan, Christian Conciliaiton: An Alternative to "Ordinary" ADR 29 Cumb. L. Rev. 583 (1998–1999).

Stephen Wodpert, Victim–Offender Reconciliation Programs in Community Mediation: A Handbook for Practitioners and Researchers (Karen Grover Duffy, et al., eds., 1991).

Howard Zehr, A New Focus for Crime and Justice, Changing Lenses (1990).

Http://www.voma.org

CHAPTER 12

DERIVATIVE, COMBINATION AND HYBRID PROCESSES

Several other dispute resolution processes resemble mediation, particularly in their theoretical basis. Yet, while sharing philosophical roots, these other dispute resolution techniques are sufficiently distinct to warrant different names. These derivative processes include consensus building, conciliation and regulatory negotiation.

Traditional mediation can also be added to another process to form a "combined" process. Even when combined, however, mediation is a distinct stage that either precedes or follows another process. The most common example is med-arb, mediation followed by arbitration. The mediation process can also be blended into another ADR process to form a "hybrid" process. The mini-trial is one such process. These derivatives, combinations and hybrids may be used in nearly any type of dispute. Many times, though, a process will have evolved to accommodate the idiosyncratic aspects of a particular type of dispute, and as a result becomes a derivative, rather than the more traditional model.

A. DERIVATIVES

Particular types of matters may call for different approaches for resolution. A number of distinctions exist between the generic mediation process and the consensus building process which is often utilized in public policy matters. Some differences are based on the type of matter and others depend on how the parties participate in the process.

1. PUBLIC POLICY CONSENSUS BUILDING

Examining the use of mediation or other ADR processes where a public entity is involved presents a number of challenges for the neutral. One of the most difficult factors is the sheer number of parties involved. While at first glance such a process appears more difficult than a classic mediation, in many ways it can be actually easier. Often a number of interests overlap. Some of the parties may also have shared goals. Consequently, there may be greater opportunities for integrative bargaining.

Another concern is the length of the process. Basic mediation is usually a one-time intervention, except in some models of family or divorce mediation. Public policy matters are often complex, and due to the number of parties involved, frequently take much longer to resolve. As its name implies, consensus building is not a one-time intervention, but by design is a building process that takes place during a number of successive meetings, spread out over weeks and even months. The pre-mediation phase is also quite lengthy. In fact, it is often the longest phase of the process.

During the pre-meeting stage, the neutral convener may meet with potential stakeholders in order to assess their positions and determine logistical requirements for the session. In some instances, the neutral(s) are actually involved in identifying the potential stakeholders and ensuring their participation. If the number of individuals involved is excessive, the neutral may meet with the parties to help them choose their representatives for the consensus building process. Protocol for the consensus building meetings is also determined in advance and may include, for instance, agreements about dealing with the media. The convener may also wish to talk to each party about agenda setting. Lastly, the convener may engage in joint fact finding, and determine whether there are any consultants, experts or advisors who may assist the consensus building process. The actual negotiation phase then begins.

A consensus process can be used at various stages and times during the existence of public policy matters, even before a dispute arises. For example, the parties may come together to discuss contingencies should a dispute or conflict arise. Procedures will be developed early on to manage the dispute; the participants may even agree on the type of process to be used should an actual dispute arise. On the other hand, consensus building is sometimes used after a dispute is well defined, yet prior to litigation. Finally, many courts refer public policy matters to mediation.

In most traditional mediations, there are two sides and two distinct views of the situation in conflict. Even though many lawsuits and disputes involve multiple parties, the parties tend to align themselves on either side of a set of issues. In consensus building, there are often many different groups with a variety of interests. Coalitions frequently form. While each group may have representatives at the mediation table, much intra-group negotiation takes place away from the table.

In public policy matters, confidentiality issues (as noted in Chapter Seven), differ from the generic model, due to the existence of sunshine laws and open meetings acts, and the fact that many times a governmental agency is a participant. Issues involving representation and decision making are matters that differ in the public arena as well. Often, no one person is able to make decisions for the group. Thus, there must be delegation of authority. Agreements which are reached at the table may need to be ratified at a later date. Finally, power imbalances are common due to availability of resources. For example, a corporate developer may have many more resources than a small, grassroots environmental group.

In many models, the issues have been identified in the pre-meeting stage. Consequently, the consensus building starts with brainstorming possible solutions. Part of building a consensus includes a "packaging" stage, where the convener meets in private sessions with each of the groups to determine which partial solutions might be able to be bargained for as a package. Due to the fact that nearly everyone participating in the process is a representative of others, another critical step is ratification. At that time, the meeting participants go back to their constituencies and "sell" the agreement so that each group's ratification can be obtained. Lastly, consensus building often involves the neutral convener in the implementation or post-negotiation phase as well. This is not true in generic mediation. However, because of the magnitude of most of these disputes and the complexities of their agreements, the parties may need assistance from the neutral, particularly if there are elected or appointed officials who must be consulted, or if there is a need for a monitor during the implementation phase. The neutral is also called upon if a need occurs for renegotiation of the agreement. Many of these processes are public, and if an agreement is reached, it is published.

Outcomes may differ ranging from an agreement concerning information exchange to an outcome which is a true consensus on the matter at hand. Consensus may also be reached on part of the issues or on the entire matter. Consensus does not mean voting, but rather signifies that all participants are able to live with and support the outcome.

2. NEGOTIATED RULEMAKING

A procedure somewhat similar to consensus build-ing, yet with its own distinctive characteristics is negotiated rulemaking. Regulatory negotiation, also known as *reg-neg* for short, is an attempt to shorten the rulemaking process for federal (as well as state and local) agencies. While the process could be considered analogous to consensus building, the pri-mary difference is that a dispute does not yet exist. In this process, the purpose is not to resolve a conflict, but rather avert one, and provide a non-adversarial collaborative process to enact a rule or regulation.

When the time is ripe for the creation of a rule or regulation, instead of the more traditional practice of the agency drafting and then sending out a proposed rule for review and comment, an attempt is made to obtain the opinions of those affected early on. Often individuals affected by the rule or their representatives are part of the drafting pro-cess. All interested or affected parties are contacted and invited to take part in the initial stages. Discus-sions continue until all reach consensus about the content of the rule or regulation. The convener, a third party neutral acting similarly to a mediator, assumes the responsibility for structuring the pro-cess.

The initial step is a determination of those affect-ed by the proposed legislation. Secondly, the con-vener decides whether it would be feasible to use negotiation among all of those affected to resolve any disputes. At the meetings, interested parties help draft the new legislation, eliminating the normal waiting period for feedback and revision.

The process of regulatory negotiation is similar to consensus building, with the primary difference being that reg-neg is more narrowly focused. In the consensus building process, usually there is an issue that needs closure or a dispute that needs resolution, but the specifics of a solution are left to the parties involved. In regulatory negotiation, however, the goal is specifically identified at the beginning of the session: to draft a regulation. Thus, the entire process is focused and structured. Likewise, in general consensus building, anyone with an interest in the outcome may participate. In regulatory negotiation, the convener may limit the number of parties to fewer than fifteen, or she may allow as many as twenty-five, but rarely more than that are included. (Harter). Moreover, in reg-neg only those parties who are directly affected by the proposed rule may attend the session. Another distinction is that in regulatory negotiation the convener rarely does any follow-up work. Once a consensus is reached, the rule is implemented.

The first work in reg-neg was at the federal level. Federal agencies are governed by the Negotiated Rulemaking Act of 1990, which outlines specific procedures for the process. 5 U.S.C.A. §§ 561–570. Early supporters of the reg-neg process claimed that it would necessarily improve rule quality, increase legitimacy, and reduce transaction costs. In many states, such as Texas and Montana, statutes encourage and direct the use of regulatory negotiation for state and local agencies.

3.   GROUP FACILITATION

Group facilitation has been described as a way to deal with problems in a collaborative manner in order to prevent conflict (Fleischer & Zumeta). It is quite similar to a consensus process, but often does not have a dispute or conflict as its central focus. Many of the skills used by the neutral, the convener, are similar to those of a mediator, but group facilitation is a more preventative process that may be used for brainstorming and problem solving where no real dispute or problem has yet surfaced. The group itself can be small (5 people) or rather large (hundreds of people). Often the process is more structured than some approaches to mediation, and use of agendas or guidelines may be helpful. The process may also be used to assist in planning. Applications range from workplace matters or government agency issues to potential problems facing a board of directors or council of a nonprofit organization.

B.   HYBRIDS

The term *hybrid* is used to indicate the blending or merging of two or more ADR procedures, which results in a composite. Rather than merely combining the mediation process with another process, there is true integration. For example, if mediation is integrated with an evaluative process, the result can be a completely new process, such as the mini-trial. Two of the more common hybrids are the mini-trial and the work of an ombudsman.

The mini-trial uses mediation concepts in the facilitation of communication between the parties. The neutral expert advisor first provides the parties with an opportunity for direct negotiations. If the principals are unable to reach an accord, then the neutral expert advisor may actually mediate. The form of mediation, however, may be non-traditional. Generally, the neutral shares her evaluation, after which facilitated discussions resembling mediation take place.

The work of an ombudsman is viewed by many experts as a separate, distinct process. It may also be considered a hybrid of sorts, due to the fact that in carrying out his work, an ombudsman assumes a variety of roles. In organizations such as universities and hospitals, the role of the ombudsman is to receive and handle complaints or grievances. There are also ombudsmen whose roles are more of an advocate for a particular group of individuals. What the ombudsman does in these instances can range from investigation and advocacy to negotiation coaching, mediation, or conciliation. Ombudsman positions may be the result of legislation, which handles complaints in general.

As the use of mediation continues to grow, opportunities to integrate it with other processes will increase, and additional hybrid processes will no doubt result.

C. COMBINED PROCESSES

Combination dispute resolution describes a situation where one distinct process may be used after another, for example, a summary jury trial followed by mediation. The most common combined form is the med-arb process in which the parties first engage in the mediation process. If an agreement is not reached in a pre-determined amount of time (or at the discretion of the mediator), the parties enter arbitration. A number of different variations of this process are now available.

In the original med–arb process, the neutral began the proceeding as a mediator, but with the understanding that any matter unresolved would be arbitrated. Because the same individual served as both a mediative and adjudicative function, the process was often criticized. The criticism included the contention that since the mediator knew that a decision might have to be made, the mediator could not remain impartial during the mediative phase. Another criticism voiced was that the type of presentations made by the parties or their advocates differs drastically in each process. Successful strategies in one process might necessarily damage the effectiveness of the other. In a recent case, a Texas appellate court reversed the trial court's appointment of an arbitrator who had been a mediator in the same matter. The court based its decision on the contention that the parties would not have disclosed information to the mediator had they known that the same individual would later act in an adjudicative capacity. (Cartwright).

As a result of these difficulties, another form of med–arb evolved. In the newer form, the parties attempt to mediate, but if a resolution is not achieved during the session, the parties begin arbitration with a *different* individual serving as the arbitrator. The difficulty in this form of med–arb is that it is repetitious when mediation fails and as a result, more time-consuming and costly. A third form of the process attempts to eliminate the defects of the other methods and still provide the benefits of both mediation and arbitration. Specifically, the co–med–arb process uses two neutrals simultaneously listening to the initial statements of the parties. The first neutral then acts as the mediator, leading a neutral, impartial mediation session. Should that effort fail to completely resolve the matter, the second neutral presents the parties with a binding arbitration decision of those issues left undecided.

Traditional forms of med-arb dictate that the mediation process be conducted prior to the arbitration. A few practitioners have experimented with arbitration first, followed by mediation. The neutral provides a non-binding suggested arbitration award and then assists the parties in mediating their dispute. This novel approach has been severely criticized by some who feel that the mediator, having rendered an award, may no longer be impartial or neutral about the outcome of the case.

Just as mediation has been combined with arbitration, it can also be joined with the evaluative

ADR processes. The order of the processes varies. In some cases, parties need certain information to assist them in the negotiation of a settlement. Evaluative processes, such as the moderated settlement conference, neutral case evaluation, or the summary jury trial, could take place prior to the mediation. The parties may also try mediation first. If the mediation does not result in a settlement (primarily because of inaccurate or incomplete evaluation or assessment of the case), the mediator may recommend that the parties participate in an evaluative process. After the evaluative process, the parties may choose to mediate again or negotiate a resolution without the assistance of a neutral. Often through mediation, a determination can be made regarding what other dispute resolution process will best assist in the settlement of the matter. Such choices may be made by the mediator, the parties or their counsel or other representatives. Knowledge of the nuances of each of the processes can be advantageous in making such selections and reaching a final resolution of the dispute.

References

Janice Fleischer & Zena Zumeta, Group Facilitation: A Way to Address Problems Collaboratively, 4 Disp. Resol. Mag. 4 (Summer 1998).

Philip J. Harter, Negotiating Regulations: A Cure for Malaise, 71 Geo. L. J. 46 (1982).

Cases

In re Cartwright, 2002 WL 501595 ___ S.W.3d ___ (Tex. App.–Houston [1st Dist.] 2002).

Bibliography

Michele Bertran, Judiciary Ombudsman: Solving Problems in the Courts, 29 Fordham U. L. J. 2099 (2002).

Jody Freeman & Laura I. Langbein, Regulatory Negotiation and the Legitimacy Benefit, 31 Envtl. L. Rep. 10811 (2001).

Matthew J. McKinney, Negotiated Rulemaking: Involving Citizens in Public Decisions, 60 Mont. L. Rev. 499 (1999).

David M. Pritzker & Deborah S. Dalton, Negotiated Rulemaking Sourcebook, Administrative Conference of the United States (1995).

Lawrence Susskind & Gerlad McMahon, The Theory and Practice of Negotiated Rulemaking, 3 Yale J. on Reg. 1 (1985).

Ellen J. Waxman & Howard Gadlin, Ombudsmen: A Buffer Between Institutions, Individuals, 4 Disp. Resol. Mag. 21 (Summer 1998).

APPENDIX A

STANDARDS OF CONDUCT

Introductory Note

The initiative for these standards came from three professional groups: the American Arbitration Association, the American Bar Association, and the Society of Professionals in Dispute Resolution.

The purpose of this initiative was to develop a set of standards to serve as a general framework for the practice of mediation. The effort is a step in the development of the field and a tool to assist practitioners in it—a beginning, not an end. The standards are intended to apply to all types of mediation. It is recognized, however, that in some cases the application of these standards may be affected by laws or contractual agreements.

Preface

The standards of conduct for mediators are intended to perform three major functions: to serve as a guide for the conduct of mediators; to inform the mediating parties; and to promote public confidence in mediation as a process for resolving disputes. The standards draw on existing codes of conduct for mediators and take into account issues and problems that have surfaced in mediation practice. They are offered in the hope that they will serve an educational function and provide assistance to individuals, organizations, and institutions involved in mediation.

Mediation is a process in which an impartial third party—a mediator—facilitates the resolution of a dispute by promoting voluntary agreement (or "self-determination") by the parties to the dispute. A mediator facilitates communications, promotes understanding, focuses the parties on their interests, and seeks creative problem solving to enable the parties to reach their own agreement. These standards give meaning to this definition of mediation.

I.   Self–Determination: A Mediator Shall Recognize that Mediation is Based on the Principle of Self–Determination by the Parties.

Self-determination is the fundamental principle of mediation. It requires that the mediation process rely upon the ability of the parties to reach a voluntary, uncoerced agreement. Any party may withdraw from mediation at any time.

COMMENTS

- The mediator may provide information about the process, raise issues, and help parties explore options. The primary role of the mediator is to facilitate a voluntary resolution of a dispute. Parties shall be given the opportunity to consider all proposed options.

- A mediator cannot personally ensure that each party has made a fully informed choice to reach a particular agreement, but it is a good practice for the mediator to make the parties aware of the importance of consulting other professionals, where appropriate, to help them make informed decisions.

II.   Impartiality: A Mediator Shall Conduct the Mediation in an Impartial Manner.

The concept of mediator impartiality is central to the mediation process. A mediator shall mediate only those matters in which she or he can remain impartial and evenhanded. If at any time the mediator is unable to conduct the process in an impartial manner, the mediator is obligated to withdraw.

COMMENTS

- A mediator shall avoid conduct that gives the appearance of partiality toward one of the parties. The quality of the mediation process is enhanced when the parties have confidence in the impartiality of the mediator.

- When mediators are appointed by a court or institution, the appointing agency shall make reasonable efforts to ensure that mediators serve impartially.

- A mediator should guard against partiality or prejudice based on the parties' personal characteristics, background or performance at the mediation.

III. Conflicts of Interest: A Mediator Shall Disclose all Actual and Potential Conflicts of Interest Reasonably Known to the Mediator. After Disclosure, the Mediator Shall Decline to Mediate Unless all Parties Choose to Retain the Mediator. The Need to Protect Against Conflicts of Interest Also Governs Conduct that Occurs During and After the Mediation.

A conflict of interest is a dealing or relationship that might create an impression of possible bias. The basic approach to questions of conflict of interest is consistent with the concept of self-determination. The mediator has a responsibility to disclose all actual and potential conflicts that are reasonably known to the mediator and could reasonably be seen as raising a question about impartiality. If all parties agree to mediate after being informed of conflicts, the mediator may proceed with the mediation. If, however, the conflict of interest casts serious doubt on the integrity of the process, the mediator shall decline to proceed.

A mediator must avoid the appearance of conflict of interest both during and after the mediation. Without the consent of all parties, a mediator shall not subsequently establish a professional relationship with one of the parties in a related matter, or in an unrelated matter under circumstances which would raise legitimate questions about the integrity of the mediation process.

COMMENTS

- A mediator shall avoid conflicts of interest in recommending the services of other professionals. A mediator may make reference to professional referral services or associations which maintain rosters of qualified professionals.

- Potential conflicts of interest may arise between administrators of mediation programs and mediators and there may be strong pressures on the mediator to settle a particular case or cases. The mediator's commitment must be to the parties and the process. Pressures from outside of the mediation process should never influence the mediator to coerce parties to settle.

IV. Competence: A Mediator Shall Mediate Only When the Mediator Has the Necessary Qualifications to Satisfy the Reasonable Expectations of the Parties.

Any person may be selected as a mediator, provided that the parties are satisfied with the mediator's qualifications. Training and experience in mediation, however, are often necessary for effective mediation. A person who offers herself or himself as available to serve as a mediator gives parties and the public the expectation that she or he has the competency to mediate effectively. In court-connected or other forms of mandated mediation, it is essential that mediators assigned to the parties have the requisite training and experience.

COMMENTS

- Mediators should have available for the parties information regarding their relevant training, education and experience.

- The requirements for appearing on a list of mediators must be made public and available to interested persons.

- When mediators are appointed by a court or institution, the appointing agency shall make reasonable efforts to ensure that each mediator is qualified for the particular mediation.

V. Confidentiality: A Mediator Shall Maintain the Reasonable Expectations of the Parties with Regard to Confidentiality.

The reasonable expectations of the parties with regard to confidentiality shall be met by the mediator. The parties' expectations of confidentiality depend on the circumstances of the mediation and any agreements they may make. A mediator shall not disclose any matter that any party expects to be confidential unless given permission by all parties or unless required by law or other public policy.

COMMENTS

- The parties may make their own rules with respect to confidentiality, or the accepted practice of an individual mediator or institution may dictate a particular set of expectations. Since the parties' expectations regarding confidentiality are important, the mediator should discuss these expectations with the parties.

- If the mediator holds private sessions with a party, the nature of these sessions with regard to confidentiality should be discussed prior to undertaking such sessions.

- In order to protect the integrity of the mediation, a mediator should avoid communicating information about how the parties acted in the mediation process, the merits of the case or settlement offers. The mediator may report, if required, whether parties appeared at a scheduled mediation.

- Where the parties have agreed that all or a portion of the information disclosed during a mediation is confidential, the parties' agreement should be respected by the mediator.

- Confidentiality should not be construed to limit or prohibit the effective monitoring, research or evaluation of mediation programs by responsible persons. Under appropriate circumstances, researchers may be permitted to obtain access to statistical data and, with permission of the parties, to individual case files, observations of live mediations and interviews with participants.

VI. Quality of the Process: The Mediator Shall Conduct the Mediation Fairly, Diligently and in a Manner Consistent with the Principle of Self–Determination by the Parties.

A mediator shall work to ensure a quality process and to encourage mutual respect among the parties.

A quality process requires a commitment by the mediator to diligence and procedural fairness. There should be adequate opportunity for each party in the mediation to participate in the discussions. The parties decide when and under what conditions they will reach an agreement or terminate a mediation.

COMMENTS

- A mediator may agree to mediate only when he or she is prepared to commit the attention essential to an effective mediation.

- The mediator may only accept cases where they can satisfy the reasonable expectations of the parties concerning the timing of the process. A mediator should not allow a mediation to be unduly delayed by the parties or their representatives.

- The presence or absence of persons at a mediation depends on the agreement of the parties and mediator. The parties and mediator may agree that others may be excluded from particular sessions or from the entire mediation process.

- The primary purpose of a mediator is to facilitate the parties' voluntary agreement. This role differs substantially from other professional-client relationships. Mixing the role of a mediator and the role of a professional advising a client is problematic, and mediators must strive to distinguish between the roles. A mediator should therefore refrain from providing professional advice. Where appropriate, a mediator should recommend that parties seek outside professional advice, or consider resolving their dispute through arbitration, counselling, neutral evaluation, or other processes. A mediator who undertakes, at the request of the parties, an additional dispute resolution role in the same matter assumes increased responsibilities and obligations that may be governed by the standards of other professions.

- A mediator shall withdraw from a mediation when incapable of serving or when unable to remain impartial.

- A mediator shall withdraw from the mediation or postpone a session if the mediation is being used to further illegal conduct, or if a party is unable to participate due to drug, alcohol, or other physical or mental incapacity.

- Mediators should not permit their behavior in the mediation process to be guided by a desire for a high settlement rate.

VII. Advertising and Solicitation: A Mediator Shall Be Truthful in Advertising and Solicitation for Mediation.

Advertising or any other communication with the public concerning services offered or regarding the education, training, and expertise of the mediator shall be truthful. Mediators shall refrain from promises and guarantees of results.

COMMENTS

- It is imperative that communication with the public educate and instill confidence in the process.

- In an advertisement or other communication to the public, a mediator may make reference to meeting state, national, or private organization qualifications only if the entity referred to has a procedure for qualifying mediators and the mediator has been duly granted the requisite status.

VIII. Fees: A Mediator Shall Fully Disclose and Explain the Basis of Compensation, Fees and Charges to the Parties.

The parties should be provided sufficient information about fees at the outset of a mediation to determine if they wish to retain the services of a mediator. If a mediator charges fees, the fees shall be reasonable considering, among other things, the mediation service, the type and complexity of the matter, the expertise of the mediator, the time required, and the rates customary in the community. The better practice in reaching an understanding about fees is to set down the arrangements in a written agreement.

COMMENTS

- A mediator who withdraws from a mediation should return any unearned fee to the parties.

- A mediator should not enter into a fee agreement which is contingent upon the result of the mediation or amount of the settlement.

- Co-mediators who share a fee should hold to standards of reasonableness in determining the allocation of fees.

- A mediator should not accept a fee for referral of a matter to another mediator or to any other person.

IX. Obligations to the Mediation Process.

Mediators have a duty to improve the practice of mediation.

COMMENTS

- Mediators are regarded as knowledgeable in the process of mediation. They have an obligation to use their knowledge to help educate the public about mediation; to make mediation accessible to those who would like to use it, to correct abuses; and to improve their professional skills and abilities.

APPENDIX B

UNIFORM MEDIATION ACT

Drafted by the

NATIONAL CONFERENCE OF COM-MISSIONERS ON UNIFORM STATE LAWS

and by it

APPROVED AND RECOMMENDED FOR ENACTMENT IN ALL THE STATES

at its

ANNUAL CONFERENCE MEETING IN ITS ONE–HUNDRED–AND–TENTH YEAR

WHITE SULPHUR SPRINGS, WEST VIRGINIA

AUGUST 10–17, 2001

WITH PREFATORY NOTE AND COMMENTS

Approved by the American Bar Association

Philadelphia, Pennsylvania, February 4, 2002

Copyright © 2001

By

NATIONAL CONFERENCE OF COM-MISSIONERS ON UNIFORM STATE LAWS

NATIONAL CONFERENCE OF COMMISSIONERS ON UNIFORM STATE LAWS DRAFTING COMMITTEE ON UNIFORM MEDIATION ACT:

MICHAEL B. GETTY, 1560 Sandburg Terrace, Suite 1104, Chicago, IL 60610, *Chair*

PHILLIP CARROLL, 120 E. Fourth Street, Little Rock, AR 72201

JOSE FELICIANO, 3200 National City Center, 1900 E. 9th Street, Cleveland, OH 44114–3485, *American Bar Association Member*

STANLEY M. FISHER, 1100 Huntington Building, 925 Euclid Avenue, Cleveland, OH 44115–1475, *Enactment Coordinator*

ROGER C. HENDERSON, University of Arizona, James E. Rogers College of Law, Mountain and Speedway Streets, Tucson, AZ 85721, *Committee on Style Liaison*

ELIZABETH KENT, P.O. Box 2560, Honolulu, HI, 96804

RICHARD C. REUBEN, University of Missouri–Columbia School of Law, Hulston Hall, Columbia, MO 65211, *Associate Reporter*

NANCY H. ROGERS, Ohio State University, Michael E. Moritz College of Law, 55 W. 12th Avenue, Columbus, OH 43210, *National Conference Reporter*

FRANK E.A. SANDER, Harvard University Law School, Cambridge, MA 02138, *American Bar Association Member*

BYRON D. SHER, State Capitol, Suite 2082, Sacramento, CA 95814

MARTHA LEE WALTERS, Suite 220, 975 Oak Street, Eugene, OR 97401

JOAN ZELDON, D.C. Superior Court, 500 Indiana Ave., Washington, DC 20001

EX OFFICIO

JOHN L. McCLAUGHERTY, P.O. Box 553, Charleston, WV 25322, *President*

LEON M. McCORKLE, JR., P.O. Box 387, Dublin, OH 43017–0387, *Division Chair*

AMERICAN BAR ASSOCIATION ADVISOR

ROBERTA COOPER RAMO, Sunwest Building, Suite 1000, 500 W. 4th Street, NW, Albuquerque, NM 87102

EXECUTIVE DIRECTOR

FRED H. MILLER, University of Oklahoma, College of Law, 300 Timberdell Road, Norman, OK 73019, *Executive Director*

WILLIAM J. PIERCE, 1505 Roxbury Road, Ann Arbor, MI 48104, *Executive Director Emeritus*

Copies of this Act may be obtained from:

NATIONAL CONFERENCE OF COMMISSIONERS ON UNIFORM STATE LAWS

211 E. Ontario Street, Suite 1300

Chicago, Illinois 60611

312/915–0195

www.nccusl.org

ABA SECTION OF DISPUTE RESOLUTION DRAFTING COMMITTEE ON UNIFORM MEDIATION ACT

THOMAS J. MOYER, *Co-Chair*, **Supreme Court of Ohio, 30 E. Broad Street, Columbus, OH 43266**

ROBERTA COOPER RAMO, *Co-Chair*, **Modrall, Sperling, Roehl, Harris & Sisk, P.A., Sunwest Building, Suite 1000, Albuquerque, NM 87102**

JAMES DIGGS, PPG Industries, 1 PPG Place, Pittsburgh, PA 15272

JOSE FELICIANO, Baker & Hostetler, 3200 National City Center, 1900 East 9th St., Cleveland, OH 44114

MICHAEL B. GETTY, 1560 Sandburg Terrace, Suite 1104, Chicago, IL 60610, *NCCUSL Representative*

EMILY STEWART HAYNES, Supreme Court of Ohio, 30 E. Broad Street, Columbus, OH 43266, *Reporting Coordinator*

RICHARD C. REUBEN, University of Missouri–Columbia School of Law, Hulston Hall, Columbia, MO 65211, *Reporter*

NANCY H. ROGERS, Ohio State University, College of Law and Office of Academic Affairs, 203 Bricker Hall, 190 N. Oval Mall, Columbus, OH 43210, *Coordinator, Faculty Advisory Committee*

FRANK E.A. SANDER, Harvard Law School, Cambridge, MA 02138

JUDITH SAUL, Community Dispute Resolution Center, 120 W. State Street., Ithaca, NY 14850

ANNICE M. WAGNER, Court of Appeals of the District of Columbia, 500 Indiana Ave., NW, Washington, DC 20001

UNIFORM MEDIATION ACT

SECTION 1. TITLE. This [Act] may be cited as the Uniform Mediation Act.

SECTION 2. DEFINITIONS. In this [Act]:

(1) "Mediation" means a process in which a mediator facilitates communication and negotiation between parties to assist them in reaching a voluntary agreement regarding their dispute.

(2) "Mediation communication" means a statement, whether oral or in a record or verbal or nonverbal, that occurs during a mediation or is made for purposes of considering, conducting, participating in, initiating, continuing, or reconvening a mediation or retaining a mediator.

(3) "Mediator" means an individual who conducts a mediation.

(4) "Nonparty participant" means a person, other than a party or mediator, that participates in a mediation.

(5) "Mediation party" means a person that participates in a mediation and whose agreement is necessary to resolve the dispute.

(6) "Person" means an individual, corporation, business trust, estate, trust, partnership, limited liability company, association, joint venture, government; governmental subdivision, agency, or instrumentality; public corpo-

ration, or any other legal or commercial entity.

(7) "Proceeding" means:

(A) a judicial, administrative, arbitral, or other adjudicative process, including related pre-hearing and post-hearing motions, conferences, and discovery; or

(B) a legislative hearing or similar process.

(8) "Record" means information that is inscribed on a tangible medium or that is stored in an electronic or other medium and is retrievable in perceivable form.

(9) "Sign" means:

(A) to execute or adopt a tangible symbol with the present intent to authenticate a record; or

(B) to attach or logically associate an electronic symbol, sound, or process to or with a record with the present intent to authenticate a record.

SECTION 3. SCOPE.

(a) Except as otherwise provided in subsection (b) or (c), this [Act] applies to a mediation in which:

(1) the mediation parties are required to mediate by statute or court or administrative agency rule or referred to mediation by

a court, administrative agency, or arbitrator;

(2) the mediation parties and the mediator agree to mediate in a record that demonstrates an expectation that mediation communications will be privileged against disclosure; or

(3) the mediation parties use as a mediator an individual who holds himself or herself out as a mediator or the mediation is provided by a person that holds itself out as providing mediation.

(b) The [Act] does not apply to a mediation:

(1) relating to the establishment, negotiation, administration, or termination of a collective bargaining relationship;

(2) relating to a dispute that is pending under or is part of the processes established by a collective bargaining agreement, except that the [Act] applies to a mediation arising out of a dispute that has been filed with an administrative agency or court;

(3) conducted by a judge who might make a ruling on the case; or

(4) conducted under the auspices of:

(A) a primary or secondary school if all the parties are students or

(B) a correctional institution for youths if all the parties are residents of that institution.

(c) If the parties agree in advance in a signed record, or a record of proceeding reflects agreement by the parties, that all or part of a mediation is not privileged, the privileges under Sections 4 through 6 do not apply to the mediation or part agreed upon. However, Sections 4 through 6 apply to a mediation communication made by a person that has not received actual notice of the agreement before the communication is made.

Legislative Note: To the extent that the Act applies to mediations conducted under the authority of a State's courts, State judiciaries should consider enacting conforming court rules.

SECTION 4. PRIVILEGE AGAINST DISCLOSURE; ADMISSIBILITY; DISCOVERY.

(a) Except as otherwise provided in Section 6, a mediation communication is privileged as provided in subsection (b) and is not subject to discovery or admissible in evidence in a proceeding unless waived or precluded as provided by Section 5.

(b) In a proceeding, the following privileges apply:

(1) A mediation party may refuse to disclose, and may prevent any other person from disclosing, a mediation communication.

(2) A mediator may refuse to disclose a mediation communication, and may prevent any other person from disclosing a mediation communication of the mediator.

(3) A nonparty participant may refuse to disclose, and may prevent any other person from disclosing, a mediation communication of the nonparty participant.

(c) Evidence or information that is otherwise admissible or subject to discovery does not become inadmissible or protected from discovery solely by reason of its disclosure or use in a mediation.

Legislative Note: The Act does not supersede existing state statutes that make mediators incompetent to testify, or that provide for costs and attorney fees to mediators who are wrongfully subpoenaed. See, e.g., Cal. Evid. Code Section 703.5 (West 1994).

SECTION 5. WAIVER AND PRECLUSION OF PRIVILEGE.

(a) A privilege under Section 4 may be waived in a record or orally during a proceeding if it is expressly waived by all parties to the mediation and:

(1) in the case of the privilege of a mediator, it is expressly waived by the mediator; and

(2) in the case of the privilege of a nonparty participant, it is expressly waived by the nonparty participant.

(b) A person that discloses or makes a representation about a mediation communication which prejudices another person in a proceeding is precluded from asserting a privilege under Section 4, but only to the extent necessary for the person prejudiced to respond to the representation or disclosure.

(c) A person that intentionally uses a mediation to plan, attempt to commit or commit a crime, or to conceal an ongoing crime or ongoing criminal activity is precluded from asserting a privilege under Section 4.

SECTION 6. EXCEPTIONS TO PRIVILEGE.

(a) There is no privilege under Section 4 for a mediation communication that is:

(1) in an agreement evidenced by a record signed by all parties to the agreement;

(2) available to the public under [insert statutory reference to open records act] or made during a session of a mediation which is open, or is required by law to be open, to the public;

(3) a threat or statement of a plan to inflict bodily injury or commit a crime of violence;

(4) intentionally used to plan a crime, attempt to commit or commit a crime, or to conceal an ongoing crime or ongoing criminal activity;

(5) sought or offered to prove or disprove a claim or complaint of professional misconduct or malpractice filed against a mediator;

(6) except as otherwise provided in subsection (c), sought or offered to prove or disprove a claim or complaint of professional misconduct or malpractice filed against a mediation party, nonparty participant, or representative of a party based on conduct occurring during a mediation; or

(7) sought or offered to prove or disprove abuse, neglect, abandonment, or exploitation in a proceeding in which a child or adult protective services agency is a party, unless the

[Alternative A: [State to insert, for example, child or adult protection] case is referred by a court to mediation and a public agency participates.]

[Alternative B: public agency participates in the [State to insert, for example, child or adult protection] mediation].

(b) There is no privilege under Section 4 if a court, administrative agency, or arbitrator finds, after a hearing in camera, that the party seeking discovery or the proponent of the evidence has shown that the evidence is not otherwise available, that there is a need for the evidence that substantially outweighs the interest in protecting confidentiality, and that the mediation communication is sought or offered in:

(1) a court proceeding involving a felony [or misdemeanor]; or

(2) except as otherwise provided in subsection (c), a proceeding to prove a claim to rescind or reform or a defense to avoid liability on a contract arising out of the mediation.

(c) A mediator may not be compelled to provide evidence of a mediation communication referred to in subsection (a)(6) or (b)(2).

(d) If a mediation communication is not privileged under subsection (a) or (b), only the portion of the communication necessary for the application of the exception from nondisclosure may be admitted. Admission of evidence under subsection (a) or (b) does not render the evidence, or any other mediation communication, discoverable or admissible for any other purpose.

Legislative Note: If the enacting state does not have an open records act, the following language in paragraph (2) of subsection (a) needs to be deleted: "available to the public under [insert statutory reference to open records act] or".

SECTION 7. PROHIBITED MEDIATOR REPORTS.

(a) Except as required in subsection (b), a mediator may not make a report, assessment, evaluation, recommendation, finding, or other communication regarding a mediation to a court, administrative agency, or other authority that may make a ruling on the dispute that is the subject of the mediation.

(b) A mediator may disclose:

(1) whether the mediation occurred or has terminated, whether a settlement was reached, and attendance;

(2) a mediation communication as permitted under Section 6; or

(3) a mediation communication evidencing abuse, neglect, abandonment, or exploitation of an individual to a public agency responsible for protecting individuals against such mistreatment.

(c) A communication made in violation of subsection (a) may not be considered by a court, administrative agency, or arbitrator.

SECTION 8. CONFIDENTIALITY. Unless subject to the [insert statutory references to open meetings act and open records act], mediation communications are confidential to the extent agreed by the parties or provided by other law or rule of this State.

SECTION 9. MEDIATOR'S DISCLOSURE OF CONFLICTS OF INTEREST; BACKGROUND.

(a) Before accepting a mediation, an individual who is requested to serve as a mediator shall:

(1) make an inquiry that is reasonable under the circumstances to determine whether there are any known facts that a reasonable individual would consider likely to affect the impartiality of the mediator, including a financial or personal interest in the outcome of the mediation and an existing or past relationship with a mediation party or foreseeable participant in the mediation; and

(2) disclose any such known fact to the mediation parties as soon as is practical before accepting a mediation.

(b) If a mediator learns any fact described in subsection (a)(1) after accepting a mediation, the mediator shall disclose it as soon as is practicable.

(c) At the request of a mediation party, an individual who is requested to serve as a mediator shall disclose the mediator's qualifications to mediate a dispute.

(d) A person that violates subsection [(a) or (b)][(a), (b), or (g)] is precluded by the violation from asserting a privilege under Section 4.

(e) Subsections (a), (b), [and] (c), [and] [(g)] do not apply to an individual acting as a judge.

(f) This [Act] does not require that a mediator have a special qualification by background or profession.

[(g) A mediator must be impartial, unless after disclosure of the facts required in subsections (a) and (b) to be disclosed, the parties agree otherwise.]

SECTION 10. PARTICIPATION IN MEDIATION. An attorney or other individual designated by a party may accompany the party to and participate in a mediation. A waiver of participation given before the mediation may be rescinded.

SECTION 11. RELATION TO ELECTRONIC SIGNATURES IN GLOBAL AND NATIONAL COMMERCE ACT. This [Act] modifies, limits, or supersedes the federal Electronic Signatures in Global and National Commerce Act, 15 U.S.C. Section 7001 et seq., but this [Act] does not modify, limit, or supersede Section 101(c) of that Act or authorize electronic delivery of any of the notices described in Section 103(b) of that Act.

SECTION 12. UNIFORMITY OF APPLICATION AND CONSTRUCTION. In applying and construing this [Act], consideration should be given to the need to promote uniformity of the law with respect to its subject matter among States that enact it.

SECTION 13. SEVERABILITY CLAUSE. If any provision of this [Act] or its application to any person or circumstance is held invalid, the invalidity does not affect other provisions or applications of this [Act] which can be given effect without the invalid provision or application, and to this end the provisions of this [Act] are severable.

SECTION 14. EFFECTIVE DATE. This [Act] takes effect ....

SECTION 15. REPEALS. The following acts and parts of acts are hereby repealed:

(1)

(2)

(3)

SECTION 16. APPLICATION TO EXISTING AGREEMENTS OR REFERRALS.

(a) This [Act] governs a mediation pursuant to a referral or an agreement to mediate made on or after [the effective date of this [Act]].

(b) On or after [a delayed date], this [Act] governs an agreement to mediate whenever made.

APPENDIX C

Related Websites

www.abanet.org/dispute

www.mediate.com

www.adr.org

www.acresolution.org

www.cpradr.org

*

Index

References are to Pages

345

MALPRACTICE
Legal, 113–114, 296
Mediator, 163, 180, 265–268

MANDATORY MEDIATION
Generally, 86–88
Court, see Court–Annexed Mediation
Legislation, 88, 106–107

MED–ARB, 8, 311–313

MEDIATED AGREEMENT
Content, 36, 209–213
Drafting, 44, 205, 209, 276
Enforceability, 44, 179, 213–219, 285

MEDIATOR
Ethics, see Ethics
Introduction, 41, 42–43
Preparation, 116–117
Qualifications, 95, 225, 233, 254–260
Role, 153–161, 206–207
Selection, 42, 95, 104–105
Skills, 46–56

MEMORANDUM OF AGREEMENT, 44
See also Mediated Agreement

MINI–TRIAL, 11, 302, 310

MODELS OF MEDIATION, 40, 41–46, 167

MODERN MEDIATION MOVEMENT
See History of Mediation

MULTI–DOOR COURTHOUSE, 5, 21

NEGLIGENCE
See Malpractice

NEIGHBORHOOD JUSTICE CENTERS, 21–22, 30, 88, 257
See also Dispute Resolution Centers

NEGOTIATED RULEMAKING, 32, 307–309

NEGOTIATION
Generally, 41, 44, 67–71
Mediator's Role in, 44, 67, 72–73, 75, 79–82, 176
Obstacles in, 75–82